LIBERTY STREET

WITHDRAWN

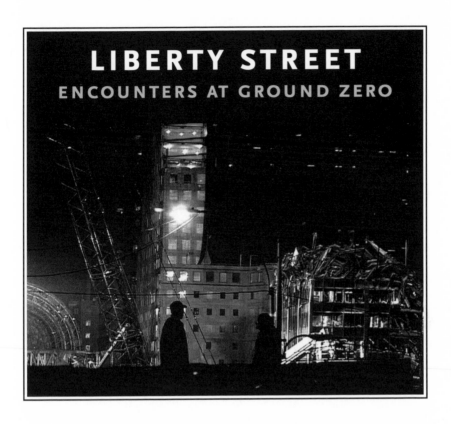

LIBERTY STREET
ENCOUNTERS AT GROUND ZERO

PETER JOSYPH

UNIVERSITY PRESS OF NEW ENGLAND   HANOVER & LONDON

Published by
University Press of New England
One Court Street, Lebanon, NH 03766
www.upne.com
© 2006 by Peter Josyph
Printed in the United States of America
5 4 3 2 1

Library of Congress Cataloging-in-Publication Data
Josyph, Peter.
Liberty Street : encounters at Ground Zero / Peter Josyph—1st ed.
p. cm.
Includes index.
ISBN–13: 978–1–58465–551–0 (cloth : alk. paper)
ISBN–10: 1–58465–551–8 (cloth : alk. paper)
1. September 11 Terrorist Attacks, 2001—Personal narratives.
2. World Trade Center Site (New York, N.Y.) I. Title.
HV6432.7.J67 2006
974.7′1044—dc22   2005030901

for Aurora, Mallory, and Elijah
with the hope of no Ground Zeros
in their future

It harrows me with fear and wonder.

—Shakespeare, *Hamlet*

CONTENTS

BEHIND THE GREEN DOOR

At the window of a lightshaft of 114 Liberty Street,
debris includes a slat of venetian blind from the Twin Towers.

1

WHAT'S BURNIN NOW

More than a grave and a ruin, Ground Zero was a new New York neighborhood that transfigured the best and the oldest part of the city, turning your head with exotic sights that lifted you and flattened you simultaneously, proving, every hour, that ordinary men are creatures of infinite interest if only you can abide them and keep from getting killed. For one historic instant the meanest of mean streets were not in Harlem, the Bronx, or Little Italy where my father was born a hundred years ago and where he brained a local bully with half a pistol, they were down at the end of the island where the air alone could kill you and your boots left prints in the dust of the dead. I was only a man with a camera having a long look around but there is no need to apologize for that. More movies should have been made there, for all that is gone now forever.

After a screening of the film *Bad Lieutenant,* I found myself in a parking lot facing its director, Abel Ferrara.

"Thanks for that movie," I said.

I had arranged the accident.

Ferrara shook my hand, leaning into my arm in a gesture of camaraderie. I told him I'd shot a movie at Ground Zero.

"You did?" he said, stopping in his tracks. "I wanted to do one too."

I had only brought it up in order to specify the gratitude I felt for that brave, X-rated explosion he had made roughly a decade ago. I said: "Trying to do something fierce, you look for other films to give you the courage."

"I understand, I understand."

"*Bad Lieutenant*'s an ally. Keep at it."

Walking away, he said: "No, listen—they're not gonna stop us," and I took *they* to mean more than foreign operatives, I took it to mean the forces against a man ever making a *Bad Lieutenant,* a *Liberty Street,* or any film that takes the camera where it isn't supposed to go.

I wish Ferrara had been there shooting. It was not only the grit, the mean-
ness, the gruff vulnerability that would have appealed to him. This was New
York life at its rarest and most typical, over the edge of the rational world—the
only place to be. It was electric, it was mysterious, it was a theological problem circumscribed by funerals in all five boroughs and it was a lot of tired
dirty guys doing their daily jobs. Men were snorting stuff all the time but it
was not cocaine, it was DNA. Breathing through respirators, philosophers
and seminarians could have held their classes there without saying a word,
and Jacques Derrida, who lived close by, could have deconstructed the very
idea of *respirator* and what it meant to absorb the event through *a mask* (pointing out that mine was made in Brazil), to at once breathe in, filter out, and
infiltrate what would seem to be a contradiction in terms: Ground Zero, a
standing on nothing, a no-thing full of things with antecedents in Hiroshima,
the first Ground Zero that was once a target-to-be, an atomic point of arrival;
the name now used for the departure of the Twins, a target-that-was which has
become a point of departure for something else—something like a century—
another—of blind fundamentalists hurling their mad deities at each other.

Among men to admire, to enjoy and to learn from there were hustlers,
thieves, nerds and blockheads of every American stripe—New York, after all,
went on New Yorking—but they did not rule the day. It was more than cir-
cumstantial that everybody invoked what an indelibly beautiful morning it
had been. The clear blue sky out of which the terror came was a primordial
vision. It might have created a city of dayfearers. It didn't. Men went abroad.
Things got done. New Yorkers who ran from those collapses didn't run from
the city. The urge to reconstitute a bearable existence was palpable—and
powerful. But amidst all the calls for perpetual remembrance, conveniently
forgot were the honest Downtowners trying to get back home—back home,
when that was a bit like sailing back to Vesuvius and more thought was given
to Afghanistan than to Liberty Street. As it cut across the island there were
places farther east—around the Federal Reserve, for instance—where it was
doing a lot better, but the three blocks of Liberty at the south end of the site
were a mess, devastated, and between Church and Greenwich streets, a
block of great resilience that included a firehouse, two residential buildings
from the teens of the last century and a few older buildings dating back to
the 1800s, Liberty Street was, to me, a national disgrace. If you think that
after September 11 residents and shopkeepers were shown a little mercy, no:
the desert men in the sky were only the first to dispossess them. Landlords,
insurers, cops, the City, environmental agencies, the president and the pres-

Glimpse of the new neighborhood from Greenwich Street, which intersects Liberty.
Trucks weighted with Trade Center steel rolled slowly down Greenwich on their way to Pier 6.

ident's people hung them out to dry. One of the nation's oldest streets (Crown Street before we left the English), Liberty was bivouacked, looted, lied to, bullied, insulted, ignored—at one point it was even written off—virtually razed and built over—in architectural renderings of the new neighborhood. Some of the men who paid for the 11th were better protected.

And yet, incredibly, in my year and a half of filming I personally encountered less anger there than ever in my New York life, perhaps because anger is good for destruction but not in it. When a proud, independent shopkeeper showed me a photograph of men in uniform enjoying the stock from his little shop—"Do you see who they are? These are the heroes! This is not the American way!"—his emotion was oddly out of place, unseemly: it made him a foreigner in the neighborhood he'd pledged his life to, for he hadn't figured out how to live there now, or how to live anywhere. When a foreman from the nightshift told me what he wanted for his birthday—his brother, who was buried, he thought, under the Tully Road—"I'm hoping to find him by Friday, I have a good feeling about it"—it was without sarcasm: he was truly looking forward to that gift of decomposed remains wrapped in a bunker coat, and in redefining the notions of finding someone, a good feeling, and celebrating your birthday he encapsulated the way September 11 and its aftermath confounded the ordinary with the macabre. As for hate, I didn't see much of that, except in myself, perhaps because a lot of it had burnt off already or was stored up for later or perhaps because it was, to say the least, rather too much in evidence gusting up your nose.

Some days I would sit on a bench in City Hall Park, where the stone fountain was empty but the triglobed gaslights were burning day and night; I would look up through the trees at the Woolworth Building, or over toward the mayor, and I would think about the ill-advised, ill-natured restriction against photography that had turned me into a spy in the house of destruction, an undercover agent for independent film, and I would hope that there were, at least, teams of oral historians coming to catch this event while it was raw, still literally in the air. It wouldn't have taken much prodding. Out of a trinity of smokers down in Bowling Green Park, which is enclosed in a cast-iron fence built in 1771 around a plot where Peter Minuit allegedly bought Manhattan Island for sixty guilders' worth of junk, a man named James Jones hit me up for a touch after a long conversation about addiction, homelessness, and the fact that more people associated his name with Jonestown than *From Here to Eternity*, which is why he was calling himself Steve. These guys were perfectly clean and they were minding their own business but from the moment I spotted them and observed their mannerisms I thought of them, affectionately, as Burroughs Boys: you could have sketched them into the margins of *Junky* or *Naked Lunch*.

"All these buildings're still full of dust," Steve said after lifting a couple of bucks from me, unconvinced—at least undeterred—by the admission that I was homeless once myself, was only a misstep away from it again, and was shooting on a shoestring. Steve proofed himself, showing me his driver's license to verify the name as identical with the author of *The Thin Red Line*. It was midsummer. It was 2002. The Red Cross tent that was here in September had picked up and gone but September was still alive. "Windy days you watch it blowing off," he said of the dust that was allegedly not traveling anymore and that allegedly wouldn't hurt you if it was. "It comes down on everybody. We see it all the time. We're in a position to notice."

Ike, a Polish-born shoeshiner who worked the Broadway fence in front of the Trinity churchyard, where obnoxious young sharps tried to hustle away his custom, told me about his brand-new box.

"Everything was falling," Ike said. "Everybody was screaming. I said: 'I better get out from here,' so I ran across the street. I wasn't even thinking about taking my box with me. I say: 'I want to save my life.' People was running so bad they pushed me down, trying to get away from the explosion, because the explosion was right here. My knees was injured and I couldn't come back to work for seven weeks. That's right. Yes. O yeah. Then a lady, a customer, she knows me, she say: 'What happen to your box?' I say: 'They broke my box from people running.' I didn't have no money at the time, so she gave me a hundred dollars, she bought me the shoeshine box because I had no box to work with. Yes. *Uh* huh. So there's nice people around."

It was spring of 2002. Site work was flying. Streets were opening. Storefronts were seeing new signs and paintjobs. Plywood departed, windows returned, restaurants and stores reopened under the guise of being clean—excepting a shop called Chelsea Jeans, which had the historical consciousness—perhaps, too, the enterprise—to leave one window as it was on the 11th, the clothing layered in World Trade dust. Ike's Broadway was crowded, so was Wall Street behind him. One of the hustlers said: "Pops—you got a sponge?" and Ike loaned him the spitshiner he used after the Kiwi. September 11 was not old Ike's first run for his life. At the age of eleven he'd been taken to Bergen-Belsen.

"Just happens to be I was Jewish," Ike told me in the midst of a thorough shine. "They say: 'We not gonna bother you, you gonna work.' But if you say you not gonna work, they pretend you gonna take a shower and they gas you to death. I saw thousands of people coming out. We had to bury them in big graves. After about six months—I was working outside—I run into the woods and I got shot running away, but some people was hiding me out and that's how I survived. But my family didn't survive. All my family died over there. Yeah. That's what happened." Ike unsnapped the right cuff of his jacket and he rolled up his sleeves to show me the scar, saying: "Right there. Yes. O yeah." The huckster next to him was probably thinking: "It's not the old man's *sponge* I need for business, it's his fucking *arm* with the Nazi bullet."

When I asked Ike whether he felt afraid of the city now, he said: "I'm not scared, no. Come out here I feel much better. I've been in New York for fifty-one years, I'm not gonna move out now." Business was picking up and people were kind to him, but it was different now. "I had a few steady customers used to come here from the World Trade Center, but I don't see them guys no more. I don't know if they gone or whatever. They don't come around here no more." In a topless joint, the Pussycat Lounge on Greenwich Street where trucks bearing the twisted steel rolled off the site on the way to Pier 6, a barmaid, Jax, had told me the same thing: steady customers were gone, but when I pressed her on whether she meant gone or *really* gone, she made it clear that she didn't mean displaced: she meant dead.

I thought about Ike when, a short time later, I read an article by a friend on the ethics of Spinoza. I said something like: "A good test for Spinoza is to ask whether he's useful to a guy who is (a) shot by Nazi guards running away from Bergen-Belsen, then (b) sixty years later, shining shoes in front of Trinity Church, he finds himself running from the collapse of the Twin Towers." As a reminder that survival is an open invitation to a future that doesn't preclude catastrophe, Ike deserved a documentary of his own, but during the three and a half years in which I composed Liberty Street: Alive at Ground Zero, a two-hour film made from more than two hundred, I would fight like a dog for even five minutes of Ike, so great is the necessity to cut until you feel as if you've cut everything.

In fact this allegedly well-documented catastrophe generated so many unanswered images, and such a tangle of questions over the double helix of plots and permissions leading up to it, that only under the narrowest definitions could you say that it was documented at all. Only one young filmmaker, Jules Naudet, was properly situated near the intersection of Lispenard and Church about fourteen blocks from the Trade Center and, although inexperienced, was sharp enough to shoot the first of the two bomber jets as it entered the North Tower. Who was shooting—who was watching—before that? Events don't begin when the networks find them. Even then, what did we see of the jumpers, the bodies and parts of bodies in the Austin Tobin Plaza and in the streets around the site? When a teenage nanny in charge of three little children told me about seeing chunks of meat on the Liberty sidewalk, and how she was confused because she couldn't recall a butcher on that block, I learned more about September 11 than all the networks had told me. As for what I saw of the people who are paid and are sworn to prevent such a disaster, the answer is: not much that mattered. That seeing was too controlled

BEHIND THE GREEN DOOR

for me. So was this. After the first few shots I had taken of Ground Zero on a chilly October morning were disrupted by National Guard, I could see that I was going to have to fight to work here and I could see that it was worth it. The City's disarmament of cameras could be seen as symptomatic of a much larger move toward concealment and the repression of prying eyes that would see into the precincts of policy and privilege; but here we are talking about a parcel of New York that was redefining civilization—hardly a small case—and if you had the stamina for it these very old streets in which the Republic had arisen were forceful places in which to consider recent events, the state of the union, and the fact that more than 767s had been hijacked. In St. Paul's Chapel, where men sipped something hot or slept on cots and pews, George Washington went to service after the first inauguration and his pew is still there, it's the one not scored by the utility belts and gear that sat with the men from the site. Thomas Paine boarded with friends on Church Street. Madison lived on Maiden Lane. Federal Hall, the first seat of government, was located on Wall Street, at the east end of which both Hamilton and Burr lived as neighbors for a time when they were building their law practices and stepping over cowshit until the street became more generally gentrified. In fact Hamilton was everywhere: Stone Street, Pine Street, Garden Street, Cedar Street, and in the graveyard at Trinity Church Hamilton was littered with the debris of both collapses. Now that the Constitution he worked so hard to ratify was being privatized by men who were thereby proving that they weren't Americans . . . now that the marble and the granite of Federal Hall had been fractured by the shock of both collapses . . . you would walk by Hamilton, with Con Ed lights at Rector Street and Broadway flashing on his monument, and even at the lowest point of midnight fatigue you would wonder how to be a citizen.

This camera that was hiding in the bag over my shoulder: was it a way to cast a vote? Was it a weapon of revolt? If, at the age of fifty-three, you are shooting what is decidedly a young man's movie, how do you meet that standard? The more I thought about the camera, the more I determined to make picking it up matter more than putting it down and to do something right for which it was worth going to jail. One could say that I was only walking around the premises, but why the *only,* as if it weren't enough? Isn't that what men of thought ought to do, walk around premises, probing them, challenging them, arranging them, perhaps, into an interesting idea, or the basis of an argument?[1]

Cocteau called film a form of confession. Bless me father for I have sinned.

Believing that, like all men, the terrorists were fashioned in His very image and likeness, I took the camera to town in order to see what constituted a good day's work for them in one of the great vineyards of the Lord. When the Koran challenges men to write their own chapters, threatening them with fire that is made of men and stones, I assume it is talking about an unbeliever like me who has seen some of that fire and is ready to start writing. But Hemingway was right in preferring to trust the names of places over the thoughts of men, even of men who were in a war with him. Ground Zero—it was really the perfect name. Like the place itself it meant too much, it explained nothing at all, and no master interpreter (not even Derrida) stepped into the light.[2] From perimeter rooftops you saw barges on the Hudson that carried more clarity about it than the *Times*. In the fractalist geometry of the pile every sign of disorder, however impressive, was just that, a sign, a marker beneath which innumerable combinations were only to be revealed in the act of being removed. The floor of one mess was the table of another: it was a long way to the bottom. There were no gross forms without nuance here, but this was a tough place for art because, beyond the technicality that artists weren't allowed, art likes to take a thing and ramify it for you. After September 11, Lower Manhattan was a fever of ramification all its own. Ironies, poignancies, absurdities, epiphanies pelted you in the face until you were glad to help lift something large, climb a ladder, trim a drillbit with a hacksaw or use the camera zoom to help locate a brick that was hiding in a façade. Fechner's Law, which is a formula for quantifying relations between external stimuli and the way that we receive them, would have been as useful here as a ruler in the ocean. If a poet had opened his mouth you would have shot him. But if you perched over the site and you watched those machines, that was some kind of art: balance, grace, rhythm, agility, tuned for improvisation, psyched for risk, braced for endurance. At least it put wonder into the thought of engineering and it showed you that, amidst all that ravenous masculinity, a few feminine verbs were necessary. Had he come to watch here, Derrida could have been taught something too: a new school of deconstruction.

Ground Zero worked something on everybody, and few were protected or prepared for what they found because none of us is educated for that. The popular formulation that we needed to do one thing or another *or else the terrorists will have won* was sophistry to honest eyes. A glance from any rooftop told you who succeeded, who failed that morning and nothing could turn that around. The very same prospect told you not to begrudge any solace to anybody within the law, and peptalk platitudes, jingoistic slogans, the silicone breasts at the Pussycat Lounge, memorials and banners from Oklahoma City, Crayola greeting cards from faceless classes of second graders, Red Bull, vodka, applause, hot food, massages, prayers, smiles from volunteers or maybe more from some of the Ground Zero groupies, even a fistfight or two seemed like leeway, like cutting a little slack, although they ought to have stopped short of a hasty war and violating the Posse Comitatus, and they ought to have shopped short of treating Downtown loyalists as if they were trespassers when, in fact, it was ten men in jets who had trespassed here and no one had done a thing to keep them out.

For me a few four-shots of Starbucks espresso hit the spot and, despite its association with upscale leisure, I couldn't find an article, a book or a film that could brace me as well as a dark draft of that brew. On the morning of the 11th several downtown Starbucks held open their doors for the stunned, the blinded, the choking, and while I was shooting they enabled me to recruit myself and the camera when we would have had to shiver in the streets. Donavin Gratz, a principal in my film whom you will meet in this book, said to me recently: "Starbucks—that was your solace, your solitude," and he was right: even the smell was sanctuary, not from being around the site, which is where I wanted to be, but from the world that had made it happen. There was a lot to be seen in that coffee. To this day a cappuccino works its memory-magic like the crumb of *petite madeleine* in Proust's spoonful of tea, only I don't see the provincial quietudes of Combray, I see the floodlit sprawls of baked Pittsburgh steel, the John Deere Gators parked at delis and pizza joints, the spotters with spades digging for flesh, the diesel excavators cleaning up after bin Laden and his Wahhabi financiers with compatriots in the White House. I see the birds, too, diving down for World Trade feed or moping around as if it were pointless to fly again, a reactive depression in which they found me complicit. Saint Francis, who adjured his feathered flocks to appreciate their birdly blessings, would have taken one look at that ragged, feeble assortment and he would have shaken his head and kept his counsel.

I envy Proust his memory, not his subject—meaning, of course, I envy him his eyes. My own eyes had a zoom that took me across Liberty Street into places my perimeter pass would not let me go—if you can't crash a gate, fly over it—but I worry, even now, that I did not see enough and should have shot more fiercely. I would like to have seen Ferrara there—or five of him. Despite the prohibition against the lens, I was surprised not to see more people dodging around, trying to capture this. Perhaps these secret shooters were hiding as well from me as from the law and their films will emerge. Perhaps movie moles were even rarer than I thought. They had to have acted fast, for Ground Zero was a disappearing act and there were no reshoots, no second takes here. Within nine months the site would be clean, the scrapped steel shipped to foreign ports—all the more necessity to have this abundance artfully extracted, preserved, and proposed as a primary cause for contemplation, rumination, investigation. I, for my part, was stocking up to build some of the wreckage of Lower Manhattan on a four-foot table in a small carpeted room, a fool's errand unless it engendered a little astonishment, never a sure thing. It might feel like life, wonderful life when you focus but the soul of the lens is not so easily animated. Hundreds of hours of footage for one handmade film mean nothing: no ratio is reasonable unless you get it right. Films, like books and like people, need to know much more than they can say.

Nothing about Ground Zero was simple, nothing about it was dull—or even its dullness was interesting—and nothing about it was clean. From the moment that I walked out of the Number 4 train at the Fulton Street station, the odor from the pile was pervasive. "Ho—Christ—is that *it? Jesus.*" I was only at the stair that brought you up to the little Keys Made, Shoe Shine shop in the first of the corridors that led to Fulton Street less than half a block from Broadway. So: the site came to meet you where a dry cleaner advertised four pairs of pants for ten bucks, and where the third rail beneath you carried an old life of yours through a long dark tunnel into oblivion. Photography had failed to render this, or even suggest it. Manhattan subway corridors are never much to breathe, and *nasty* can be used in New York all the time, but as I walked past the barber's to the short second stair that faces an arrowed Twin Towers sign pointing you, improbably, downward again toward the World Trade Copiers, it smelled like the burning of things that shouldn't ever burn but were burning at their essence and with fiendish energy, as if the fire could be fed forever. It told you, instantly, of something at work here that was equal to the might of the city itself. It made you wonder what it looked like. It also made you wonder whether you ought not to have stayed on the train. To borrow Shakespeare, it was an odor *at which my nose was in great indignation.*

I am sure that in the forested New York of Cooper's *Deerslayer,* an old American smoked a pipe, lowered into the old earth and dreamed a long pre-

     BEHIND THE GREEN DOOR

monitory dream of this odor, the hawks full of fire, the rills of black water, the forts falling down, and the warriors from the country of silver sand, but he could not think how to communicate it. He groped for the power of tongue but was muted by the endeavor, saying only: "You will each have to dream it for yourself." And so we have.

"Bury your face in the embers of a smoldering fireplace." That is how I once tried to suggest the sensation, but the likeness was lame for this was a compound odor that derived from the burning not of paper and wood merely but of everything the city has accrued and placed within the reach of its enemies. For me the odor was not corporeal—I was to sample that later from a roof on Liberty Street, where parts of people were rotting in drains and flies rested comfortably on your hand or on car-size remnants of the Towers— but it was electrical, it was metallic, it was plastic, it was rubbery, and as close to a solid entity as scent could attain. With a little more strength it would emanate fists that would pummel you in the chest and the face. It did that anyway when the wind blew hard, which it knows how to do in between two rivers that are running a short sail from the Atlantic.

I say that the odor came to greet you. For what? If it did not come to destroy you it certainly came to defeat you. If you had to attach a participle, *drifting* and *wafturing* would not qualify. *Drilling* is more like it, but what kind of an odor drills? Aggressive, pernicious, it attached itself to you, penetrating the fibers of your clothing, the pores of your skin, the ways into your lungs and your heart. Terrorism. In a phone conversation tapped by federal authorities, a Yemeni terrorist said: "The fire has been lit and is awaiting only the wind." The wind he was talking about carried it that Tuesday, but less partisan winds continued to carry the fire for months. Well into November that vile stifling odor still dominated the air, fuming its way up the island. Everyone in New York must have smelled it and, thinking about the liars at the EPA and all the other complicitous agencies, must have said, at least once: "*Safe* levels? Safe levels of *what?*" If I had gone back to Montmartre in order to write another novel about Matisse I'd have found *safe levels,* not here. Because of that odor, no one in Lower Manhattan could escape intimate knowledge of the disaster that changed the temperature of a beautiful day by two thousand degrees.

Amazing. Here is an urban environment so supremely smoke-conscious that, half a year later, the board of a luxury co-op on West End Avenue, close to Lincoln Center, would deny new dwellers the right to smoke in their own apartments, and yet ten men have, in a sense, arranged to smoke in everybody's apartment. I do not mean to be frivolous in making this connection, I simply could not get over the fact that such a season of homicide, hysteria, despair, dislocation, toxicity, insomnia, unemployment, and daily consternation could have been visited on Manhattan by a small pack of monomaniacs.

On the 1st of December I was photographing a section of Twin Tower being hoisted into a barge on the East River. As it was necessary to work without a tripod, I was trailing the smooth trajectory of the big Weeks crane as it swept out over the water by seating the camera on my scarf and sliding the scarf along the surface of a marbled composition book. A fire broke out toward the south end of the island—it was around Moore Street—sending smoke clouds billowing toward the water. Fire trucks sped down the FDR Drive. Knots of people gathered. Cops redirected traffic. I was trying to stay focused and did not want to become a journalist who chases fires, but it occurred to me that I would be a moax if I neglected a new nightmare erupting down the street in order to shoot the detritus of an old one. Blowback, the CIA's gift to the population, isn't a temporary endowment: it will rule and shape this country with the constancy of the Constitution, and as little was being done to forestall a fresh assault as was done to impede the last one. Division between the acts of anticipation and remembrance had been narrowed down to nothing. Everybody working around the site, or living there, looked up whenever a jet sounded above them. The wheels of a Mack could turn a steel streetplate into a thundersheet re-creating the ten-second storms of 9:59 and 10:28. Even the sirens and the bleats of fire engines, cop cars and ambulances were plangent quotations from September. So I went to have a look, camera ready, feeling as if I were working at someone else's occupation.

I think it was on Broad Street that I passed a black woman in her sixties who was walking out of her building. With a calm, almost whimsical dismay that made me wish I'd had the camera turned on, she said to herself: "O lord—what's burnin now?" That sentence carried a history, and you can bet that the odor I have labored to evoke was central to it. If I were another director I would record that line with an actress and insert it into my film as if it were part of a wild track. One could position it anywhere, use it repeatedly as a refrain: "O lord—what's burnin now?" But my sketch of this woman needs revision. She was alone, but she was not really talking to herself. I doubt that it was the Lord she was talking to either. I think she was talking to the world in which madmen burn New York or any city in which people are trying to live a decent life. It was almost as if she had said:

BEHIND THE GREEN DOOR

"O lord—what're *they* burnin now?" The hinge of that verb, that *burnin,* to the events of September 11 interested me. The Towers were punched open, the Towers gave, the Towers fell, and as they fell they rose again as two huge black hands coming to choke and smother and sweep the streets of anybody in them. The fact that it was all in the blink of an eye doesn't matter because time adjusts to catastrophe: brief, sudden traumas are allowed to repeat themselves and reverberate forever. But the Towers also burned, and they did so unforgettably. Everyone, even New Yorkers who weren't in town that Tuesday, smelled it interminably, an odor that even attacked lamentation itself, granting it no quarter in which to breathe. Heraclitus was right: *in the abysmal darkness, things are known by their scent.*

Seven months later I asked David Stanke, a resident of 114 Liberty Street, which is directly opposite the site, about the effects of the odor on his life. David's small white building, constructed around 1913, has had a lucky star above it, for it survived the wide brute demolition of the area when the Towers were put up, and survived it once again when the Towers were put down, although all of its Liberty windows were fatally blasted; a beam of the South Tower had gouged a section of its façade; and its homes had been bombarded with a rubble of office equipment, shards of tinted window glass, slats of venetian blinds, bricks, aluminum, cameras, pottery, paper, steel, photographs, furniture, sheetrock, ceiling tiles, spaceage plastics, portland cement, foam insulation, and organic illustrations of *Gray's Anatomy*—all of it coated with lethal dust. Dumpsters full of Twin Tower and 767 had to be craned off its roof. In a small central fire-escaped lightshaft between 114 and the neighboring 120 (125 Cedar), you could see, even in May, a display of articles that could make you wish you hadn't gone to the window. As 114 was not yet habitable, the Stankes and their four little children—all of whom were directly under the Towers during the tumult, with David in the same mad streets trying to find them—had lived in five locations since the attack.

David's reaction to my query was charged with his adversary relation to the odor.

"It was a cloud on my life," he said, "and a cloud on everyone's life. It impacted you physically and immediately. You had to think: 'I shouldn't be breathing this.' But you couldn't move to the other side of the room and you couldn't get rid of it. You couldn't do *anything.* When I went through the subways the first time, I thought: 'O my God, this is the smell from when it happened—it just stayed down here because there's not enough air to clear it out.' I didn't realize it was ongoing smoke. It took me a while to see that it was a *living* odor, not merely a *lingering* one. We had moved to a temporary apartment in TriBeCa, thinking: 'It can't smoke down there forever. The fires will all go out—they can't last that much longer—they *can't*—the smoke will stop, and we'll all feel better.' But the smoke just kept pouring out. You would sit there thinking: 'God, what can we do?' We couldn't close the windows because the air *in* the building was really bad, so we ran air conditioners and heaters at the same time to get some filtered air and yet not be frozen. It wasn't until December that you finally stopped smelling it everywhere."

The apartment in which David had been staying was near the Holland Tunnel, which is three subway stops north of the site.

"Any car coming into Manhattan out of that tunnel," he said, "the first thing that hit them was the odor. I had a friend in Soho who was in a serious funk about it. She wore a mask, she didn't like going back to her house, and she kept saying to me: 'Don't go back, don't go back—that odor is too much.' The odor was a reminder: it kept September 11 in everybody's face. You could look away, but you couldn't turn your nose off."

Donavin Gratz, a carpenter who converted old Liberty from a commercial to a residential building and who, after September 11, was hired by the co-op to secure it from looters and to retrieve it from the city and make it habitable again, said: "Not really knowing *what* you were breathing. *All the time*. Green smoke comin up everywhere out of these shafts. Unforgettable. Days it was blowing into the building I gave everybody off because we just couldn't *breathe* that shit."

Donavin and I were on the filthy black overhang of the Liberty rooftop with the huge gape of the site directly below us. Although he has a lively, charismatic presence, the stats on Donavin are nothing extraordinary: medium height, medium build, medium-length brown hair; but Donavin is one of the toughest men I know, and in his scrappier moods he has faced off with FBI, advanced upon construction men three times his size, and climbed out of his truck to treat with any breathing portion of Lower Manhattan that tried to thwart his objectives at Ground Zero. Mayor Bloomberg referred to him as "that guy from Liberty Street." But the odor was beyond him. You couldn't scrap with that, and Donavin exhibited a tangle of two frustrations: one with the memory of the discomfiture, the other with the task of describing the indescribable, which could not be separated from believing the unbelievable.

"Horrible," he said. It was 2002 and the odor was mostly gone but he was suddenly transfixed, as if he were *seeing* the odor as it advanced across the roof at him, hating it all over again. "Days it would come directly at us on the wind, it was: 'What the hell is *that?*' It was . . . *plastic,* it was . . . I don't know *what* it was. Ten thousand ballasts that were all melted together from fluorescent lights, computers, everything that was in there."

The first time he walked me around at 114, Donavin and his men slid a plank of plywood from one of the walls that were hammered by the collapse, so that the grapplers and dumptrucks were visible from the room where you stood around dusty red couches and stacks of window panes that retained only jagged filthy perimeters of glass. Going to look out, he said: "Is it a good day or a bad day?" This was in December, but Donavin wasn't talking about the look of Ground Zero—it was pretty much looking progressively cleaner to everybody—he was talking about the smell.

At the start of my first morning with the camera, the first sight to capture me the moment I reached the frozen zone, beyond which a citizen couldn't stray without a pass, was a cop who was walking with an apple in one hand, a respirator in the other. He wasn't dusted or disheveled. He walked slowly to a squad car and climbed into the back seat. The car made a three-point turn and drove north up Broadway, a one-way street going south. Nothing spectacular there, or worthy of comment, excepting the fact that a respirator was walking through the Financial District of New York City, a placement of object that should not be seen in a civilized world. In that entire day, however, the only respirator I saw doing the job for which it was made was on the face of a photographer on West Street who looked as if he'd been shooting since the 11th. A loudmouthed cop threatened someone with arrest for having turned around and taken another picture after she'd told him not to shoot in that direction—"Don't you play with *me!*"—but the guy with the respirator must have had it customized to filter sound out as well, for he ignored the altercation and continued to shoot around it as if he were working in a world, albeit a subworld, to which his entitlements were every much in order as any worker with a badge and a uniform, an attitude I found characteristic of anybody who worked the site successfully. I was going to try it myself until a troop of National Guard marching up from Battery Park made me think that maybe this was not the time. That day a few Downtowners, very few, wore those white paper wafers-on-a-string that carry labels warning you of their worthlessness. Psychologically they must have helped people who had had enough of thinking rationally about danger for a while, and they might have degraded the odor, but the only relief *I* could imagine was to split. Splitting, though, was not enough. It was dawn when I arrived at the site, but late that night on Long Island it would be there in my nostrils, making them bleed, sickening every breath. The room in which I quarantined my clothing reeked of the site for more than a week, as if my jacket, my cap, and my scarf had started a fire of their own. One did not need to enter the room to smell it: it would find you as you passed the door. Mark Wagner, an architect engaged in tagging items from the site for an historical archive, told me that he went to California for a vacation, opened his suitcase, and realized the coat he had worn to Ground Zero was unwearably permeated with the stench of the pile, which had followed him cross-country and was setting up house on the West Coast.

When David Stanke invited Stefania Masoni, a feng shui master, to cleanse his apartment and to liberate the spirits she had located there, she coaxed her own ceremonial plumes everywhere, including the keyhole of a cabinet she couldn't open, displacing the odor of one smoke with that of another. With a trancelike purpose she moved her scents around swiftly, but witnessing was good, she said, so I followed her room to room, playing the part of three cameras, inhaling more smoke than any cupboard or any transient dwellers there. It was interesting to watch her in this peaceful act of cleansing while there were hundreds of men across the street cleansing another way; interesting, too, to watch David. Formally trained for business, David was smart enough to know that to give this experiment a fair enough shake it was best for him to bracket skepticism and surrender to the motion of the procedure. He has a tall, slender frame, close-cropped white hair, the most perfect skin I have seen on any man, and the handsome youthful face of a print model—hardly inscrutable; but zooming in on it, it was hard even to tell if he was looking at the present, the future, or the past on Liberty Street. This was good for the film: the face neither demeaned nor extolled the ceremony. It watched. Or so it seemed. As I chased behind Stefania, I recalled what David had said to me a week before: "I'd hate to think that there were souls trapped here who were waiting to be released." A slight catch in his voice told me as much about David as the keen observations I was hearing in many hours of conversation at Ground Zero. But the truth is that no manner of incense, however infused with prayer or invocation, was proof against the meridians of dark rancorous energy that had crossed Liberty Street.

When I asked Stefania, hesitantly, whether feng shui could ever be applied to the site itself, she answered instantly: "That's my dream." She wanted to tackle it with a team, although she did not say *tackle* and her method, more esoteric than the one she used for David, was not clear to me. I didn't pursue it because I knew it would never happen, but we did entertain various means of getting a feng shui squad into the pit. The image of a half-dozen monks or other masters spreading out across the site, like Oriental ghost-busters, in workboots, hardhats, and respirators with flashlights and feng shui paraphernalia was no more mad than anything else in Lower Manhattan during the time I was shooting. Tex McCrary, a storied oldtimer you will meet in another chapter, called Lower Manhattan "the last great frontier town in America for a good idea." At this time especially, jokers were wild: almost anybody could make things happen that made a difference, or at least made sense.

During the first few weeks, 114 was a command post for firefighters who used it as a means of watching the pile from the Liberty windows. Out of a speaker on the sixth floor an alert signal blasted to evacuate the site in the event of instability. That dust-impacted speaker, now a historical artifact, was left lying around just waiting to be claimed for a museum since the day Donavin took it out of the window. One day, before their own building had been repaired, the firefighters of Ladder 10, Engine 10, who are housed at the intersection of Liberty and Greenwich, hung a big new sign above the door of the Ten House:

TEN

ENGINE TRUCK

OPEN FOR BUSINESS

Never mind that they didn't have a truck, and if they did they couldn't have brought it into the house or into the street. The will was there, the fight was in them. But there were hollowed-out dreams on that street, along with fractured hearts, falls from grace, suicidal predilections, heated correspondences, fights—fights everywhere—fights with City officials, with federal agencies, with unions, with cops, with insurers, with the mayor—threats of demolition, protracted nightmares, water leaks, byzantine bureaucracies, and toxic infestations at 114 in the face of which fire hoses were useless. Whether feng shui fared any better is hard to say.

One morning in mid-May we were sitting in some of the chairs that had been left in David's place when David spoke about the odor as if it were something out of *Alien*. "When the people doing repairs began to investigate the ductwork, opening vents, drilling, checking for contamination, the odor of September 11—and this was January, February—rushed right back out again. The air, with the odor of that day, had been lurking up there in exactly the same shape and form." In late July, going to meet Donavin at his apartment on Pearl Street, I was turning the corner at Maiden Lane and Broadway when the odor of the site, which had left me alone for half a year, halted me, spun me around, and turned me into a nose with a man attached. Given the animal urgency with which I sniffed the corner in circles, trying to situate the odor, it surprised me that no one else was similarly engaged. Had some Broadway renovation, or a new excavation in the construction of the PATH train in front of Liberty Street, exposed some subsurface fire that was burning beyond the official limit, or otherwise dislodged a lost pocket of the 11th? When I mentioned it to Donavin he answered with a single word— "*Where?*"—and it was charged with the intensity of interest and the immediacy with which two people will discuss an old foe. You'd rather not see him again, but if he is around you need to know exactly where, and you want the higher ground.

When I discussed this phenomenon with Owen Burdick, director of music at Trinity Church, he said: "They could put you anywhere on the planet and if you smelled that odor again, you would know it *instantly*. You'll know it for the rest of your life. The burnt wire, the burnt steel, the burnt flesh, that had almost a sweet, sickening, acrid . . . there was a kind of a . . . it just . . ." His reach for articulation was familiar. "I don't remember the day the odor turned off," Owen said, "but we were down here in our offices and the smell was just *constant*."

The odor, like the dust from both collapses, entered Trinity Church by invisible means, for apart from a few pieces none of its stained glass had broken, and the windows hadn't been open because they aren't openable.

One morning I was walking along Exchange Place, approaching the intersection of New Street, when a woman who was coming up behind me started singing in a brave, clear, incredibly relaxed gospel voice: "I am washed in the blood of the lamb."

No one in the Wall Street crowd seemed to care, or even to notice her. Perhaps they were used to her, perhaps they were lost in the start of their own day. I hung back to let her pass, then I followed along behind her, listening to her sing until she entered a jewelry store. It was morning. It was September. It was bright. It was summery. It was much like that terrible Tuesday, people told me, as they looked up into the sky. The woman appeared to be on her way to work. I wanted to follow her farther and to record at least a refrain or two by turning the camera on, but it was a rather intensely federal day, for Wall Street was hosting, at Federal Hall, the first joint session of Congress there since 1789, and tailing a gospel woman felt mildly imprudent. If even the thought of congressional oversight can turn me toward the criminal class, three hundred senators and reps a block away made me want to run for cover, which is exactly what I did. But like the woman I overheard on Broad Street, this voice wouldn't leave me.

"I am washed in the blood of the lamb."

She had to be singing about the 11th. If she weren't, I would not have been able to hear her. But what did she mean by that? *Washed in the blood of the lamb*. Could the power of religion that helped propel some of the savages into the World Trade Center have carried this woman back to work? I wondered how soon after the hour of the catastrophe this woman was able to sing. I wanted her to come out of the store, wanted to ask her, politely: "When the streets stank to hell were you singing the same way?" I wondered, stupidly: *Can you be cleansed by toxic dust if the blood of the lamb is in it?* I wondered whether her words might not be taken literally. "I am washed in the blood of the lamb" could be a simple statement of fact, meaning: "Today is September 11. Every day is September 11," in the way that a Christian would say: "Today is Easter Sunday. Every day is Easter Sunday." If what was burnin now was the blood of the lamb for her, perhaps she had welcomed, with open arms, the storm of whirling ash as it pushed across Exchange Place, much the way the bookwoman in *Fahrenheit 451*—Truffaut's film of the Bradbury novel—takes a stand within the flames as the firemen, the book police, burn her library. The flames and the woman embrace each other: ecstasy, evoking Joan of Arc. I wondered whether there mightn't have been one single person, someone in the Towers, someone in the streets, whose life could have been saved but who decided their deliverance had come and let it take them. If, as Hamlet says, there is a special providence in the fall of a sparrow, there must be one in the fall of those towering Rockefellers and the souls who went with them, but I was not convinced by the people who were stepping up to claim it as theirs. "It was a miracle," "God was with me," as if omnipotence picks and plays its little favorites by the hour. This song, though, this testimony— it made an irrational sense to me. *Washed in the blood of the lamb*. I didn't know about blood, blood from any source, but I wouldn't have minded a cleansing myself. I was as much to blame for those attacks as anybody.

A Wilfred Owen verse, "Spring Offensive," about young English soldiers who, *knowing their feet had come to the end of the world*, were mowed down in France during World War I, contains this line: *Some say God caught them even before they fell.* We shouldn't have to be God to do that; or, if we have to be, well then we should be God. The least I should have done was to catch them as they fell: the Towers, the jumpers, the men and women for whom, like the soldiers in Owen's poem, *instantly the whole sky burned with fury / Against them.* What if the dust and the stench you were trying to shake off were there to purify your soul? "I am washed in the blood of the lamb." *What the hell does that mean on New Street in Lower Manhattan?*

I didn't know who to ask. I only asked Owen Burdick, as we sat in his small Trinity office, to sing a hymn for me, one that is woven around the twenty-third Psalm, which he sang for the dying when the Twin Towers were burning, an act of compassion that I wouldn't have imagined: singing beautiful verses, offering them up, not to save your own skin but to sanctify the painful separation of body and soul—a way that Owen, perhaps, was able to catch them before they fell.

During that first October night, as I screened the first footage I had shot in the neighborhood, I tried, repeatedly, to blow the smoldering out of my nose, but the fact is, *I* was in the process of becoming Ground Zero. So was Ray, my companion during the first half-year of these excursions; so was everybody down there. And becoming Ground Zero meant, of course, becoming the World Trade Center. Often, over the course of the following months, sitting in front of the monitor, chronicling my footage, scratching out the notations that would serve as steppingstones when it was time to cut the two hundred hours into a picture, I would smell it quite clearly but without knowing why. Was it there on my person—was it a bag, a piece of clothing, a patch of carpet—or had something in the tape stirred a memory of the senses? I could not pin it down but it could never be confused with anything else, and it is mystifying to me that the World Trade Center should have possessed me through the odor of its demise.

I have juxtaposed the odor of the site with the word *terrorism* because the odor was malicious enough to bear the identification. And, after all, if it hadn't been for terrorists we wouldn't have smelled anything. For one malodorous atmosphere to signify the attacker and the attacked does not entail a fault in logic, for they were burning together. Still, no one thought of the odor as *them*, the terrorists; one thought of it as *a result of what they did.* But this morning I happened to hear an Elizabethan madrigal by the composer John Weelkes that includes this phrase: *we die in earnest.* If men and women

BEHIND THE GREEN DOOR

do, can't our buildings do it too? Thanks to a few bright words by a Chichester musician four centuries ago, it now strikes me as peculiar to have expected the Twin Towers to have died any the less earnestly than any other American giants, or that I should have expected the dying to be any the less intrusive into the life of Lower Manhattan than the buildings themselves. "Ho—Christ—is that *it*?" I should have answered my own question: "That's it, that's the World Trade Center dying in earnest." I hate to think of this but the phrase can be equally attached to the deviled adventurers who piloted those planes.

It isn't entirely accurate to say that everybody remembered the odor of the site with great discomfort and a sense of the indescribable. When I mentioned it to Gautam Patel, proprietor of Smoker's Choice, a small cigar store with an oldstyle plaster Indian Chief by its door, which is a few paces east of Park Row on Beekman Street, it brought to mind something else. "The starting smell," Gautam said in his high, gentle voice, "we are very used to this smell because we are Hindu and we burn the body."

I was taken by surprise.

"When our relatives die," he said, "we go to Bangkok River or we go to cemetery and we burn them. And that smell, when the body burning, we know, because we are standing there for two hours, three while the body burns, then we get the ashes and go home. And in India we live wall-to-wall—Hindu, Muslim, Hindu—very close, so a lot of times trouble comes, riot comes, fighting—sticks, beatings—and a lot of people die together—fifty, hundred—and we go collect the bodies into a pile in the woods and we burn them. Because Hindu people they don't bury the dead in the land. So that smell that I smell here is not a strange smell for me."

Before managing cigar stores, including one down in the subway under the World Trade Center where his nephew, its proprietor, felt the earthquake of American Flight 11 pounding the North Tower, Gautam was a journalist in India. After September 11 he wrote, in his native language, a series of poems—"Two Tears," "The Death of New York"—which he published in newspapers in New Jersey and in India, displaying linguistic talents not as evident in his conversational English.

"How many bodies we consider?" he asked.

We were standing in the humidor in which he kept his best cigars, including the Don Diegos I would smoke occasionally in refreshment from the scent off the pile. I had talked in this cramped olfactorium with a young firefighter who, from under the black brim of his enameled leather helmet, told me about his cigar of choice, which was big, vanilla flavored and not cheap. I was giving money to Stephen, Gautam's assistant, when the firefighter returned to get another pack of matches. The pack with which he had tried to light his cigar out on the street had combusted in his hand, as if a hand off the site would have retained sufficient heat to ignite it.

"In India," Gautam said, "one thousand and two hundred bodies in one place, and that smell is very worse than this place. Month, it comes, slow by slow, everybody's nose is used to. Go home Friday, Monday you come back you smell like this for up to three months. You put a mask, but later on we quit the mask also. Ten, fifteen days you use it, but working in the store it feels weird. Good for your body, but you don't work with the mask."

"So," I said, "inside that odor that had the burning of the chemicals, the steel and the rubber you could smell, through that—"

"The bodies. I smell the bodies."

Owen Burdick recalls a walk in the St. Paul's churchyard amongst pieces of clothing, half-buried file cabinets and body parts that were later taken away by federal agents, but only once did the odor of death assert itself to him (Owen used the word *assault*), and that was not around either of Trinity's churches but in the Fulton Street station from which I first approached the site. It was a morning in September before the station was closed for cleaning, at a time when Owen occasionally assumed the garb of a priest in order to pass the checkpoints and get to his business in the church, where his great Aeolian Skinner, with pipes like an array of artillery shells, now contained some of the dead for whom he had played it. When the doors of the subway opened, Owen stepped onto the platform with a woman on each side of him, one older, one younger. The unmistakable odor of rotting flesh was so severe that the women vomited simultaneously.

In mentioning the sign in the Fulton Street subway with the Twin Towers on it and the arrow directing you downward, I neglected the green door standing beside it.

That door . . .

If Hawthorne were here he would build a novel around it, a little gray punisher full of antithetical wonderments, mysterious provocations, suffocative atmospheres. Whenever I trudged along Fulton Street, tied up in bags full of equipment like a burro, I was drawn to try the handle on this archetypal dreamdoor—tall, wide, heavy—but I resisted the invitation to make the descent, perhaps out of respect for the thought, if not the reality, of the netherworld behind it. I have stood in the bedrock bottom of the site and I have seen, up close, on a beautiful May evening, the long Druidic rite in which the last column of steel from the foundation of Tower Two was quite formally deflagged with a symbolic spray of fire ("For all the trades!"), a salute, and a trumpeted taps before it was hoisted out and dressed in black on the bed of a Mack truck, graced with a wreath of flowers, and draped with a flag again at a time when the site seemed miraculously quiet, clean, and uncompromised by the commotion that had shaped its identity for months. The huge rusty brown beam, totemically brightened now with a patchwork of pasted insignias, photographs fixed with multicolored strips of tape, and commemorative graffiti, some of it signifying the lost, painted in freehand or stenciled— **PAPD 37** — **FR. MIKE**—**CARPENTERS 18**—**FDNY 343**—**NYPD 23**—was still dripping dust, as it was lowered slowly down, from those places where bolted brackets and jagged chunks of concrete testified that it had attached to a larger body. But thus appointed to represent a diversity of interests—dressed up and accoutreed, so to speak, for the occasion—the Last Beam, genuine though it was, wore an aspect of theater compared with the inscrutably mute and unadorned power of the Bathtub itself. Those walls. O mercy. I ought not to have seen them. No one should have seen them: they were made to stay buried. Their faces were studded with tiebacks and you could see from everywhere the cast-iron hole from the old Hudson-Manhattan subway tunnel that brought the first Jersey passengers into an underground mall beneath the original Twin Towers—the huge Hudson Terminal, two redbrick skyscrapers, twenty-two stories each, between Church and Greenwich streets—but more than one person, myself included, remarked on a resemblance in these walls to something Roman, old Roman, exactly what didn't matter, for theirs was an unnatural power that was not of this city or this age, and comparisons were fundamentally cries of astonishment. You could be sure that anybody who said "To me it's just a hole in the ground" hadn't looked into it in any of its stages. Walking down into its ponderous atmosphere was something else again. *Where is Hart Crane?* I thought. *Where's old Walt? Where's Poe? Where the hell is Charlie Parker? Kerouac? Henry Miller? Don't leave me alone, boys, in this diabolical place, shoulder to shoulder with Donavin, holding this goddamned camera.* But Donavin, who barely said a word, *was* the ally

Dust pours off the last big beam of the Twin Towers as it lowers onto a long flatbed during a ceremony in May, 2002. Windows on Liberty Street are visible behind it.

for me—*was* Whitman, *was* Miller, *was* Bird—a flawed, brave, independent American spirit who, surrounded by every uniform, hardhat and badge on the island of Manhattan, told me to take out the camera.

"But that detective."

"Forget it—he's a blowjob."

"But this is not the place to make trouble."

"Take it out, turn it on, I promise you'll thank me for it."

So I shot the ceremony, but my fear of being dragged away could not hold a candle to my fear of those monster gray walls that comprised what was known as the Bathtub, although its purpose was to keep the Hudson *out* of the Twin Towers. The World Trade Center was now a vast open cellar of which we were standing on the floor and in which Scotch pipes were playing and time itself appeared to be sorely confused. Despite one spontaneous outburst—"U! S! A!"—there was a motion toward serenity that I found disquieting, but I was disquieted anyway, pressured by poltergeists over the fact that the pride of building the Twin Towers here was superseded by the pride of having hauled them out as junk.

BEHIND THE GREEN DOOR

Still, it *was* a splendid spring evening and, at seven stories under, the noise of Lower Manhattan was inaudible. Every inch of videotape from any space around the site, even when the microphone aimed due south in the direction of Battery Park from the far back room of a Liberty Street apartment, was tracked with the harsh metallic turbulence of the work, and pierced by the ubiquitous backup beeps of grapplers and trucks. Not now. Not tonight. Not one gear turned except to take that beam down. It even smelled remarkably ordinary, almost fresh, something I thought I'd never encounter. Two things seemed certain. One: *the Twin Towers were totally gone.* Two: *the burning was over.* Technically speaking the World Trade fires burned for precisely a hundred days until, on December 19, they were formally declared to have been extinguished. I could believe it. Nevertheless I am convinced that the green door at Fulton Street, taken by the right man at the wrong time, will lead to that furious subterranean hellfire that began one Tuesday morning and is still, for some people, burning, and with the door locked behind them.

WORSE FOR THEM

Despite the burning, the smoke, and the engines of deconstruction it was cold in Lower Manhattan from mid-October to mid-March, even cold, sometimes, for men whose workboots and steel-toed safety shoes were softened and burnt through by the ferocity of the rubble, in which temperatures ranged from 400 to 2,800 degrees. For my friend Ray and I the phrase *down there freezing our asses off* started many a sentence about these excursions in Lower Manhattan. That we were vagrants with nowhere to go—when people asked us who we were *with*, which they did compulsively, I would tell them we were *without*—kept us at a disadvantage. Cold for an hour or two is not the same as cold for ten. After a long night shooting through a cold Christmas Eve I was walking up Broadway, dining on a container of mashed potatoes, puzzled as to why every New Yorker in the streets appeared to be coping with the weather while my own teeth clattered like a cartoon character. Then I realized an elemental fact: *they are all going from one place to another.* I was seldom in that position. Unlike journalists or crews on assignment, I worked for nobody and I had no appointments to draw me into congenial spaces. That came later, and intermittently. My task was in the streets, on rooftops, or in the unheated rooms of evacuated buildings. That was how I wanted it. You could say that I spent a year and a half trying to get closer to the least congenial spaces down there.

Nor was anybody complicit in cutting me loose in that deranged neighborhood that turned everyone into anthropophagi and made every spectator, every passing traveler, a participant as long as they drew a breath. I went there uninvited, unencouraged, and no one would have cared if I never went again. Naturally, most of the people that I knew wanted to have a normal day, a normal day despite the fact that the city was on fire and its citizens, commingled with their Arab annihilators, were scattered to the feathers of fucked-out pigeons, the tire treads of Macks, Kenworths, Peterbilts and Freightliners, the grids of **DONT WALK** signs and subway mezzanines, the bed of the Hudson River, as far north as Rochester where some of the ash was found, and as far east as India where some of the scrap was freighted free of export restrictions on contaminants that may have clung to it. When the Rockefellers tore down fourteen blocks in order to build the Trade Center, they ruined a lot of life in Lower Manhattan, starting in 1966 when the Ajax Wrecking Company went to work on what had been an entire neighborhood, one that included the Washington Market and Radio Row. How it was destroyed and what it meant should be better excavated, especially as the world that summarily displaced it is gone now as well. Historian Mike Wallace has suggested that the loss of Radio Row—that funky little electronic city—is symbolic of a missed opportunity for Manhattan to develop its own Silicon Valley (Silicon Alley, as he puts it), but one need not subscribe to this notion, or even care about it, to see it as a distinctive neighborhood.[3] The World Trade Center was a neighborhood as well. "It was a unique community," Tex McCrary told me, "I would say unique in history, but it was *my* community." Now the World Trade cornerstone that Tex, at least notionally, had once helped to lay was stashed away in a man's garage . . . and in my own garage at home there were clots of Trade Center forming little gray mounds where I kept my workboots . . . but it was *a normal day*, not to be disrupted by the fact that Peter was peering, perversely, into a hole. Not until late spring of 2005 did another human being sit me down across from him with a series of pointed questions, and that was another filmmaker, Eric Eason (director of *Manito*), before he looked at *Liberty Street,* which I had just completed. During the time I was shooting there was only one question from the people that I met: "What *kind* of a movie—is this fiction, or documentary?" However often it was put it always took me by surprise, making me wonder whether they knew, even, what Ground Zero was. Did they think it was an option to bring Matt Damon down there to shoot a love story? Perhaps the question arose out of a feeling that a love story would have been preferable.

The movie *is* a love story ("the lens of the little Sony starts to fall for this incredible neighborhood, but it's a love that has to hide," etc), only you couldn't love the weather. Between the cold, the odor, and the hailstorms of particles that were flying out of the site, the wind off those waters was a mean aggravator. Despite what was said, early on, about the weather having favored firefighting, one could not escape the feeling that Nature, who bestowed on the terrorists a balmy blue morning in which to kill, was being spiteful to the recovery and the removal. The teams of underslept firefighters who came after a shift at their own firehouses to stand another in that disjunctive wasteland, examining every clawful of rank ashen earth for even a slither of remains, often on their knees digging with trowels or with their ungloved hands, were undertaking the worst of jobs in the worst kinds of weather. When I first met a sturdy hulk of a firefighter they nicknamed ATV Mike because he traveled everywhere on a muddy green John Deere Gator, the word *weathered* applied to him in every way. The combination of safety glasses, wide dark beard extenuated by a gray-filtered respirator hanging just below it, and a pair of yellow flashlights bolted to the sides of his red hardhat put me in mind of Wagner—Wagner as staged by the director of *Mad Max*— but ATV Mike was, in fact, softspoken, understated, not at all operatic. When you saw him taking a break in one of the pews under the gay-colored support banners and Waterford chandeliers in the city's oldest church, little St. Paul's Chapel, where he also went to sleep, you understood that he was as much wearing his church as sitting in one, and when he referred to his Gator— "It's been through *all* of it—it's holdin up—I take care of it"—it wasn't much different from how he spoke about himself: "I'm here every day, yeah. I'm holdin up fine. Until my mission's complete." When I asked him when he was leaving Ground Zero he answered me without a trace of bravado: "When the last person is taken out of there and there's nothing left. It's seven days a week, twenty-four hours, whether we're here or whether we're not. We're all here emotionally." The image of ATV Mike was, to me, so symbolic of a type of dedication to the site and indifference to (defiance of) discomfort and fatigue that when I saw him in July and we nodded to each other as he passed me on Cedar Street, which is a block south of Liberty, he and his trusted Gator looking rested and clean and the respirator gone now from his chest, I could not quite imagine what he was doing in the world, a world that had moved toward renewal and reconstruction. One could say that he was himself again but I saw it differently. When you fit into a transitory world so perfectly perhaps there is no place for you ever again. Donavin, who was in Brooklyn that day, must have felt the lasting power of his presence, for when I tried to tell him about it and I misplaced the name, saying: "Guess who I saw driving by? It was Frank," Donavin said: "No. You mean ATV Mike," as if Mike were the only man I could have seen in the busy streets.

As for the cleanup, that staggering enterprise never shut down, not for rain, not for snow, not for anything at all save a severe electrical storm, a ceremony, or a photo opportunity for the executive branch of government. But

BEHIND THE GREEN DOOR

I never heard anybody complain, not even where the weather was the fiercest: at the Weeks Marine sites, where the big beams—Pier 6 on the East River—and the tangles of trash and rebar spaghetti—Pier 25 on the Hudson—were being loaded onto barges and tugged off the island. The media kept away from these ancillary locations, perhaps regarding them as insufficiently graphic or just too fucking cold to be worth the bother, but for me these geographically marginal waterfronts were pivotal factors in the story. I returned to Pier 6 regularly and with fresh anticipation, not caring that the picture there tonight was much the same as the night before. A truck would emerge from the underpass adjacent the Governor's Island Ferry, it would lumber up South Street, pass the heliport at the place where the FDR Drive originates, and stop for long enough, only long enough, for its cargo, sometimes a single huge beam, to be unchained and hoisted, perhaps still steaming, into one of the two barges on either side of a big red crane that was labeled, in white letters over the red: **WEEKS 504.** After a pause of a second or two you would hear the weighty drop, one of the last sounds that the Towers were going to make until the scrap was transformed into nuclear reactors, warships, Toyotas, razor blades, whatever they make from punished steel. When the crane operator tested his grip, opening and closing the teeth of his twenty-ton Esco bucket, or if a beam dropped back down a foot or two, the bed of the truck would sink and rumble, reminding you of the weight—twenty-five, thirty-five, forty-five tons—and of why, in each case, the shape of the flatbed—normally rising upward like the arc of a suspension bridge—was totally reversed so that it sagged into the street, and of why, at any time, at least one or two brokeback Macks were incapacitated along West Street. One teamster bragged to me about the number of trucks that were forced to bite the dust under his usage. One dockbuilder, Tom, said: "It's hard to finesse this stuff off a flatbed. It's hard enough off the ground. We have walkie-talkies—and there's a lot of yelling." Another dockbuilder, Anthony, expanded upon the difficulties. "It's demolition steel," he said. "It doesn't have pickeyes. A pickeye is a hole you blow through the steel that you can shackle up with spreader cables, or a hook, to safely swing the steel. Without it, you try to take as good a bite as you can and hope for the best. We try not to beat up on the trailers too much. But the crane operator can't see the back of the truck and the bucket can twist them up pretty hard. We're basically here to keep the operator honest. But this area is really beaten up from steel dropping and all the trucks driving through. The road's damaged, and the bulkheads are sinking."

Rudy Wohl, a port captain in the towing division of Weeks Marine who was there within forty-eight hours of the attacks, told me about the very first night at Pier 6, Friday the 14th, when sixty-eight trucks were offloaded.

"I loaded the first barge," Rudy said. "Those pieces with three beams and a plate that connects them? They would come in with other pieces wedged into that. A couple of times I watched the back wheels of the crane creep up off the track. A crane will tilt up occasionally, but there is a counterweight, a big huge block, that gives it its center of gravity, keeps it from toppling—but there's nothing to hold the crane *on*. Cranes aren't complicated equipment: a bunch of moving parts. So that night I'm telling the operator: 'Yeah . . . you know . . . you can do it, but . . .' Crane ratings have built-in safety factors, but if you reach that limit all bets are off. The result could be devastating, so it's important to measure the pieces and find out the density of the material. You also look to see how many feet a barge is drawing and you calculate the tonnage. You use a displacement formula. You should've seen me in those first five days with the loading books, figuring everything out with all these tables. 'Okay, let's see . . .'"

Occasionally an item that was brought to Pier 6 by mistake—an elevator engine, or some squashed twist of a thing that you guessed had been a truck—would be sitting on the sidelines waiting to be carried to the Fresh Kills detectives. Often the *Kathleen*, a handsome red tug whose lights were used, on the night of the 11th, to shine on the makeshift morgue that was waiting, just beneath the North Cove, along the Hudson River, to take in corpses that never came, sat in the glacial rough water with a stoical dignity until the steel had submerged one of the barges far enough to indicate, at the draftline, that it was ready to be towed. Scott Murray, the *Kathleen*'s master, then took the load on a ten-minute run to the Brooklyn staging area, from which the debris was transported by larger boats—the *Shelby*, the *Elizabeth*—to scrapyards and the Fresh Kills site on Staten Island. Knowing when a barge was full and how to fill it properly constituted a science in itself.

"A huge piece sinks the barge an inch or two," Rudy told me, "but an inch here is not an inch there: you've got to keep it level so it doesn't develop a list. You also have to keep the water pumped out or it's like an icicle tray: things will move. And the pieces have to be stacked, interlocked. When the barge moves, you can't have it loaded so loosely that a piece will fall on a man or a tug if a tug bumps it." And there were draft issues. "There's not much water here. If the tide was coming in I'd be looking at how many trucks I had. If the barge wasn't sinking faster than the tide was rising, and if I had a lot of trucks, I'd hold it a little longer to load another two or three hundred tons."

I was never not cold and never not mesmerized when I went to Pier 6, even if there were no trucks at all and the crane was sound asleep, for there was always a voice of gulls, always a pile of beams rising and falling with the waves, always the Brooklyn Bridge to the north and to the south the old green ferry terminal for backdrop. I never forgot for a second that the trash heap before me was the building from which my mother phoned my brother in the excitement of being up there in the clouds and it was the most incomprehensible lesson of my life, more so even than the death of my own father. Scott Murray had a similar feeling of awe about it.

"It could have been anything we were haulin around," he later told me. "That's what we do with the *Kathleen*—the work itself was no different. But I was never unaware of the contents of those barges. I'd look out all the time and say: 'My God—look at what I'm lookin at here. That's the World Trade Center.'"

Anthony, who spent thirty-six hours volunteering in the hole, starting on the morning of the 11th, knew firsthand—literally—the transporting power of the steel he was moving. "In the beginning, going down there," he said about the site, "you could put your hands on the steel and fuse with it, from when the plane made that impact with the building and all those people were killed. You could hold the steel and feel it." Rudy was able to read the beams as he guided them into the bucket. "Look at some of these larger pieces," he said as we stood on the pier. "You can see the force from how they're bent. And a lot of the steel is totally clean of concrete. You'll see small pieces [of concrete] no bigger than a foot. You can also see how well this building was constructed. If you look at the bolts you see that the bolts didn't fail: the steel itself, in many cases, was simply stripped away. The part that man put together, for joining the sections, really held up. It's a testimonial to the craftsmanship."

Pier 6: a place to study, a university for only the cost of the cold. But nobody walked there. No one much cared. Behind the tall glassy office building at 55 Water Street, an elevated plaza just south of Old Slip gave the pier its own superb viewing stand. Unlike the stand they belatedly built for seeing the site—the one situated beside the St. Paul cemetery, the one for which they lined up at a South Street kiosk for a time-stamped ticket with which to wait in line again in order to see practically nothing—the view of Pier 6 and the Manhattan world around it was never less than breathtaking.

Old New York used to face in this direction and much of the bold, unstoppable Nietzschean energy that has informed New York arrived here, came to its best and its worst expression here, loitered and marveled here, ran from here, died here, and with its three old bridges connecting the islands, its diverse water traffic, its busy streets and its elevated highway, its helicopters, its seaport, its spectacular range of architecture, its promise of high velocity, its transcendent mapping of American aspiration at every stage of its advance, it is one of the most exciting urban places in the world. Writers who have called Lower Manhattan a sleepy place must have gone there on a Sunday to cash a check. Even at its calmest it is tremendous. From the floor of the two stock exchanges alone there is a rumble. In late spring, early summer of 2002, before going to Liberty Street, I would climb to the empty mezzanine at South Street Seaport, sit in a deckchair and watch the boats, the gulls, the sun coming up over Brooklyn. No tourists or daytrippers, not at that hour. Chinese women would be dancing without music, some of them with a flag or a sword. A guy hosing down the pier, another guy sweeping up. Dogwalkers around the *Peking* and the *Ambrose*. Tai Chi. Police boat backing up to case the camera. Not much more. But I could feel, over my shoulder, the absence of the Towers; or, rather, I could feel a terrific presence and the destruction that took it away and transplanted it to the pier just a little south of me. As I looked over the wall of the plaza at Old Slip just below the First Precinct, an old limestone stationhouse of Florentine design and imposing aspect (where Popeye Doyle comes and goes in *The French Connection*), it was plain that if there were anywhere in the world for this job—managing the ruins of the World Trade Center—Pier 6 would be it. It had to have happened here. And yet in all the time I spent there I met only one other person who stopped to look, a young Brooklynite who descended from his office up in 55 Water to smoke a troubled cigarette as he talked about his view of the Twin Towers on the 11th and the way his building shook with the force of the first collapse. One sunny afternoon there the wind was so severe that Ray and I had to hide from it behind a brick wall. January, midnight, icebladed winds severed heads off shoulders and spun them around for soccer practice. The men of Pier 6, firebreathers, were undaunted. Their jobs were important, they were working long hours in a week that wouldn't end, in some cases, for three months, and they found it honorable that the truckloads of World Trade rumbling off the site, streams of them on every shift, were floating across the water because of them. On one shift alone they off-loaded 126 of the 13,000 it would take to do the job. From the first of the

BEHIND THE GREEN DOOR

Macks that rolled off the site, the blunt push onward had an enticing clarity to it: *remove more,* and it attached to the best of reasons: they were putting New York and the country back to order. It made them more American, made America more them. It was a war effort. To work was to fight. "Great job, guys," they would say into the lens as a shout out to their military counterparts, their hardhats sitting atop the hoods of sweatshirts, stocking caps and earpads. On the low wall under the FDR Drive where the teamsters stood their trucks for unloading, there was a white-painted sign facing the river:

ICE STATION
ZEBRA
EST. 09-18-01

Alongside that it said:

GOOD MORNING AMERICA

Pride won't warm you but it does tell the cold to go chase itself. Rudy, a hulk of a man with a round face, red hair and a full red beard, was patently excited by the smoothness, safety and efficiency of the removal. "The day after it happened I'd have bet my life's savings that this mess would have shut the city down, around here, for at least a year. When I first went to the site with some FEMA engineers when the fires were still burning and it was just a few workers and volunteers, I wasn't prepared for what I saw—the devastation, the carnage. Video imaging can't capture the enormity. The boom on those cranes is 220 to 250 feet. You stand next to them and they are *enormous.* But on television they look like they belong to some kid in a sandbox."

This is why, in trying to capture the crane at Pier 6 by shooting it from the East River, shooting it from boats and bridges, shooting it at dawn, and shooting it at night, I had to then shoot it from beneath the huge bucket and then climb into the cab and have the operator, an Irish master, Mickey Quinn ("You get a great view . . . Brooklyn Bridge . . . helicopters . . . I've seen the president comin in"), show me the simple controls ("Once in a while you get a visitor, not many"), turn it around for me, pick a thirty-ton beam ("Steel is steel. I always worry about the men that's underneath"), and deposit it quite neatly into a barge as the small cab shook like a paintmixer ("Feel it comin up?"). Afraid of heights, afraid of water and the East River especially, having had recurrent nightmares of falling into it, I had to ask, at each rung of the

At Pier 6 on the East River, a barge full of World Trade Center.

ladder: "This is good for the movie, right?" Ray, who watched from sealevel, said: "You looked like Jimmy Stewart in *Vertigo*." From a Weeks Marine site on the Hudson, Mickey, like Scott, had seen the second plane when it entered the South Tower, and he was on the job here, climbing his steep white ladder at dawn, the gulls gliding around him, only three days later. When I walked out of the cab and positioned myself again on the ladder, I clung to his advice: "Hang onta all them steps goin down."

"It's a rough-and-tumble industry," Rudy said, "but it pulled together to do this. Within three weeks I couldn't believe the progress. It's short of a miracle here for *all* the companies involved. Nothing is routine on this operation. People will look back in amazement at what was done, and in such a timely manner. I don't think it'll ever be over, not for the people who are involved, but the foundation of what'll be said is that it really was a tremendous group effort."

Rudy was right, but I could never see it that way. I would see a guy here, a guy there, I'd see the spotters in the hole, each with his own hoe, a restless dog sniffing around them, I would see the excavators with one seat, I would see pairs of ironworkers in small yellow cabins, I'd see the trucks with one driver leaving the site along Greenwich Street and coming to Pier 6 with one beam at a time that would be guided, sometimes by hand, by one man making gestures to Mickey Quinn, one guy up in the cab perched above the barges that were waiting for one tug with one man at the helm.

For some men, worksites helped put *them* back to order, or, at least, kept them from unraveling completely.

One night I was sipping a pint of Guinness in O'Hara's, an Irish pub on Cedar Street that faces the back of David's building. It had been closed for six months after the Towers shut it down. I had spent the day, as I spent many a day at Ground Zero, in the company of Donavin, whom I ought not to have introduced as a carpenter, for he is more than that—philosopher, daredevil, badboy, motionmaster, designer, *ébéniste*, raconteur. But my carpenter friend Donavin put down his Black and Tan, looked out the window, and set his sharp eyes on the building across the street that, in a short space of time, had swallowed a huge portion of his life and that had nearly gotten him killed, for he was there that Tuesday, anointed with exquisitely fine mists of Tower glass, running through the streets under both burning death-traps, trying to help David to find his children. "That building saved me," he said, referring to 114. "It gave me life when I was really down."

When he took a long weekend to see his wife in Santa Fe, I told him that, after a taste of that austere New Mexico beauty, he would not easily fly back to New York—but I was wrong. Donavin had liked Santa Fe, but: "I couldn't wait to get back," he said. "The plane wasn't fast enough." His complex attachment to the building was verified when, in the spring of 2002, they opened up Church and Liberty streets. Suddenly pedestrian traffic. Civilians. Ice cream. Taxis and limousines. A bicycle rickshaw. Singing Uncle Sams. "America" on a flute. Pirated portfolios: "Twin Towers! Twin Towers! Before, during, *and* after!"

"I'm a lost soul," he said.

This return to normalcy was an illusion, for nothing on that block was normal at all, and every slightest encroachment toward appearance of the normal had to be fought for, paid for, fretted over, argued. Donavin had told me: "Sometimes I stand in the shower and I'm thinking about everything that's going on and I completely forget to wash my hair or soap myself. I turn off the shower, I get out, and I haven't done anything at all—I've just stood there for ten minutes." Still, this illusion of normalcy so unmanned him that the next morning he woke up and vomited in the shower. For many men, the level of wantedness and the emotional engagement they had enjoyed at the site fell dramatically as the mess began to clear. On one of the colder winter days at Pier 6, one solicitous older man gave me a thin pair of gloves so I could thaw my frozen fingers and still operate the camera. He insisted that his little floating cabin was there to warm me any time, any day. "Unless you *like* freezing your ass off." (Ray, who was never mad to be there, probably thought: "Well, he *does*.") He explained to me that he was there to oil the crane as a therapy to bear the loss of his nephew, a bright young accountant with an office in the sky who was killed trying to help people down. "I was in bad shape," he said. "I've been going to talk to someone and it helps, but I needed to do *something*."

"You should tell me with the camera on."

"No, this is for you. *You* say it. You can put it in your narration."

He respected the fact that I was trying to do a thorough job, but his use of the word *narration* surprised and disturbed me. The film wasn't to have even a word of narration, but what if it did? How do you *narrate* the man in this room? At least his was a grief that was eased by the sway of the pier beneath him, protected by the commotion surrounding him, tempered by the prospect of kindness. Go there today, you will see that his warm little closet, the barges, the crane, the entire operation has disappeared without a trace and there is only the East River and the gulls or the descendants of the gulls that had perched upon the beams of the Towers. What will temper his grief now?

Hector, another dockbuilder I met at Pier 6 and who was diving on the 11th *under* the World Financial Center, told me that he volunteered to swim beneath the ruins. "I told them they could probably access the mound, or pockets of it, through tunnels that were going across West Street, outfalls for cooling the air-conditioning in the complex. I called my buddy up, practically crying. 'Man, we've got to do something. Maybe we can get in there, start burning some holes, maybe access some people.' I got some numbers, made some calls. They finally did send divers through the tunnels, but the debris was so compacted they couldn't get in. At least they checked that out. Then they called us to start on removing the debris." Scott Murray told me: "Weeks Marine could've said: 'Okay, nice job that day, now you guys're goin to Florida.' But I would've very much not liked that. I felt an obligation to stay there and do something—as everybody did." For Scott there was another, simpler act that gave meaning to the situation: a nightly constitutional culminating in— well, not much more than sitting down, but that was enough, for it was a walk through the floodlit darkness into a gentler kind of light. Scott found solace in St. Paul's Chapel, which had become a relief station after the tremors across the street shook sandstone names off some of its older graves. It was a place where people such as ATV Mike could have a cup of tea, pray, take a nap, sleep the night, hear a hymn, get a chiropractic adjustment . . . stare into space.

"During the early days of recovery," Scott said, "when it was still pretty raw down there, I used to walk across the entire span of the site, from the southwest corner, around Liberty Street, to the northeast end, up by Church and Vesey streets. This was around midnight when I got off work. I spent four years in the navy, I worked on an aircraft carrier, I've been in potentially life-threatening situations. In all my life I've never had the sense of a situation that we, as a country, couldn't handle. Maybe *I* couldn't, but someone could. America could respond. Being there that first night I felt, for the first time, that this was something we've never seen and don't know how to re- spond to. *We don't have this under control.* I could see it in the faces of the firefighters. Those nights it was like walking through a little piece of Hell that was delivered to the earth. People crawling all over the site, like an anthill, tearing away at it. That immediate urgency settled into a constant rhythm— less a response to an emergency, more an ongoing project—but it never changed completely. As it got progressively more cleaned up and organized, the pace stayed several notches up from any ordinary construction. But right from the beginning I would get off watch and take a walk through the site. I don't know why I kept doing it. It began to feel like an obligation almost. Some nights I'd be tired but I'd walk up to St. Paul's and sit there for ten, twenty minutes, half an hour. The feeling in there—it became a little refuge, a place to catch your breath, mentally and physically. They had food and mas- sage therapists and pastors were there for people who wanted to talk, but you could simply go to unwind. You could do that anywhere, but the fact that it was in that chapel, an incredible old church from before the Revolution, gave it a special feeling. I never ate anything there. They kept wanting to give me gloves, all sorts of things, but I figured no, it's for the people in the hole, I felt guilty about taking *any* of that and I didn't. Like a lot of people I just went to sit. It was a little oasis in the middle of all that commotion. I'm not a reli- gious person but I would feel this compunction, this obligation to make that round and sit in one of the pews at St. Paul's."

When Scott told this story to a friend, David Munn—a blacksmith in Charlottesville, Virginia, where Scott lives—David's fiancée, Amy, had a reaction that struck a chord: "Maybe you were carrying lost souls with you into the church."

"This is something that hadn't occurred to me," Scott said. "She caught the feeling perfectly without my even knowing it." When I told him about the feng shui experiment at Liberty Street, Scott understood. I think he also understood, as David Stanke did, that if there were souls which in any way were trapped at Ground Zero, his and David's counted among them.

Scott became part of a plan to thank St. Paul's. When David Munn and David's partner, Fred Crist, who have a sculpture studio called Metalsmiths, wanted to make a cross for an elderly black woman they had met in Charlottesville—she'd lost her sister on the 11th and was sad that she couldn't have a remembrance from the site—Scott brought them two strips of steel from which they fashioned a few crosses, including a small cross for the woman and a larger one for Paul's, which is displayed there now across the street from where it had served as part of the World Trade Center. The base to which they secured it is a chunk of concrete, also from the site. When I drove down to Virginia to shoot the steel that was making this interesting round—from Pennsylvania or Japan to New Jersey and over the river into one of the Twin Towers, down to Waynesboro, Virginia and back to Lower Manhattan again—being hammered, now, another way, and fired another way, perhaps not for the last time—David took a break from the forging. "There's something strange about the concrete," he said. He showed me minuscule flecks of something white embedded in it. Tiny bits of legal paper. If you pried one out, turned it about and scrutinized it on the tip of your finger, you could see that it contained a letter of type.

One wicked winter's night I was standing in front of the 10 & 10 Fire House on Liberty Street, a few doors down from 114. I was talking to Stephan Mueller, a German-born New Yorker who reported Ground Zero for a European network based in Berlin. His videographer was with him, shouldering one of those big Beta cameras that, because you couldn't hide it, would have prevented me from shooting most of my movie. Together we had been taking some remarkable shots of the site from the Ten House roof, which is three stories up and directly across the street, a great vantage from which to view it and an access not easily gained. It was Super Bowl Sunday. I said something about the cold. Stephan's response was: "Yeah, but it's okay, I don't like to complain, hmm? It's much worse for them," and his *them* did not need to be specified. It was a sentiment that would have made sense to anybody who attended the aftermath of September 11: there were people everywhere for whom everything was worse.

As for the insignificant operatives roaming the ghostworld for video prospects and democratic vistas, we complained to each other all the time. It was a kind of worksong, but worksongs have their foundations in pain and for us it was the weather. The first day was not as bad as the second, when by midafternoon I could work the camera only after lifting up my left hand with the right, for the left was paralyzed, but this proved helpful (seriously) when I needed to angle the camera off a wall an inch or two, for my hand, stiff as a board, steadied the frame perfectly. And I succeeded in photographing the tarped and patched and boarded-up World Financial Center looking more like the South Bronx than an annex of Wall Street; disabled subway stations; construction workers from Tully, Turner, AMEC and Bovis; guys from FEMA, guys from OSHA, guys from the DDC; guys hoisted in cages to deconstruct the barren cathedrals that were built when the Towers fell; huge Kubrickian klieg lights; old Barthman's Jewelers looking cleaned out, heisted; a Connecticut car encrusted with the cementy gray deathdust; earthworn grapplers, dumptrucks and cranes; and the lines of long slow sagging flatbed trucks that could not reemerge without a trim and a shower and that groaned as they carried out the tonnage of tormented steel. But after a day of sauntering such as I had never known, Ray could barely work his frozen legs, my ribs were knocking against each other, and neither of us could stand to smell one more hour of the World Trade Center on fire.

I would be lying if I didn't mention another kind of discomfort that had nothing to do with the weather. One did not need to be a political scientist to see that it was not only the sand of foreign deserts in which sinister imperatives had grown. The D.C. desert had been cultivating its own. Brother, I did not know what to do about the mess they had made of New York, did not know, even, who *they* were, for whoever defined the enemy were enemies themselves.

Fifteen bodies were taken out that day.

It was a hard mystery.

But no one was waiting for me to sort this out. By the time I made it home with my first day of film the United States had gone to war.

3

Big business buildings, ashbaked and wounded, wrapped like packages in black and red . . . camouflaged soldiers in the New York streets with G-men and flatbeds . . . dust under every heel . . . acetylene torches spraying fountains of spark and steel . . . open spaces, like the island that divides West Street, strewn with toxic contracts, copycards, parking stubs dated that morning. If this is the spectacle for starting the new century, don't call me to it: I am devastated enough. Eager as I am to walk the world, I have drawn a wide margin between myself and the battlefield. I report back from fronts of a different order. And I am the last man you would ever see driving to a catastrophe. How, then, did I come to be poking my nose and a video lens into the ruins of the World Trade Center?

"No, not cut out for this," I would say in emotional moments. "I'm a mess." Half a year later my reaction was still the same, but I had grown fond of it, fond enough to miss it and to feel solidarity with men I had come to admire at the far end of a zoom. I even developed a sense of belonging in Manhattan, where my father, an MP during World War II, had patrolled its lower streets from a base on Governor's Island; where my mother had danced in clubs; and where I had gone to school, played music, earned a living, published stories, directed plays, shown pictures, and had never, for five minutes, felt at home in any way.

The way that I first phrased it was that I wanted to go and examine some of the evidence for myself.

"Are you saying it didn't happen?" a friend asked testily. "Are you saying they're lying about it?"

We are lied to about practically everything by everyone but that was not my point. It was not that one doubted a catastrophe had roared into Manhattan at five hundred miles per hour, or that the measure and the means of the carnage were historic. For that, if little more, one could trust television.

But if, as Jefferson said, the price of democracy is vigilance, the least one could do was to pack the camera into a leather bag and see the destruction for oneself. Without the stake to purchase indulgences from our elected officials, citizens such as myself are obliged to parse out what it means to be a democratic man. I work at it daily. Progress is slow. Meanwhile, one is still one's country. You might not be caught up in politics, but in every American lifetime politics will, sooner or later, catch up to you. This would appear to be an instance. Whoever *they* were, they had driven to the airport, skated through security checks, boarded according to seating assignments, abided the empty announcements, left the earth for the last time, shown the crew who was boss, flown to New York, done the most thrilling thing any man has ever done and then pulverized well near three thousand people and two of the world's architectural immensities. Hearing, additionally, about the loss of World Trade Center Three, Four, Five, Six and Seven reinforced the idea that a small city was gone.

Actually, not so small.

Gone, but not entirely.

Webster defines a raid as *a hostile or predatory incursion,* and as *a surprise attack by a small force.* Over the last fifty years, *small force* has secured itself a new ambiguity. Since 1947 we have had to recognize that a craft flown by a team of ten can carry in its fuselage power enough to prove that no allegedly small force can ever be trusted as small again. Hiroshima would have appealed to Napoleon, who regarded it as a principle of warfare that thunderbolts are preferable to cannons. The thunderbolts of September 11 were not nuclear fission, and direct damage of impact lasted less than a second (0.7 and 0.6), but those jets with their wingtanks half full of fuel factored into a simple equation that would multiply the threat to the stability of the Towers and the Republic itself: their energy increased in proportion as the square of their velocities, and they were traveling fast, for their velocities were still being squared in the burning, and squared in the motivation to mobilize a response, so that the burning that would last a hundred days at the site was sure to continue, around the world, for at least a hundred years. To have their tallest buildings being slammed in the face with twenty million pounds of force was more than a piece of bad luck for the people of New York, and it was more than Saudi millionaires putting up a show with their brothers who were willing to carry their souls in their hands. When André Breton said that the true surrealist act was to fire into a street randomly with a loaded revolver, he couldn't have dreamed that ten sectarian thugs would call his bluff and then raise him by changing the weapon of choice, leaving behind ruins that, for me at least, threatened to render a lifetime, the chronicle of a city, even the course of civilization meaningless.

The mere thought, say, of Herman Melville's "Bartleby the Scrivener: A Story of Wall Street," which I had adapted for the stage and in which Ray had played Bartleby and I had played his boss, left me cold and confused, as if the affectionate adaptation mounted by Josyph and his comrades, the high art of Melville, the characters he created while he worked for the Customs Office, the busy black tophatted street on which it was set, the stages on which it bodied forth, the critic who came to review it for the *Times*, the *Times* itself and all its thousands of Metro sections and the wide advancing world that used to be New York had come to nothing and was all a pathetic mistake.

Has it all led to this?

Go to see, at the bottom of Pearl Street about a block from Battery Park, close to the Staten Island Ferry, a bronze bust of Melville in a Plexiglas case. A plaque identifies the author of *Moby Dick, Billy Budd,* and "Bartleby." The wall to which the case and the plaque are affixed faces a plaza that was swept by the clouds of September 11, leaving the tribute to Melville as DNA dusted as anything else around the Battery . . . and leaving me to revisit my character, the Lawyer, who wondered why Bartleby, his scrivener, would only say "I prefer not to," until one morning, walking on Wall Street, the mystery opens up when he, too, partakes of Bartleby's premonition: he looks up into the sky and he sees a Boeing jetliner roaring up West Street . . . and leaving me to feel, about the human enterprise, that Bartleby had the right answer: "I prefer not to." Even the feeble explanation that is tacked to the end of the story, positing that Bartleby was thrown into a funk for having worked, previously, in a dead letter office, now made perfect sense to me, for all of Lower Manhattan was a dead letter office, inundated with letters to a phantom zip code, all sent to people who were suddenly removed.

Has it all led to this?

The word *miraculous* was common in people's stories of survival, but for me it appeared as if the victims were multiplying like the loaves and the fishes in the tale about Jesus, for no one didn't know someone connected to someone who died. That morning Sarah Stanke, David's wife, had emailed her friend on the 102nd floor of Tower One. That floor was not destroyed by the plane instantly, but Sarah was led to believe that her friend *went fast.* "If she was at her computer she might have seen the plane coming but she wouldn't have felt anything," Sarah said. "So: thank God for small favors. Because I knew of some people that were on her floor but had time to call out to family—which is even worse, I think—saying we can't get out, we're burning up here." I have mentioned the *Times* Metro section. Dining with one of its editors, I tried doing something I have never done before: complimenting a newspaper, praising that section for having found, every day, some unexplored angle from which to view the impact of the 11th on Lower Manhattan. I had thought to set us up for a little chat about journalism. "You know I lost my son-in-law," the editor said, but I wasn't hearing right. "What's that?" And he told me that his daughter had been married for a month when her husband disappeared in Tower One.

Has it all led to this?

And yet the airstrike itself had a Homeric simplicity.

One day the angry jets rushed across the sky and knocked the big buildings down.

Legendary, but this was not six thousand years ago, it was this morning. What does it mean to be alive at such a time? What constitutes responsive behavior? Or, to phrase it differently, who should one become in order to not feel totally ashamed? I had just finished a script about the Hamilton-Burr duel in which some of the scenes are set in this neighborhood, fine; now there were scenes in my own life that had to be set in this neighborhood. I needed to take a walk. Did I say that I was looking for democracy? Look, then. If you can't find democracy at the end of a good walk, maybe it's in the walk itself—or maybe it's gone for good. Thoreau suggested that the only true walk is that walk from which there is no going back. As it happened, the walk that I took on my very first day at Ground Zero was precisely of this nature: I have never returned from it, which is why I intimated that I left a former self in the Number 4 train at Fulton Street. There are times when the right thing to do is to disappear. The old self is antiquated and keeps you out of the action of your time, the adventure that is your birthright. Here is a motto: *Are you afraid? Go closer.* Here is another: *Is it forbidden to you? Find out why. Worst that happens is that it kills you.*

In an inspired meditation on the differences between human knowledge and understanding, Aldous Huxley defined the latter in this way: a naked contact with reality. From this perspective, I wanted to understand, viscerally, at least a thing or two about the events of September 11 by getting in touch with what remained. The air was toxic in Lower Manhattan, but I needed to breathe it awhile. The streets were dirty down there, but I needed to carry home some of the ash in my hair. If the confetti of lives and businesses that were blown out of the Towers were still littering the ground, I might have to reach under the yellow police tape and touch a sad piece of that. If the streets were full of tears, some should be mine so I could examine what there was to cry about and how deep down the crying had to go. If the Trades were knocked down, so should I be. If I thought that I was knocked down already—"I am devastated enough"—I was asking to be rudely disabused of that presumption. The tortured installations that were sculpted by the blasts and the falling of the Towers were exquisite to behold, but I wondered whether I wasn't a little too mesmerized, wondered whether it wasn't, perhaps, important to see them contextualized by what was still standing in this old American city that was built around an Algonquin trading trail. To say Mohamed Atta had an advanced degree in urban planning isn't a sick joke; sadly, it's a fact, but it's a sick fact. In a book about the American architect Cass Gilbert, a book published in 2001 before the attacks, Dennis Jacobs, a judge who sits on the U.S. Court of Appeals, Second Circuit, said that the Woolworth Building "acts as if it is still the tallest building in the world."[4] When it appears in my film it certainly looks that way. With a Gilbert courthouse just a little north of it (the Thurgood Marshall), his U.S. Custom House a little south of it (now the National Museum of the American Indian), and his 90 West Street below the now empty lot toward the end of Liberty Street, Gilbert, who was born before the Civil War and died in 1934, could rank once again as Lower Manhattan's most commanding architect. I admire Gilbert's work but this is not the way to revive or enhance a reputation—it was too demented for me. The events that took the Towers, all those lives, and over eleven thousand businesses were more than great shocks, upheavals: they were contraventions of reality. The island of Manhattan has seen its share of transformations, but mountains of man and steel are not meant to disperse within the space of a few hours.

Once you broke through the border of big buildings that dominated the Ground Zero perimeter—chiefly the huge monolithic Deutsche Bank, the green-topped towers of the World Financial Center, 90 West Street, the old Barclay-Vesey (now Verizon) and Federal buildings, the Millennium Hotel, Century 21, and One Liberty Plaza—the success of the attackers was instantly apparent in the profound lack of New Yorkness about the site. It was as much the moon as Manhattan. As a result, few of the pictures I was viewing resembled the city in which they were taken. To *see* where it happened, rather than simply to presuppose it, my assumption was that you needed to look around from every vantage in all directions, triangulating oneself with the cities of the living and the dead. The seemingly simple act of seeing the Woolworth Building wasn't a simple act at all, especially in places where you were not supposed to see it. I, who had ascended the Twin Towers only twice in thirty years and had only photographed them accidentally, was drawn now to study them in pieces and to wander around their footprints and explore the absence of things, for this was a rare case: a very great city significantly reversing itself, collapsing into chaos over the slurry foundations of its largest landmarks.

How would it feel to walk around the bend of Maiden Lane, to pause at Barthman's Jewelers at the corner of Broadway, to plant one's feet on the glass of Barthman's clock—a clock which, in a quintessential gesture of American enterprise, they imbedded in the sidewalk a century ago, a bright idea whose glow I had seen from the top of the South Tower—to look across the street toward the place where a world once began, and to see—nothing? Jersey angles on the Twins that dissolved into identical views without them were a way of representing the transformation—now you see them, now you don't—but seeing and not-seeing are both harder to do than that. I could not afford to leave it to a network editor. If Aristotle thought that Nature hated a vacuum, he ought to have seen television. Faced with one of the great abysmal voids in all of history, television couldn't wait to fill it with a sentimental piano, flag graphics, glory-trumpets. You could say that I wanted to see both more and less than what I was being shown. Perhaps, too, I could earn the right, although I had the right already, to criticize the national response to this event without suffering the accusation of distance.

This is what had agitated my friend about my *seeing the evidence*. Evidence *of* can also be construed as evidence *for*, and it annoyed him to contemplate the twisted case a man without investments could make of it. He was not unresponsive to the human tragedy. In fact to meet the emergency he had donated equipment, which is more than I could do. But the rhetoric of shoring up *the economy* had stirred him into defending great monetary rewards for two of the guilty groups—airline executives, intelligence officials—and as an engineer who loved to watch the way things work, he doted on the differences, and the effects on caves, between one smart bomb and another. "It's not the explosion that does the job, it's the vibration." A patron of war movies, here he was—here we all were—producing one for television. Like most of my dear friends he was a patriot preferring propaganda to reality because it made Wall Street sing and enabled him to play war games in his den. "Easy for you," he said about my excursions at the site. "You enjoy making trouble." *Manhattan is torn apart,* I thought, *and it's my trouble he's worried about!* But of course it wasn't really. If he was jumpy, bellicose, so was half the world. His city was on fire and so he was on fire.

But no, I wasn't there to make trouble, not yet. Thinking as a citizen within the strict bounds of my profession—art—I had contemplated appealing to the best minds in America to shine a little light on that darkest of days, for I certainly couldn't rely on my own capacities or the plumbing and PR that passes for news and commentary. Whatever else it denoted, September 11 was a fundamental failure of the state in the duty of protecting its citizenry, and in addressing this failure it was failing even further by implying that an investigation, or after-action review such as the military would call for a debacle of lesser impact, was unpatriotic. President Bush had been to Ground Zero, and I would like to have left the investigation to him, to Congress—to all our well-paid employees at the top, but I was not reassured by their posturing and promises. Like a trope out of medieval theology, *national security* was tossed out to deflect such a multitude of charges and to obscure such a multitude of sins that the term, at least in the hands of its abusers, was rendered practically meaningless. Which is perhaps just as well, for *national security* didn't exist on the 11th, neither as a reality nor, apparently, as a primary concern, and the situation wasn't improving at all. James Woolsey, former director of the CIA, was a member of Donald Rumsfeld's Defense Policy Board. Like others on that committee, Woolsey was a speculator, poised and positioned to prosper from the so-called *war on terror.* His equity firm, Paladin Capital Group, promoted investments in that exciting, explosive field, and as Webster defines *paladin* as the champion of a medieval prince, the name suits men who look to the Borgian realpolitik of Machiavelli's *Prince* in the way honest men might consult the Constitution. "We need a little bit of Machiavelli," Woolsey has said.[5] When they dispatched him to Europe it wasn't to troubleshoot lapses in our *national security* but to drum up support for taking Baghdad. Well, if Defense Secretary Rumsfeld said, on the afternoon of the 11th: "Go massive. Sweep it all up. Things related and not," then why *not* go to Baghdad—or anywhere else around?[6] All expenses would be paid. The horizon was bright.

But there was a different kind of sweeping up at Ground Zero where the horizon, the sky itself, had disappeared, and President Bush did not deserve to be down there. If Bush's appearance was a boost for the men on the site, of course they had earned that moment of proud relief; but he was exploiting an event that he, commander in chief of the armed forces, had done

BEHIND THE GREEN DOOR

nothing to prevent and in the midst of which he had strolled into a Sarasota schoolroom and, with press cameras clicking in back of the class, observed a reading lesson as a photo op to foster the illusion that he cares about education, blacks, children. Nothing altered that agenda, not even the fact that if the nation was under attack this preannounced visit was endangering schoolchildren. President Bush sat with them, then he hid from sight and invented a silly story about the reason that he hid, a fair description of his leadership. And he invented a silly story about seeing the first attack on the school TV before he entered the classroom, allegedly saying: "There's one terrible pilot," a story that is progressively more bizarre when you consider that (a) Bush was in his limo when the North Tower was hit; (b) Bush was told about it before he entered the school; (c) no TV was on in the school for him to see; (d) there was no live footage of the attack on the North Tower; (e) he was in the classroom at the time of the second strike; (f) if, however incredibly, the president confused seeing a tape of the second strike with seeing real-time footage of the first, the remarks he has made about viewing it as an accident are equally troublesome.[7] Respecting September 11, the president of the United States has told a short story that is gratuitous, inane, a tale meant to place him at a point of innocence and (in its own crippled way) on a ground with New Yorkers, such as those in my film, who did in fact face that event as it happened. "Anyway, it was an interesting day," was his unscripted summary of the 11th.[8] It goes without saying that his policies were calculated to hurt most of the men who were cheering at his feet when he said, at Ground Zero, "I can hear you," hurt their wives, their children, their grandchildren all. If they thought this executive's protectionism included them—in other words, if they thought they were being heard at all— they hadn't been paying attention.[9]

Serious situation. I wanted to think well about it, I needed help with that, and I thought it might be good to put the help into a movie. I would go talk to people: philosophers and generals, investigative reporters, statesmen and poets, scholars, ex-presidents, revolutionaries—it would be grand if I could find even half dozen people who were willing to stop lying for at least half an hour. But when I called my friend Ray, suggesting that we go to Ground Zero and that I take along the camera, it was not with any thought of making a picture in New York or making a case for any partisan point of view; it was only to have a record of my own pictorial memory in the event that I needed it for background (background!), something to lend texture and credence to a movie that I might decide to make and to help keep the film, and the filmmaker, honest. Like my agitated friend, I was interested in Wall Street, but it was the street itself for which I had headed downtown . . . the street that used to face a Dutch palisade of stone and wood that stood to keep the English out . . . the street that, on September 11, saw a monster cloud overtake Trinity Church and push down that hallowed corridor of business without regard for the traders from the Exchange who were scrambling for their lives in front of it. In a season of such congressional condescension and indifference to the Bill of Rights, a citizen should, at least, show sufficient stamina to stroll the streets of his city, looking at the event they were already starting to use against him. "Even if we can't take the camera out of the case," I said. "Even if we can't get close enough to see. Here is an event that will influence the course of this century—it'll be used as an occasion for *everything*—and it happened, not at the other end of the world, but thirty-five miles down the street. We should go. We have no excuse not to."

I was lying to myself—lying, at least, a little—when I said this. I had seen the menacing sky, the portraiture in dust, and you didn't need a doctorate from MIT to see through the deceptive assurances of EPA officials, who are the last people you'd want to consult about your personal safety. It was no surprise at all when I heard, much later, that as they were abating their own Downtown building, the EPA *mis*tested the rest of Lower Manhattan and misinformed the citizenry about the danger. That Bush's own Council on Environmental Quality, chaired by the corrupt James Connaughton, guided the EPA in the arts of deception is well documented.[10] The wonder is that anybody believed the EPA about anything at all. September 15, 25 . . . October, November . . . even into December or 2002, let me give you three guesses where it's not good for your lungs, see what *you* would say. And the way some people fear flying, rats, or East Coast liberals, my fear of asbestos was practically pathologic. For someone to say: "The air was toxic in Lower Manhattan, but I needed to breathe it awhile," would, for me, qualify the speaker as insane. Here is what you do with any hazardous material: *keep as far away as you can*. What sense did it make for me to call up a friend and say: "Let's go get some"? I cannot answer that, except to say that in life, as in art, there are times when you need to peel the white gloves off, take pieces of your nightmare into your bare hands, and gulp them for breakfast. After all, it's only a day. Fate couldn't penalize me too much more for that—could it?

A lot of people living in New York, even those in Lower Manhattan, working a few blocks away, would never look at the site. They had their reasons. Those that I heard were mostly smokescreens for fear, but one of the solid truths about Ground Zero was this: everybody ought to be allowed to be afraid of it. A Viet Nam veteran sobbed when he contemplated the loss of the Twin Towers, and when I offered to take him down to see the site from Liberty Street he reacted as if I were offering to have his head drilled. Another Viet Nam vet who worked at the South Street Seaport went to volunteer during the days of recovery but he left the site forever after finding a severed arm with a bloody shirt and a watch on it, saying it was worse, for him, than anything in Nam. I was afraid of the site—I am afraid of *everything*—but I accommodated the fear by going as close to it and looking at it as clearly as I could. It is said of ideographs that they mean what they look like. Another solid truth about Ground Zero is this: whatever more it meant, it meant what it looked like, and videography could, at least, communicate that. But although it was important to bring the camera and to determine whether any kind of work was feasible there, it was not, at first, the lens and what it would see that interested me at Ground Zero, it was this old familiar myopic and astigmatic pair of eyes, looking into the corners and the crevices of chaos for clues that would help me to become a better man.

I was also interested, as anybody would be, in standing in the vicinity of the impossible.

I had not gone to the site as a filmmaker, but I started to shoot it immediately. If I hadn't brought the camera I might not have missed it: I'd have settled for observation, maybe jotting a few notes. I was even uneasy about the fact that I was looking into the LCD screen. I envied Ray's position as a lookout. He didn't have the zoom that brought me into the teeth of the grapplers, but he, at least, was not observing this awesome imagery as a digital re-creation on a two-inch screen. *Doomed to television,* I thought, *even in the thick of it.* What kind of understanding was this?

Then I zoomed in to shoot the great detrusions of tangled steel at the south side of World Trade Five. You could choose your verb: it was caked with Twin Tower, harpooned by it, wrapped in it like a shaggy suit of mail. On September 11 radiant heat from this building, called the Northeast Plaza—which had housed the Lower Manhattan Cultural Council, a State Claims Court, a daycare, a Borders, a Port Authority Police desk—crossed Church Street, where it threatened to burn the Millennium Hilton and probably would have burned it if resourceful firefighters hadn't plowed through the debris and pumped a protective curtain of water between them. Months later I met a fire lieutenant, Rudy, who was instrumental in making this happen. He rolled out a big map of the site on the trunk of his car, and through Rudy's eyes I was able to see this court-house renounce the role of arbitration to recklessly attack another building. Even now, World Trade Five, a burnt-out, bashed-in, nine-story building that was shaped like a stately and reversed capital L and that, over the following months, I would shoot until there was nothing left standing aboveground, was not totally disempowered. I was over a block away shooting across Dey Street but through the lens of the camera I was climbing over the barricades, floating past the cops and the kids in camouflage, scaling its burnt and broken walls, inspecting it in remarkable detail while it spoke to me with a wordless eloquence. *This seared black and battered block of steaming useless junk is New York,* I thought.

That stupefied thought was the beginning of something for me. Look: a dream deconstructed, a heedless ambition meeting its match in ruthlessness and learning an old, unimpeachable lesson: fire to fire, ash to ash. What if I could capture some of this sad, mangled world that was vanishing by the hour? If I could shoot it decently, maybe I could make some small contribution to telling the story of the city on its knees, a city I had never seen so brutalized and, at the same time, so compellingly beautiful. Half an hour at Ground Zero made me more of a New Yorker than the previous half century. Perhaps one reason is that it was more beat than I was. Maybe I felt, too, this was such a tragic place that every man was obligated to be his best here. This meant that I would have to be an artist, even though I wasn't at all practiced with the lens and would have to reinvent myself accordingly. I shot greedily, I shot passionately because I don't exist well unless I am making a piece of art, and I must have thought, after the first astonishing frames began to form before my eyes: *I have to work with this.* And working with something well means finding it in yourself and vice versa. It means clearing a way for love. It means closing down distances between you, or relinquishing the delusion that there is separation at all. As a painter I had learned that as you try to see a thing in order to paint it, you are also trying to paint it in order to see it. I had never seen a bottle until I painted a series of them. Never had seen a clock. Never had seen a vase of flowers. Never had seen the shape of a woman, which I really thought I had. If I had never become a painter I might never have seen at all. Just so, I might never have seen the site had I not tried to capture it on tape.

This thought carries a tinge of poetical inversion, so let me ground it with a story about Ray.

Building Five of the World Trade Center.

Six months later, around the time his participation ended, Ray confided to me that he had felt nothing at all about the site. "Completely numb about it." It was no secret to me that he hadn't felt that much enthusiasm for going. There were practical concerns. We were broke, we were badgered, these excursions were stretching us past the breaking point. So what? For Ray there was a *what*. Essentially he was being a good sport to come along on these thankless knockingsabout, and he expressed more ardor over a shorthaired blonde fetch of a waitress in Quartino, an Italian café under the spell of the Brooklyn Bridge, than for any of the marvels that were bordered by West, Vesey, Church and Liberty streets. During the time we were together he never asked, even once, to look at the footage I had shot. It was a different affair for me. I would screen the day's take, then the site would vividly complicate my bed until morning, haunting my half dreams, conjuring nightmares, guilting me for absences, berating me for the stream of stupid mistakes I was making, anticipating fresh ones tomorrow. James Creedon, a young paramedic who was on Liberty Street directly under the South Tower when it started to come down, was blown off his feet running for cover under the South Bridge, with shrapnel penetrating his scalp and the skin on his back. Four of the men in his squad were killed, and James, like many survivors, was sure that he would die, and that certitude expressed itself in nightmares for months. Likewise, for two or three months, whenever he closed his eyes, Donavin, who ran from the collapse of Tower Two on Maiden Lane, and peeled away from Tower One with his tires skidding on snow-slippery dustdrifts and his month-old son wrapped like a parcel in the back of his toxic truck, was transported to one of the burning floors above the impact.

"*No fucking way* I'm going to settle for either option—being roasted, or jumping down to die," Donavin told me about his dreams. "But it's getting hotter and hotter and I'm trying to find the track for the window washers, as if somehow I'll climb down on that, or ride the washer device, or grab a curtain or a blind and try to hang glide. Because it's always been my way to get as close to the edge as possible, then pull myself out at the last second. I would rig up a parachute quick—McGyver myself to the point of feeling good about jumping, not just jump to die. If there was even a sheet of plywood . . ." Even as he spoke to me, Donavin was looking for a way out of the fire he had witnessed that morning. He was serious. He was upset. "I can't find a fucking way to deal with it. I go through *so* many scenarios, over and over. And these dreams . . ."

My own dreams didn't test me, they taunted me by not letting me look away from the site. If the odor came to greet me in the Fulton Street subway, the site came to bed with me in Huntington, Long Island, making me say to myself, aloud: "I shouldn't be doing this. It's ruining me." With these nocturnal apocalypses I was seeing as much of the site on Long Island as I was in Lower Manhattan. People would say: "I think you're becoming obsessed with this," as if rubble were unworthy of intense enthusiasm and artistic concentration. Or as if boyish Peter wanted to play Bob the Builder. Or as if the sensitive man were psychologically scarred and it was time for the spy to come in out of the cold. I wondered whether, during the Great Fire of London, which ruined twelve thousand homes and put sixty-five thousand Londoners into the streets, the diarist Samuel Pepys was troubled in this way, so I looked it up in his entries for 1666. On September 15, about two weeks after the city started to burn, Pepys wrote: *Much terrified in the nights now-a-days with dreams of fire, and falling down of houses.* Ten days later, on September 25, he wrote: *So home to bed, and all night still mightily troubled in my sleepe with fire and houses pulling down.* On September 27, nearly a month after the fire started at one of the King's bakers in Pudding Lane, Pepys, who was Secretary to the Admiralty, wrote: *A very furious blowing night all the night; and my mind still mightily perplexed with dreams, and burning the rest of the town, and waking in much pain for the fleete.*

No bad dreams for Ray. If the situation owned him at all he never showed it. Nothing wrong with that, but his confession was so emphatically categorical—not shook with a single sob, not at all attached to the subject—that even he felt obligated to posit an explanation. He initially ascribed it to the emotional distancing—the lack of passion or enterprise for anything at all—that he inherited from his father. In writing a book about Ray and his father I had become an authority on how alike they were, so I could not quarrel with this. But then Ray put forth a more telling explanation: "Maybe it's because I wasn't seeing it through the camera."

On the morning of the 11th Howell Raines, who six days earlier had become chief editor of the *New York Times,* walked out of his building at Seventh Avenue and Eleventh Street and looked down at the Twin Towers burning. His initial impulse, one that he overcame, was to dash back for a camera with which to record the catastrophe. Imagine the fascination of an event that so mesmerized the editor of the *Times* that he could forget—or disregard—for even a moment that he was captain, now, of some of the best photographers in the world. *He* was going to shoot this. In a televised interview he said: "There are certain events that can only be depicted as they are."[11] This would seem to be the right approach, and his paper was amply honored for its pictures. On the 12th the *Times,* at least, showed a jumper on page 7. That was important but it was not enough for me. Nothing in the *Times* or any paper was enough. They all moved on, and off to war, too soon. But the Raines anecdote has always made me wonder whether he might have managed it differently, pictured it more fiercely, urged an investigation into how it could have happened and who, in this country, working for this nation, should have been censured, fired, prosecuted, impeached, if the editor of the *Times* had done the *wrong* thing, *not* taken a taxi up to 43rd Street, walked the 30 blocks down Seventh until it became West Broadway, and viewed the dread spectacle through the lens of his own camera.

JUST DON'T LET A COP SEE YOU

In a move that was represented as sensible and righteous but that was, in fact, a monumental mistake and might have broken the Fourth Amendment, the site that was treated as a signifier of war and the justification for mobilizing the troops was designated a crime scene of which no photography was permitted. The order came from the mayor's office, it made no sense, it shocked and opposed every responsible impulse, but it was announced publicly on September 25 and it was enforced long after the mayor rescinded his own order, almost as if it weren't rescinded at all. As this meant that no one who wasn't connected could shoot the site (no rule in Manhattan is enforced consistently), for nine months at least I was constantly at risk of confiscation or arrest. After my apprenticeship without an identity, the perimeter pass that led me to Liberty Street did not include the camera, which could seldom show itself obviously. History had lost a lot in those collapses. Beyond the living memories lost in all those people and in all that architecture . . . beyond the Miró tapestry, the big red Calder, Rodin's *Three Shades,* close to a million artifacts from the Five Points District, even the relics of three saints . . . lost too were a frightening number of texts and photographs: over twenty libraries; parts of the Broadway Theatre Archive; archives of the Helen Keller Foundation and of the Port Authority; forty thousand negatives of Jacques Lowe's chronicle of JFK; and documentation of the African Burial Ground. Entire worlds of lost imagery: of all places to say **NO PHOTO**—here? Now history itself as an ambulatory act, as spontaneous archeology, as cinema verité, had gone into hiding. It has had to hide before, but hiding in the heart of Lower Manhattan, where so much of the nation originated and where it was now transformed, made it all too obvious that something was drastically wrong. Which, of course, you knew already from the morning of the 11th and you knew even better as you probed into how such a calamity could have happened, so that the interdiction was more than an inconvenience: it was an outrage. My little Sony VX 2000: with what conceit did they dare disallow that intrusion after allowing the intrusion of those 767s? If I was out of line in wanting the world to see this, the line itself was out of line, for it was a critical entitlement for anybody touched by the news of the 11th.

But even the press were hustled off. Photographers with press passes who hadn't been issued a pass to the site—which was a different deal entirely— were often denied access, and those who gained access were not necessarily professionals. If they were, they were easily dismissed. How a person with a camera, whether professional or not, was able to shoot the site at all depended on who they knew, who they were working for, whether they were having a lucky day or, in some cases, whether they were willing to pay cash for the privilege. I can vouch for the latter claim because the offer, which I declined, was made to me by a man who would put me in touch with another man who would address all my needs in return for what he referred to as *something*, which we assume was not a cigar or a box of candy. One man was so accustomed to bribes that he couldn't abide the fact that, having earned the solicitude of his employers, I had been welcomed into their building in order to shoot its interior free of charge. Bellowing insults and threats, "I'm tired of all this illegal shit," he said, meaning: *you owe me a piece of this action.*

A man I liked to call Big Frank—Frank Silecchia—a union worker who achieved notoriety for finding and promoting a huge steel cross that was formed out of pieces that had tumbled into World Trade Six from Tower One, took me to see the proud rusty structure, twenty feet tall, that was taken from what he called God's House. As we stood in the rain at the northwest corner of the site, Big Frank reached into his pocket, drew out a fold of bills, and handed me two twenties. "That's my contribution to the movie." Earlier that day I was sitting with him in the Taj Mahal, the EPA's big white washdown tent that was erected on a parkinglot at West and Murray streets. By big I mean fifty feet high and thirty-five thousand square feet around. The EPA, which had spent over eight million dollars on it, donated half of it to the Salvation Army, which was serving food to six thousand workers per day. At my refusal to take even a snack out of the offering, which I felt should go exclusively to laborers, Big Frank gently grabbed the pale blue perimeter pass hanging on my chest. "This pass means you've earned the right to be here," he said. "Go get some hot food, and put plenty of fruit into your pockets for later. You're an actor. Pretend you're on location. Craft Services, right? There's the food trucks. Go. Unless you're trying to make me angry."

Big Frank, for one, would have believed that I was shooting through the money I had borrowed for an infected front tooth ("Just be sure you don't use it for a movie," the lender said), but I didn't have to explain: he had an exceptional intuition about these mad movie guys. More common, though, was the willful misperception that a man with a handsome camera must be making a killing with it. One spring morning I was working around the Stage Door Deli near the corner of Church and Vesey streets. A seatbelt had landed around here from Tower Two. A landing gear assembly, a wheel and an engine had been thrown several blocks farther north. On the other side of Church, diagonally across the street, fuselage had landed on the roof of Building Five. Now men arrived on Gators, stamped a little Ground Zero dust off their boots, and went amongst the public for sandwiches. I was shooting a big police copter circling the site when a maintenance guy from one of the buildings started a conversation.

"Lookin for *someone*," he said.

"Scary, huh? Really hovering up there."

"I thought it might be out of fuel. Wasn goin back to my building till I'm sure it don't crash. Ever see the choppers they used to use in Viet Nam? Might be one of those."

"Converted?"

"Yeah. Nice camera. Whoo. What's a camera like that cost?"

"It's expensive, but it's good," I said. "You should see it at night."

"*How* much?"

"More than I can afford."

"Look at that. Ever get any roof shots?"

Then he volunteered to take me on his roof.

"For a fee."

With those three words, which are easy to justify but not to me, this guy had disgraced himself. But when the site was cleaner, the deli advertised its own view of Ground Zero from its upstairs window, an honest enough promotion, for if you wanted to sit with a sandwich you'd be sitting at the upstairs tables anyway—and there was no one taking tickets. As for the site itself, nobody working on the pile or, later, in the pit, could honestly dispute that there were cameras in use. Why not? One union worker was even shooting a documentary, which I can tell you all about because we exchanged information under the sweep of the monster crane over at Pier 25 almost as if we were at a screening—after all, we were just two filmmakers using the same location—excepting we wore hardhats and needed to outshout the racket of the World Trade refuse pouring out of trucks into huge scale-pans that were swung around deftly, blowing contaminated kisses at the windows of Stuyvesant High, and dropped into barges on the Hudson—a place where the barges of a century ago meant the innocence of New York oysters, not the detritus of New York itself. "What're you using, the VX 2000? Good camera. I've been using the 1000. What's your editing—Final Cut?" This is not to say that firefighters, volunteers or union men digging out remains were down there snapping photographs. The fact is, though, that from the morning of the 11th shutters were clicking across the site but if you respected the barricades, stood behind the perimeter and pointed a camera toward Ground Zero, you could lose it. Michael Cook, a painter who lived at 120 Liberty Street (125 Cedar, next door to David Stanke) for over two decades, was threatened with arrest and had a roll of film stolen from him for shooting his neighborhood from the vantage of his own toxic dump of a livingroom. There were remains on that street that weren't discovered until June because the City wasn't interested in residential affairs, but Michael Cook's roll of inflammatory Kodak was confiscated to make the city safe for democracy.

"There is the hallowed viewing platform for families of victims, but they don't like the fact that *we're* here," Michael told me in the wreckage of his home. "I said: 'This is my film, my personal property—and this is my neighborhood,' but with cops on either side of him this firefighter was ready to haul off and beat me. He gave me a lecture about photographing the site when people had died there. Meanwhile tourists were taking video and vendors were selling albums of ripped-off pictures and pirated videotapes and they were a big sell. I said: 'I'll send you the relevant frames,' but he said: 'I'm not going to listen to one more argument—just give me the goddamn film right now.' He could have beat me, carted me off, had me arrested, so I opened up the camera and gave him the film."

On my first day alone, keeping out of the frozen zone, I was stopped three times and in none of those cases was I pressing for access: I was out of everyone's way excepting the mayor's. But I wasn't singled out. For *any* unconnected person with a camera, no view of the site was permitted.

NO CAMERAS
NO PHOTO

These **NO PHOTO** signs were posted even beyond the perimeter. They were along Rector Street, from Broadway to Greenwich by the Trinity churchyard, where it was being excavated for Con Ed repairs. Such work can be seen every day around Manhattan, work safe enough for people to pass it all the time, for the Rector Street sidewalk was open to pedestrians; but if, at one in the morning, you pointed a camera toward a floodlit crevice in which there was nothing but pipes and cables, you could have been jailed. People were, in fact, jailed, and they were held, in some cases, for days without charges, their film lost forever. But the number of arrests doesn't matter. Given the circumstances surrounding the destruction, it was an odd group—men and women with cameras—to target for incarceration, especially after airborne Saudis, including bin Ladens, had been spirited out of the country at the indulgence of the White House. In the parlance of the Pentagon, photographers were nothing if not *spurious targets*. Even above the site, after the ban against rotocraft and planes had been lifted, it remained in force for all ENGs (electronic-news-gathering helicopters) until the National Security Council allowed the FAA to rescind it in mid-December. Until then an amateur on a passenger flight, or someone posing as one, would have had better access. Too bad. If ever there was a disaster that needed chronicling from the clouds this was it, for the burning would not stop reaching up to them. But by the time cameras could fly, the fire had gone out.

At one of the entrances to the site, on South End Avenue, a large hand-lettered sign announced that confiscated cameras would contribute to 9/11 relief. It might have been effective in dissuading you from aiming at the floodlit commotion, but in hinting that the confiscation converted voyeurism into healthy altruism, it inspired sarcasm as to what it would really mean, in the rumble of city life, if they took your camera away, and how far it would travel from the hand that did the taking. Reflecting on my camera as an object, I recalled that the expression *in camera,* which denotes an official meeting that is adjourned to private quarters—litigants, for instance, seeing a judge in his chambers are said to be meeting *in camera*—is based on a Latin word for an arched vault or keep: a secret space. Putting into your camera something you've seen at Ground Zero is more than examining the evidence: it is to stow it in your keep, make it your own private property. To take a picture is to collect and to take home the evidence: tampering—all of us with cameras were tampering, which is why it was not merely videotape and film but cameras themselves that were so obnoxiously threatened with confiscation. As federal agents specializing in evidence recovery—thirteen of the FBI's trusted travelers—have been cited by the Justice Department for carrying off World Trade mementos . . . and a manager at the City Morgue confessed to selling coffins that were donated for victims . . . and a retired police sergeant, then head of the Secret Service motor pool at World Trade

BEHIND THE GREEN DOOR

Seven, confessed to stealing cars allegedly crushed on the 11th ... and in Secretary Rumsfeld's office there is a piece of the 757 that penetrated the Pentagon ... you can italicize *obnoxiously*. Of course, how the restriction against photography protected or respected a crime scene from which a million and a half tons of evidence were rapidly removed on a round-the-clock schedule has never been explained.

And yet it was much to their credit that, with some exceptions, the cops on the beat and other workzone controllers did not appear excessively zealous about enforcement. Not far from the sign in question on South End Avenue we asked one policeman about my shooting toward the site from an obscure quiet corner between World Financial One and Two, an alcove half a block away from any building, one that was furnished with an empty toxic waste pail, an empty old dumpster, and an EPA monitor braced to a fencepost. I was a short walk from the Hudson. It was November and it was cold. There was never much to shoot from that perspective anyway but I was eager to shoot everything: the biggest of the big red crawler cranes, a Manitowoc 21000 that could hoist a thousand tons and that flew from its lattice boom a flag from the Iowa State House in Des Moines; glimpses of the rooms in which loans had been approved that were visible through disintegrated walls in the black-wrapped Deutsche Bank; or simply the dust that was dancing in the glare of the floodlights.

"Go ahead," the cop said. "Just don't let a cop see you."

Another night, when I needed to take a shot from the center of Greenwich Street just above the interzone, I asked a cop if it was going to start trouble.

"Technically," he said, "you're not supposed to do it. But *I'm* standing *here,* and if *you* were standing *there* and I wasn't looking your way ..."

One cop told me that his captain would make him take away my camera if I did not make myself inconspicuous, but he went the additional step of estimating the cost of the camera—"What's that, around fifteen hundred?"—as a way of encouraging me not to lose it. And not a day went by without my seeing a couple of cops or firefighters posing for tourists in front of the site that wasn't supposed to be photographed. Of course there were news reports. C-SPAN aired and re-aired a walkaround. Other crews were granted permission. And FEMA shot everything (what they judged to be everything). But the intimidation of cameras was in the atmosphere, it didn't dissipate as the removal raced toward its conclusion, and not every day was a lucky one. As far along as March 2002, I was on one of the rooftops in Gateway Plaza, a complex of dwellings at the west end of Liberty Street in Battery Park City, looking at the site with two of Gateway's residents, one of whom was Kevin McCrary, whose father, Tex, was instrumental in the inception of Battery Park City and was the first man to live there. Tex had also taken the first team of Western photographers into Hiroshima after the bomb. Kevin and his father, who was ninety-one at the time, were there when the Twins fell, and since that morning Kevin had offered himself as generously as anybody around, driving an electric Taylor-Dunn transporter, a handy little personnel carrier—like an oversize golf cart—with seats in the back that folded down for freight. Like me, Kevin had the wrong answer—no answer—as to who he was *with*, but he was *with* everybody and he helped them indiscriminately: cops, clergy, construction workers, volunteers, students, restaurateurs, firefighters, film crews and journalists from everywhere. He helped *me*, a testament to the democratic nature of his mission, which was based, in part, on his father having decided that the pictures from Hiroshima were not publishable. Kevin did not want the story of Ground Zero to be lost like that. "It's often the outsiders," he told me, "the people on the fringes, who have the real story, the real truth," and we were on the fringes together a lot. "Bringing the world to Ground Zero and Ground Zero to the world," is how he put it. But Kevin and I, in the company of a girl who had moved to Ground Zero from an apartment in which she had seen the Pentagon enveloped in flames, were chased off that roof for shooting a tragic interlude in American life, a phase that was entitled to all the chroniclers it could get and that, in terms of its most graphic imagery, was just about to end. It was one of the few times I was angry at someone there but it was someone I couldn't see, for they were pushing us around by remote control, running us off intellectual property they weren't entitled to own: the story of a broken neighborhood. If I was being asked, as we all were, to respect The Narrative that was dominating mainstream media and to forgive—or, better, to forget—less than admirable behaviors around and about the site, some of which were seamy, some of which were cruel, some of which were truly scandalous . . . and if I was being asked to respect The Narrative issuing out of the White House and every other federal building about the events that morning—how they couldn't have been predicted, couldn't have been prevented, couldn't have been *imagined* . . . then I ought to have been permitted to constitute my own narrative based, as it was, on wanting to see and wanting to shoot some of the city of New York from a peaceable perspective.

I have been asked the question: "What were they afraid you would find?" But I do not think the concern was for any finding at all, I think the subver-

sion was in the seeing, the shooting, the tampering in and of itself. Whatever its pretexts, control of this sort is a hysterical symptom, a domineering,
even dictatorial impulse that signifies the weakness of the men in City Hall
and all the way up the command to Pennsylvania Avenue. You make a movie
like this with your eardrums, too. With headphones on, the surveilled is a
surveillant. With Mr. Karl Rove as the Voice of America, I was entitled, obligated, to listen to a noise more honest and meaningful.

"But these people *live* here," I said to the guard. "My friend's father's lived
here for thirty years. They were here September 11. My friend was one of the
first volunteers."

"Sorry I can't do nothin about it. They call me, say you have to come
down."

"Because of the camera?"

"Because of the camera. They said you have to come down," *they* being
men with binoculars who were scanning the site's perimeter, protecting it
and, of course, history from the hazards of unconnected photography.

I talked about the balance of interest in documenting history in situations
of danger, grief, and opposition with a photographer from the *New York Post*,
Bolivar Arellano, who came to New York from Ecuador in 1971 after some of
his photographs had landed him on a hit list. On the 11th he was on another
hit list, for he was directly underneath both collapses.

"I've been in civil wars in Nicaragua and El Salvador," Bolivar told me.
"I was kidnapped by the Contras. The death squads used to throw children
into the air and wait with the machete. I have seen shootouts. I have seen
students in Guayaquil massacred by their government. After that I thought:
I will never see anything as horrible as this. I had passed the worst that one
human being can do to another. But everything I saw is like a kid's game
compared to this. It's painful, it's sad, and sometimes people are angry at the
press, but like the police, the firemen, the doctors who have a job to do, the
same is true for photographers. We have to shoot these pictures. I cannot
edit myself before I take the picture, I cannot say no, it's too horrible. There
is no way we can cover it up. This is history, as painful as it is. We have to
show these horrible things so that one day, maybe, someone who will become the next president, or prime minister, can see the sort of things that
have happened, like September 11, and maybe they will help it not to happen
again."

Another staff photographer for the *New York Post*, Brigitte Stelzer, who
took some of her pictures with the camera aimed back over her shoulder as

*View of Ground Zero, facing east toward Church Street, from Tex McCrary's apartment
in Battery Park City. To the right, Liberty Street runs along the south side of the site.*

she raced from the fall of the South Tower, talked to me with passion about
the prohibition against trying to shoot Ground Zero. "There's a big shame
to it," she said, "because it cut us off from our documentation of history. We
weren't allowed access at all. It was mostly based on stealth, smartness,
friendships. Someone with a connection to something giving you, at most,
maybe an hour somewhere. We couldn't *really* cover it, day by day, week by
week. So, *in your own city,* you can't cover it. What more do you need to be?
For recovery workers it was easier. If you had a point-and-shoot camera, a
little autofocus thing, you were allowed to take pictures. And so many doctors, nurses, rescue workers of various types called us at the *Post* wanting to
sell us their pictures, and yet they might have come from just that position
where they chase a press photographer, rip his pass off his neck. It would
have been *so* important to show our world what we are doing right now to
make this better, to make this go away, to heal—whatever was appropriate to
the death of all those thousands of people. Big mistake."

One press photographer who had been shooting at Ground Zero since
September said to me: "I don't like to be around it." We were sitting in a Starbucks behind the wonderful old Maine granite Custom House across the
street from Battery Park, exactly on the spot where the Dutch West India

BEHIND THE GREEN DOOR

Company founded Nieuw Amsterdam. As we conversed, a cable from his longlensed Cannon to his desktop enabled him to transmit pictures he had shot that morning to his agency. "It's the cops," he said, so disgusted he could barely muster the energy to say it. "I've had it to here with them. No consistency—none. They do whatever they want. That business of a crime scene is such a load of crap. Crime scene! It's meaningless. I think they hate the press. They think we're making all this money. Absurd. They're bored with their jobs, they've been given carte blanche, so they exercise it being rude, pushing people around. It makes them feel better, as if they're doing something, but it's just a bad attitude. It's an outrage. I can't stand to see them anymore."

I did not have that severe a problem with anybody, but I was not the press, and I worked overtime to keep the fact that I was shooting to myself. When I say that Ray was a lookout I do not mean to suggest that he did nothing else, but the task of looking out for a man with a camera at Ground Zero was not a trivial occupation. Over the course of nine months, wearing a hardhat, allweather boots, and my pass and respirator I was more self-conscious, harried, suspicious, than in all the years of a lifetime, and I take no pleasure, not even a sly smile, in being furtive for any end. If profound relaxation is a key to any art, this was a terrible situation in which to enter the art of the lens. So often did I need to turn the camera off, replace the lenscap, and stash it in its case only to take it out and crank it up again a minute later, that I started to feel a tingling and numbness in my hand and my wrist. After weeks of anxiety and an increasingly useless hand, I noticed a pinch of nerve in the turn-and-squeeze motion by which, whenever I was inspired by an intimation of law, I reached the lenscap to the front of the camera and clicked it on. NO CAMERAS NO PHOTO was decommissioning me with carpal tunnel syndrome. When I learned to perform the action slower, turning the camera to meet my hand halfway, the syndrome relaxed and disappeared.

I saw the interdiction in its barest, truest form in front of the firehouse for Engine 10, Ladder 10. It was posted on a bridge erected to shield the Liberty sidewalk, where someone, perhaps a firefighter, had handlettered a sign: NO LOOKING.

Abstracted into its broadest social sense, NO LOOKING summarizes what the nation has been told about the worlds behind the worlds of September 11, and it indispensably complements the move toward a condition in which all of us are looked at, surveilled, all the time; a condition manifested in the tripling of spy cameras on the streets of New York; in the proliferation of helicopters, police boats, armed street squads; and in the rush to confound dissent with disloyalty and to neutralize it with COINTELPRO[12] tactics—domestic infiltration, agitation, intimidation—freshly vitalized by provisions in Title II of H.R. 3162, the virtually unreadable *Uniting and Strengthening America by Providing Appropriate Tools Required to Intercept and Obstruct Terrorism Act*, known as the USA PATRIOT Act, to which *one* patriotic senator, Senator Feingold, registered opposition in a way that really counted: he voted against it.[13] What was strangely out of place about this notion of **NO LOOKING,** as it applied to Ground Zero, was that if the statesmen we hire were doing their jobs half as well as most of the men on the site, they wouldn't need to tell us not to look, and we would be encouraged to disobey and disrespect such a sign wherever we see it. And, of course, those buildings would not have been knocked down.

This is not to criticize the men of the Ten House. That firehouse, which lost six of its men on the 11th (one retired captain, two lieutenants, three firefighters), had suffered enough to last it a lifetime. Glance to the left as you walk toward the stair and notice that piece of ruined truck against the wall. When you see a group of spotters sitting down at the lunch table, notice the posture of the men, as I did one day when Kevin McCrary brought them a typical McCrary combination: aluminum pans of hot Italian food he had driven down from Nino's on Canal Street, and tapes in which you could hear—a rare thing—as well as see the second plane as it plowed into the building that once stood across the street.

"Watch the upper right of the frame," I said, touching the TV screen. "It's coming now. First you'll hear it, then you'll see it."

But I could not bear to look at their faces when it struck. If anybody in or around the Ten could be regarded as responsible for a sign that demanded **NO LOOKING,** they themselves had looked enough, more than was fit for any man. And the guarded generosity with which the Ten House shared the astonishing view from its rooftop enabled as much looking as any space around the site. When they printed up FDNY T-shirts saying **DEFENDING LIBERTY STREET,** Donavin and I had to smile over the brave superior charm of the motto, for Liberty Street, as the focus and the title of my movie, and as a shorthand for 114 ("I'm goin over t'Liberty"), was totally *our* street, and we were each, in different ways, defending it. On the other hand, beyond its practical use to decongest pedestrian traffic, that unfortunate phrase—**NO LOOKING**—symbolized an unhealthy measure of control over a moment of historical consequence, and in a purely political sense, **NO LOOKING** is a way *not* to defend Liberty Street.

BEHIND THE GREEN DOOR

5

CATS' CLAWS, TWISTED BEAMS, BIG RED CRANE

I am not ashamed to say that I loved shooting the site and the commotion surrounding it. It was a privilege being there and I never took it for granted. One day turned to two, two turned to twenty, forty; before I knew it I was setting a deadline in order to make myself stop, but the deadline passed, the borrowed money dried up, the inked signatures on my hardhat faded, my battered perimeter pass had to be taped back together, the weather turned nice, the world turned more mad, my friend Ray departed, and I was still going down. The more I shot, the more acute was the longing to snake my way in closer, do it some kind of justice. Robert Capa, cofounder of Magnum, the great cooperative agency for photojournalists, used to say that if your picture wasn't good enough you weren't close enough. There was not a single vantage on any street around the perimeter where I hadn't held the camera, and in trying to get closer I relied on the zoom, but to zoom is to wobble, so to stabilize my shots without the help of a tripod I used everything around. I used Ray's shoulders, I used the spurs of fire hydrants, standpipes and sprinklers; the scotias, the angles, the bases of lampposts; the handles, the hoods, the bumpers of trucks and cars; the concrete, the castiron, the woodwork of benches. I used the barricades themselves, I used my own hardhat, I used nitrogen containers, I used traffic control boxes, I used rails of polished brass and dirty iron, I used the moorings of piers, stray lumber, caution cones, mailboxes, dumpsters, stacked old cardboard, window ledges, fences, ladders, gates, trees, stakes, chains, barrels and fountains. I used the stone of stoops and cobbled streets, I used the slanted silver rims of metropolitan garbage pails with people tossing their trash toward the lens. I held my breath until I was blue. I lied for shots. I walked in circles for shots. I espresso'd myself stupid in order to stay awake for shots. I disgraced myself for money to buy more tape for shots. I worked for months with a faulty camera I wanted to toss into the Hudson—one night I fought it for an hour before it ran—but at least I made the sonofabitching piece of shit shoot. I shot in the rain and in the snow with a plastic bag over the camera. I shot at two in the morning when the lens could hardly see but it was seeing better than me. I shot when the zoom was frozen. I shot when Ray was plotting his assassination of me and an escape to Fantasy Island over a quiet cup of coffee. I shot when the camera told me there was nothing to shoot on. When there was no better option I held the camera at my side as if I were merely passing by and I would let the camera run to get a surreptitious second I could use in slow motion or freeze-frame.

I started without a clue to what I was doing with the camera—it was a foreign body to me—but as I shot I came to respect it and appreciate its power. It was only a "sonofabitching piece of shit" if I was having trouble with it; otherwise, it was a minor miracle. As you grow older with glasses nothing helps you to see better. This helped me to see better, and I saw what it meant to cradle an image—to hold a world—in your hands.

When Kevin McCrary sneaked me through an evacuated redzone in Gateway Plaza—this is the building where, once it reopened, we were escorted off the roof by those who had the law of us—he brought me up to a short roofladder, where I needed to raise the hatch with my head to keep a hand free for the camera, and I was able to see the entire sprawl of the site for the first time. It was comparable to standing at the rim of the Grand Canyon, but as I was only afforded about a minute in which to shoot, I was practically in tears over my own incompetence. *Why'd you keep to that longshot? What's the good of a sloppy pan? Why didn't you zoom?* I recall having to turn away from Ray to hide the emotion when, sitting in my car later, I glanced over the footage. Uh! *History and this is how I handle it.* I would have given anything to steal another chance, and when Kevin, good man, gave it to me, I shot for two days until the camera itself ran out of steam.

Once I started to meet more survivors of the attacks I came to know exceptional people. A few of them, such as Kevin, Donavin, David, became my guides and compatriots. But as a filmmaker I sometimes wished that I had never talked to anybody, for no one spoke truer about the events of September 11, no one was more engrossing or instructive than the site. Like New York's Picassos, like the Brooklyn Bridge, like most of what has attracted me to the city, the site was what it was and not at all another thing and it was interesting to me in every way.

I was interested in the ironworkers, the way their sparks lit the night and shielded faces that were working, as they did in Oklahoma City, to take down what they or their fathers or grandfathers had put up.

I was interested in the remarkable reach of the Abbel Aerial water trucks that sprayed down the dust, their bright blue rounded forms the chipperest things on the site.

I was interested in the bent weighted look of the firefighters in their high-crowned, widebrimmed hats ("cowboys in overalls," someone called them), and the scrape and drag of their boots as they trudged off the site, shoulderers of a million and a half tons of wreckage, the weightiest men I have ever seen, so weighted you expected their coats to push them, face-first, into the street; weighted enough to walk the moon; weighted enough to not stand straight ever again.

I was interested in the wrecker's ball, really a wrecker's cylinder—or a rectangle resembling a suitcase—with a big tire above it, and the way it simply hung there, looking as if it needed to rest its neck for five minutes, the silence as it rose up slowly, and the unforgettable sound when it pounded through the floors of a building, like a few dozen dumptrucks unloading themselves at once, the sound of the World Trade Center still falling down.

I was interested in the smoke and steam that danced and distorted the shadows of men moving under the floods.

I was interested in the inconspicuous midnight loners who, when the cold streets had emptied of their business and amusement, would stand behind a barricade and smoke cigarettes while they looked toward the site with a calm, unswerving concentration that half a pack of Marlboros brings to restless men, an act that was anything but prurient or trivial: the opposite of loitering, or, if it was loitering, it made that action beautiful, an act of great dignity, sadness, and hope, an act that I saw as both a verse from a blues and a page from the quintessential New York novel, a necessary act that completed the great picture of recovery and removal, a note in the margin of the Constitution that states: "In tobacco and the doing of nothing, there is freedom too," whether you're reading the *Daily News* or watching operating engineers from Local 15 whose equipment just partly appears over a fence.

I was interested in the small steel unadorned boxes sitting alone and unnameable in the beds of pickup trucks that were driven, without ceremony, up the long steep slope of the Tully Road and through the streets of Lower Manhattan, going to add a part of another body to the widening grim assortment (there would be nineteen thousand) at the morgue on Thirtieth Street, an image so intensely compressed with hard meaning one would not be surprised if the pickups exploded before making it off the site, but it also resembled a getaway: here is the little prize, in the capture of which all this commotion was, for so long, directed, and yet it departs, by necessity, unannounced, unattended.

I was interested in the silvery white allnight glow of Ground Zero, the way it illuminated the terminus of streets that used to run continuously north to south, east to west, until they were severed by the World Trade Center and now this, a catastrophic brilliance that lightwashed the corners of façades, haloed rooftops, and found you, as you walked away, by piercing through a window, a chink in a wall, a gap between buildings, calling out to the camera, coaxing it closer, like a vision of holiness.

I was interested in the walls of smoke that floated toward the Battery or up to Chambers Street, as if a World Trade ember at the site's epicenter had been fanned too fast and set the fires ablaze again.

I was interested in the signage that marked the walls and doors of buildings everywhere around the site with handpainted (and sometimes misspelled) words, phrases, and symbols out of spray cans—1ST AID CEDER— MED TRAUA—TRIAGE—9/15 CHECKED—WFC2—MORGUE—EVACUATE— NYPD TEMP. HQ.—and which added, in bold bright strokes that were to linger, in some cases, for over two years, a story of improvisation to one of the great anthologies of styles and traditions that coexist in city signage, an anthology to which this phase would be a footnote, for where, except in photographs or films such as mine, would these signatures of emergency be preserved? And yet one small white paper sign, DOW JONES & COMPANY, that was scotchtaped to a doorway could tell you an awful lot about the great upheaval that had occurred on the 11th.

I was interested in that even more temporal breed of signage, texts that were written in gray films of deathdust, graffiti by which survivors, workmen, and visitors alike expressed a feeling of solidarity and transferred particles of the World Trade Center into their eyes, their beds, their pockets, their sandwiches, and the focus rings of their Nikons.

I was interested in the commercial advertisements partly visible in the shambled wreckage of trucks—EMPIRE 1-800-WAY-AHEAD—vehicles that were smashed into sinuous skeletons, often with only their tires intact, and yet they wouldn't stop speaking, wouldn't stop advertising, and I wondered whether the drivers were dead and where you would be calling if you dialed.

Signage on a Burger King at the corner of Church and Liberty streets, where Donavin Gratz saw the fireball from the second strike. Not visible is a sign on the window: MED TRAUMA, misspelled TRAUA.

I was interested in the birds that were all over my earliest frames, flesh-eaters flocking to the feed, competing with firefighters, making it look as if I were trying to compose scenic shots.

I was interested in the disturbing interludes in which the activity of the site temporarily subsided, disturbing not because you didn't have an explanation but because, emotionally, the scale of destruction seemed to call for commotion *without* pause or conclusion, and this feeling helped me later to understand why the site made increasingly less sense when it was clean and constructive than it did when an army of siege engines were toiling noisily over its hills, voids, and furrows of ashen steel.

I was interested in the fact that after you learned how to look you could turn in any direction anywhere on any street and you could see the total destruction of the World Trade Center and the lives that flashed away imprinted upon the neighborhood: a black wall that should be white; a white window that ought to be clear; a gash in a block of impervious limestone;

a sign with its meaning sheared off or else twisted into a half obscenity; clots of those September clouds in such overt places no one would ever think to clean them because no one would care to notice; bent bars of iron that looked as if Superman had made an impromptu demonstration before jumping the E train; a business paper that slapped against the wall of a rooftop or was tapped, absently, under the toe of your boot, insisting on another of the countless eulogies for the disenrolled ledgers of Aon or Cantor Fitzgerald, lines of disembodied finance mumbled into the wind, sad little ceremonies that happened a hundred times a day.

I was interested in the agile one-man Gators that would appear out of the corner of my frame and reduce the ungovernable diversity of the site to the wonder of one soul, a wonder that the camera could never resist, as if a solution to that isolated mystery—*Where the hell can he be going?*—*What has he seen today?*—*What is the look on his face?*—*What's he thinking down there?*—would unlock the larger, multiform secrets of the site, or as if the camera were saying to me: *This is what we ought to be doing, following one man, more than that's the way to madness,* but I did go mad in my own modest way and the camera came with me.

I was interested in the irreversible arc of perfect grace in which a fused stack of beams the length of a flatbed truck would float nobly through the air in slow motion over the street, the pier, the river and then mournfully disappear into the hollow of a barge, each performance less than a minute, each one different and engaging in appearance, each one as fated as the next, each one a taking apart, a picking up, a giving back, a shipping away, a stark indicator that the sleek tall walls with all those windows couldn't cut it, couldn't stand in the world of men: an indisputable failure that you, who never saw the pieces coming in, now observe going out, one by one, the rust glowing orange and gold in the early sun, a last gleaming of the Trades as the scrapping of old unfortunate Pittsburgh steel that didn't last in its purpose a fifth as long as some of the four-story buildings that were here in old times when the bowsprits of schooners jutted out into the street, buildings that are lucky now to earn a glance of contempt, so that I wondered whether the speed of removal might have partaken of a subterranean drive to disperse these weighty evidences: the sooner it's all out of here, the sooner it didn't happen.

I was interested in the bucket itself, the one at Pier 6 with the number of the crane, 540, handpainted on it, a beautiful old Esco bucket that single-handedly lifted the bulk of the World Trade Center off the island of Manhattan, a bucket that touched more of the Twin Towers than anybody or anything else in New York City; and how the crane operators would make this gap-toothed rustbucket take a test bite, gently rocking twenty tons side to side to get a feel for how the pick was going to hoist; and how, in the hands of operators like Mickey Quinn, the bucket became a gentle thing in lifting and laying down these scarred and scored and bent and seared victims of such violence; and how occasionally, despite an array of hand signals reminiscent of baseball by which the crane and the pier communicated, a dockworker would grip one of the teeth of the great bucket and try to guide it into position manually, moving you to wonder whether the next logical step was to reach up and carry the steel himself.

I was interested in the fact that if you viewed them from the west under the noonday sun, bucket and beam appeared to have exactly the same texture, the same tone, so that the bite became a protective embrace; more than that, a possession, a momentary claiming that said: "You, beam, being one with this machine, have built something else now, if only for a moment, if only for whoever might be standing across the street;" or if you focused on a barge that was piled into the air and the beams thrust forward as it moved out majestically toward Brooklyn, you were looking at a ship, imposing, monster-made, and you imagined that the captain, the Nemo, the noname, was the spirit of steel itself and there were barges for each load, thousands of them waiting on the water all at once, a fleet of Tower beams that would search the seven seas for a place to put themselves together again.

I was interested in the way those beams were like fragments from a presocratic philosopher, unadorned expressions of elemental truths that so well suggest the beginnings of civilization that one can easily imagine them applying to its destruction, only the beams wheeled past me, or flew over my head, without translation, and everybody I turned to for help seemed to be saying: "Yes, I know the Greek of that steel and the meaning is this: *I am a beam*," so that I wondered whether that was what they were saying after all.

I was interested in the way the steel spoke literally . . . emitting a short, sharp, highpitched cry when a Maztec Enviro, a grappler that would serve double-duty with the crane, would fasten its five steel teeth into one of the smaller beams before whipping it around, tossing it into the barge, and opening its jaws in a voiceless victory yawn . . . or when the steel folded down under the pounding of the wrecker and it would roar like an animal that, like the disembodied catless Cheshire grin in *Alice in Wonderland*, existed *only* as a sound but was animal nonetheless, made *out of* steel but not *of* it.

At Pier 6, steel from the Trade Center is craned into a barge before the Kathleen *tugs it across the East River to Brooklyn.*

I was interested in the sad stirring sight of the *Kathleen,* hauling those pieces, barge after barge like a boat in a Grimms' tale, the little red tug that towed a whole city away.

I was interested in the fact that those beams—Pennsylvanians, Japanese, some of them carrying empty cans of Bud or Rheingold or Viet Nam headlines in copies of the *Daily Mirror*—were shipping out to build again in Turkey, for instance, where the mementos hid within them would be discovered and discarded—or maybe a young Turk would take home a Schaefer beer opener, a yellowed newspaper, a crumpled Hershey's wrapper, a phrase from Morgan Stanley, a wedge of dried paste or a jetseared bolt and keep it on his night table to find out how it skews or attacks or haunts his dreams, or to study it the way men ponder postcards, coins, or stamps from distant places that can be contemplated only when you hold them in your hands.

I was interested in how, if you sighted along the south side of World Trade Five toward the World Financial Center, the perfectly squared clean white corner of World Financial Three would play, artistically, against the shafts of North Tower that were flung into the face of Building Five, so that it seemed an almost diagrammatic assemblage evoking the clashing geometries of Order and Chaos.

I was interested in the drillers, I was interested in the trenchers, I was interested in the path that was followed by the trucks and I wanted to shoot them driving in, shoot them making their slow determined way across the site, shoot them at the washdown, shoot them in the streets with their headlights crawling ominously toward the lens, shoot them pulling up to the waterfronts. The washdowns themselves were remarkable, their backlit showers embracing every truck with vivid Vegas-like fountains that left the vehicles, their gnarled steel cargo and their wheels to drip toxically for blocks as they rolled toward the river, the drops appearing in slow motion through the lens as if they were dense with a dust that was grudgingly relinquished by the pieces of the building from which it had formed. I was especially fond of the diesel excavators with their tanklike tracks, that sturdy breed of busy earthbeasts whose stuttering ravenous movements made them appear to be descendants not of actual dinosaurs but of special-effects pioneers like Ray Harryhausen, while a closer look revealed a quite beautiful contradiction in these metal machine monsters of orange and yellow skin: they laid their materials in front of the spotting crews with such extreme care, such precision and such grace that it was touching to behold of a machine so crude and you marveled at the finesse of the men at the controls. One grappler bit, tossed, and rebit the chassis of a vehicle till the wheels were shaken off and there was nothing but a tight crush of steel that would fit into the small space of a truck. When they wrestled out of the pile great mouthfuls of steel, yanking and shaking them free of entangled strands, it easily justified the term *spaghetti* for the debris that went to Pier 25, and if sometimes they fought, fussed, and fumbled with a single strand at a time it was from knowing that, sooner or later, it *all* had to be loaded and removed.

I shot the site at sunrise, I shot it at magic hour, I shot it in moonlight, I shot it in a blizzard with Master Gilbert's ageless aristocrat, the Woolworth Building, towering in the background. I shot it from the churchyard of old St. Paul's, where the trees still fluttered with ghostly rags from September and where more people fell as dust on its old graveled walks than were buried there in 250 years. I shot it from the streets and from the forty-third floor and from every in-between I could maneuver myself into. I shot it from cars, boats, vans, ferries, stores, roofs, bridges, and I shot it from the site itself. I shot the sky above because I regarded the Towerless air, free now for clouds, cranes, choppers, and birds as part of the site as well. I hated Ray for not showing sufficient initiative for getting me into better prospects, and *hate* is not an overstatement: the importance of the site was turning my friend into my enemy. This distinctive one-time-only universe was doing a disappearing act, changing significantly from day to day. I needed a hurryup man. That was not Ray's style, he has a lifetime to lose, you have to be willing to wait forever—but the site would not wait for half an hour. When I say that I fought for an hour with the camera, that hour was important: I can still feel the loss. To catch something, *anything* related to Ground Zero, *now* was the only time to do it. It gnawed at me, and I wondered what I was missing when I was gone for several days. What was coming down? What had dispersed forever? What wall, what pile, what prospect might have become briefly observable? Once I had begun to visit the site regularly, I contemplated with paroxysms of horror and contempt the gap of three or four weeks between my first and second excursions. I could not believe the stupidity of a man who had seen what I had seen and hadn't raced right back the next day. Entire chapters had been opened and closed without me. Lock me up? Do it, but not for using the camera: lock me up for not using it more often. I recall what I said to Ray on each of those early excursions: "We can stop pretty soon. I don't need to obsess about it. We've been lucky. We oughtn't to lose the camera for a shot." No, especially as the camera was uninsured— it wasn't even paid for—but I hear these words of mine and I think: *Amateur. Fraud. Moax.* I needed not to lose Ray's useful cooperation—he, no one else, was with me in those days and he was soaking up pathogens and coughing up cash for a venture that was not of any vital concern to him— but I ought to have said: *I don't know what we're doing here, but I know we have to do it, man. Hang out as long as it takes. Screw the clock. Screw the cold. Screw the cost. Screw the camera. Screw the cops. Screw the feds. Screw the family. Screw the stench. And screw you, too!* Eventually I did say it, but by then I was standing there alone.

6
MINUTEMAN

It was Kevin McCrary who first brought me to Liberty Street. That December night he introduced me to 114, a devastated building which, from the moment it opened its doors to me, drew me into a vision of daily life at Ground Zero, a dust-driven world of collateral damage that constituted a liberal education for me. After Kevin's intervention the lens of my camera, which had roamed the random streets uninformed and uninvited, found an ideal perch for zooming into the site, and it earned the referred protection of a WTC perimeter pass that was registered in my name. This enabled me to follow two personal perspectives: David, who was fixed upon resuming his life on Liberty Street; and Donavin, the resilient contractor who was entrusted to make it happen and who secured a pass for me because he knew, as David did, that it was important to document the transformation.

David and Donavin, different as day and night, were sometimes at odds over the Liberty enterprise, but as they persevered I developed durable friendships with both of these men. With Kevin it is hard to quite conceive what that would look like. Perhaps it looks like this: editing him, staying in touch, grateful to have counted among his compatriots in the post-September odyssey of life in Lower Manhattan.

That first night at Liberty Street could not be photographed, although I did shoot Kevin in a ground-floor commercial space formerly called Miami Sub, a sandwich spot that had gone out of business before the attacks. Pausing here, Kevin reminisced about one of his Ground Zero icons, David Bouley. A Manhattan chef with a three-star bakery and a four-star restaurant, Bouley, by an arrangement with the Red Cross, had improvised an eatery there known, by its frontage, as the Green Tarp Restaurant or the Green Tarp Café, enabling the men to mess on quality hot food without trooping uptown. Celebrities came to serve. People I met in the building would have a jolt of recognition: "Wait a minute—this was the Green Tarp, wasn't it?"

When I mentioned the controversy spurred by other restaurateurs who had complained that Bouley wrongly accepted relief money while he utilized donated food and volunteers (charges that the Red Cross itself did not support), Kevin said, with his usual half shrug: "They could've come helped out too." When I mentioned it to Donavin a year and a half later, he said: "People shouldn't even have a right to say that. We had grills out on Cedar, right in the street, when it was still fuckin *ash* out there. *All night long* they were going. We fed *thousands* every day, and they were *amazing* meals. David Bouley's a great man. I never met one person who would have taken a cent from him. These people—no one knows a fucking thing about it."

On short notice, Kevin had arranged to pick us up this evening on South End Avenue by the westside entrance to the site. When the call came through we were just around the corner at the first of his original volunteer headquarters, St. Joseph's Chapel, which is on the ground floor of the Gateway Plaza building in which he and his father, Tex, had awakened on the 11th. We were at our rendezvous in no time, but we had learned that for Kevin there was never a shortest distance between any two points. Three blocks could easily consume three hours. Kevin was so resistant to doing any one task when he could interpose another that you wondered whether he ever wanted to do what he'd planned. Donavin, whose own sense of time was not exactly military, was at the far end of his rope waiting for Kevin one night when he said to him, over the phone, pacing the lobby of 114: "Man, you know, you've got to really . . . you need to definitely . . . I don't know—*something*." A master of compulsive indirection, Kevin was such a supreme sidetracker that Time itself wanted to wash its hands of him—there were certainly people who did—but Kevin made it work for the purpose he'd been serving since he walked into the cloud of the North Tower, liberated Sloan's supermarket of any item that would support the firelines, and in a volatile mix of grunting labor, grieving sensibilities, security concerns and proprietary emotions, began to carve out an identity that few people understood and no one, himself included, could have predicted.

"I could have joined the guys on the pile but I thought I could be more useful in Sloan's," Kevin told me. "I just got caught up in the moment. The power had gone off and I knew that anybody who was in there for the first time wouldn't know their way around. I knew it like the back of my hand. People were looking for flashlights but there were none to be had, so I started lighting candles and I directed people to where the water was. We pretty much got the last drop. Guys were pouring into the site without the

BEHIND THE GREEN DOOR

basic essentials, so we set up assembly lines for taking things out, we made a makeshift table out of police barricades, and we started turning out those peanut butter and jelly sandwiches, just trying to keep the dust off of them as best we could."

It was in front of Sloan's, now closed and boarded up with a large American flag across the front, that we were going to meet Kevin—if he came. As we waited for him I remembered what he'd said about the start of what he called "my tour down here."

"We set up a second stand," he told me, "under the overpass to Dow Jones on Liberty Street, which is barely a hundred yards from the Marriott [WTC 3]. We had a bunch of shopping carts and anything else that would roll and we would push them in as far as they would go, in the direction of the Towers— or what used to be the Towers—without running into obstructions of debris or I-beams. Then we'd carry the stuff in buckets to where the guys were burrowing in, trying to recover something, or someone, with very little success. I think they knew, deep down, they weren't going to save anybody. Everyone wanted to work round the clock until they dropped, working twenty-four on, two off, catching a nap standing up, sitting down, crashing in a medic tent— wherever you could—so we just kept going out there. You just had to worry about impaling yourself on some sharp object. Everything was protruding from everywhere. You had to maneuver through these bucket lines with hundreds of firefighters, cops, volunteers who were hauling out one piece after another, and the steel was all twisted and mangled every which way. Occasionally a guy would be torching off a piece and you had to have your wits about you to not put your hand on a chunk that was still glowing."

Tonight Kevin was uncharacteristically punctual and we drove to Liberty Street without deviation. Probably *we* were the deviation and frustrated people were waiting elsewhere. That little drive, which lasted less than five minutes, was uneventful. We climbed into a filthy borrowed van (all of his transports were crowded and grungy), we rolled slowly through picketed checkpoints to Cedar Street a block south of the site, and we entered 114 Liberty from behind. Kevin knew the guards in the streets and he passed them with brief polite banter. As we were crossing Washington Street between two wounded buildings—the menacing Deutsche Bank above us on Albany Street and Cass Gilbert's sturdy old stone sentry, 90 West, burnt and broken, a little behind us—he paused to ask a pair of firefighters whether they'd gotten their posters yet. These were posters of the Twins that were printed from a panoramic photograph by Everen T. Brown and which Kevin helped dis-

Donavin Gratz, left, and Kevin McCrary, right, on Liberty Street.

tribute to the guys on the site (that was Kevin's phrase for everybody there: *the guys*). On some printings of these posters Kevin had the white margins crowded with the signatures of people he had met, including firefighters, police, National Guard, air force, rescue workers, politicians, performers and sports stars. I was always uneasy when Kevin brought these posters out, or brought them up, but they were received enthusiastically and some of the firehouses framed and hung them on their walls. Obviously Kevin was more in tune with the prevailing attitude toward those vanished monoliths. I was

BEHIND THE GREEN DOOR

always expecting to hear: "What do I want with a fucking *poster*—those build-ings're in my *lungs,* and my *brother's* in that pile." If it was said I never heard it. These men had not received their posters yet, so Kevin promised to see to it and the promise pleased them. We drove on. I wasn't able to shoot because I'd pledged, at Kevin's behest, to lay the camera low, a reasonable precaution for which I was nonetheless sorry. There weren't any astonishing revelations of ruin or relic, but if the gods of videography had granted a few minutes out of all the time the camera had to close itself down, that drive would have been it. Even Ray, who seldom expressed wonder, was memorably absorbed by the feel, the look, the implication of that drive.

I doubt, though, that aiming one camera out the window would have cap-tured it. You can only do a thing for the first time once, but it might take a measure of repetition to render it. Picasso said that if you want to be a painter you should poke out your eyes, and Giacometti said that when Picasso was in your studio he looked around not with two eyes, but two cameras. Well: I am a painter and I *have* poked my eyes out. To look with two cameras I need two cameras. Still, I'd have settled for one small spy that I could have, by turns, put to work and put away. All I have now is this reflective testimony, based, as it is, upon lenses that won't zoom, focus that softens and blurs, memory that falters. But I remember well enough. Soldiers. Police. Red lights flashing. Doors boarded up. Shopsigns blasted. Streetlamps dark. Sidewalks deserted. Residences abandoned. Piles of unswept debris that were dangling, like dirty paper vines, over the sides of fire escapes. Hard-hats. Badges. Boots. Guns. Mud. Dust. Goggles. The rumble of big trucks. Gators scooting around us. A huge red spraypainted **EVACUATE**. A black **TRIAGE** with an arrow beneath it pointing west, toward O'Hara's Pub & Restaurant. Clusters of men, each of them a solitude bleeding from unreach-able places, men whom Fate had sent to see the worst of the world in a roof-less crematorium, conceived at 54 Marienstrasse in Hamburg and erected by young men infatuated with death, medieval zealots in modern missile-machines who were gone before Chaos enacted its masterpiece.

No. This is what you had to think about it: No. The night had gotten the city all wrong. It was a page from an apocalyptic fantasy of the future where the life of a great city has been drastically deranged, the rules reordered, law and lawlessness practically indistinguishable. To live, to work, even to wan-der there awhile you will have to become a guerrilla, exercising faculties you never thought you'd need, at least not here. But this was not pulp fiction, this is how historic Lower Manhattan had entered the new century. From that

night on, the idea of Ground Zero included, for me, the streets within the restricted zone that constituted the margins of the Trade site itself. If upon
their collapse the Twin Towers had dispersed to far corners of the earth, they
easily expanded their immediate neighborhood and they left no quarter unmolested. If the drive to Liberty Street was uneventful, the neighborhood
itself was all event, a set for a noir tale, lit sensationally for sharp urban contrasts, floods flaring the lens, washed-down streets, gigantic shadows, butt-
thumping sound. This comparison to a film set is apt, for the response to
September 11 did for Lower Manhattan what a team of Hollywood filmmakers do to a section of city: it scouted a neighborhood, converged with a large,
bustling crew that went to work with impressive speed to transform it into
an alternate reality (without quite replacing the original), it locked off its
streets, it made sure everybody was fed, it inconvenienced and aggravated
outsiders—people who live there—and it consistently displayed the keen
efficiency of people who are adept at converting a public space into a workshop. Walt Whitman, who lived here awhile (as did Poe and Washington Irv-
ing), who loved to walk these neighborhoods, who sold *Leaves of Grass* at the
Fowler and Wells Phrenological Cabinet at the corner of Beekman and Nassau streets, could not have predicted this for his beloved Mannahatta, but
young Walt, who would have versefully mourned the loss of life, would also
have found it transporting, and he'd have come here all the time—it would
have been his court of miracles. *Lover of populous pavements,* he'd have spoken to all the firefighters, the teamsters, the cops, the midnight foremen, the
equipment operators. You'd have seen him on the rigs, probably sitting on
the steel itself, or standing, impossibly, on the ropes above the scale pans
that swung out over the Hudson in order to give a voice, beyond the piercing screech of the big red crane on its tracks, to the loop of continuous motion, barely broken by a brief bow of the pan, by which were dumped into a
barge, in a trip that lasted a minute, the jumbles of garbage that were once
the Trade Center. The earthshaking thump of the huge pan as it landed on the
fresh road millings of ground asphalt, the thunk and rattle of its chains—
he'd have wanted you to hear it and appreciate a beauty that also, for him,
signified democracy . . . America . . . life at its peak and within it death too.
He'd have loitered on rooftops, smoking, extrapolating, drinking black
coffee and cans of Red Bull. I know that I said, in chapter 1, that if a poet had
opened his mouth you would have shot him but you wouldn't have shot
Whitman. *I do not ask the wounded person how he feels, I myself become the
wounded person.* He'd have befriended the Irish gent who owns O'Hara's on

Cedar Street and the bartender Mike and from the hour it opened again he'd have missed not a day, *tasting the sweets of the brown mash,* perfect place for him to embrace coats of dust, to memorize faces, to hand out two-dollar bills for good luck, to work out *the meal equally set.* He'd have inscribed every brogue of a young waitress, every Ground Zero cough in a volunteer, every dark-skinned accent in every kiosk that sold coffee and buttered bagels. With his comrade Donavin he'd have driven to his workshop in Williamsburg, Brooklyn by the Newtown Creek and he'd have smoked and shared the news with Pat Tallon, the elevator operator whose son, Sean, a "probie," was one of the firefighters of the Ten House on Liberty Street who died that morning. To Walt, as to Donavin, who did this in Whitman's stead, Pat would have said: "You be careful." And surely Walt would have written a *Specimen Days* about this time of anguish, urgency, and secret sharing the way he did about the Civil War. As it is, some of what he said about that conflict applies to Ground Zero. "Future years," he wrote, "will never know the seething hell and the black infernal background of countless minor scenes and interiors."

Kevin McCrary was no poet—lyrical lungpower is not his strongpoint— but there was something Whitmanesque in his vision of democracy; or, at least, in the ripples of it around his behavior at Ground Zero. If there is something in American behavior that looks anarchic it is probably an unfamiliar semblance of democracy. Certainly Kevin was Whitmanesque in being at home in these environs. At a time when its residents and businesses were thrown out, some of them literally, Kevin had taken possession. I understood this best when, although he is a tall darkhaired man with a handsome friendly face, he reminded me, one day, of Quasimodo. I will not attempt a paragraph connecting Ground Zero, Kevin McCrary, Walt Whitman and the Hunchback of Notre Dame, but for me they are intimately connected. We were on the rooftop at 114. Kevin had climbed a ladder and was clearing off pieces of the Towers that were at the edge of a housed cooling unit called a chiller. His actions were generating gusts of September dust that whirled up into his face before drifting elsewhere, panicking other people on the roof. "Don't throw it—don't throw it!" Kevin continued to rummage about, and because he was moving in a squat some of the time, I saw, momentarily, a dwarf, a jester, a knave who was self-dispensated beyond reproach. It was a melancholy enchantment, a queer misrule that was sanctioned by the gargoyles stationed in the Church Street façade of a city landmark, the U.S. Realty Building, which I could see from where I stood. Then it came together for me: the Hunchback.

Kevin, it seemed to me, was as much in his element living—I will not say cavorting—at Ground Zero as Quasimodo was in Notre Dame Cathedral. He unabashedly, unselfconsciously explored its inferno, walked its filthy streets alone, and climbed and clamored around its evacuated rooftops, preserving artifacts, making little repairs, taking photographs, talking to everybody, introducing strangers, postulating ideas, drawing diagrams, channeling information, distributing gloves and Gatorade, delivering newspapers, collaging and copying and giving out his pictures, verifying stories, transporting Sterno stoves, rain gear, tools and detergents, hauling water out of the Hudson to flush a toilet in the office of the VIP Yacht Cruises ("That was the only running water—walking it up in buckets from the marina"), transiting volunteers, giving firefighters a lift, serving paper plates of food, favoring photographers, commandeering film crews, tipping off journalists with leads and leadlines, running ubiquitous errands, procrastinating appointments, trying all patiences, infuriating residents, enduring interrogation by the FBI, suffering the Red Cross and other entities that wanted to foul up his method or pollute his enthusiasm or dispose him to heel under the shadow of the law or the weight of bureaucracy, and generally coming to own the neighborhood the way Victor Hugo's Hunchback owned his great cathedral, a dark city of wonders that was technically not his but that more belonged to him than to anyone else around.

Kevin is not an animated speaker, but it made sense to me that he guided celebrities—Kevin Costner and Jason Alexander—on their unannounced tours, with some of them hanging around to cheer up the guys. "I thought it was constructive," Kevin said, "even though the mayor might have criticized it. I saw how it moved the people I brought in here: it changed their life, and it gave an emotional lift to the guys who were working round the clock, digging out. It was some of the first smiles they'd had on their faces. When John Travolta was here my cart was off somewhere, so we had a walking tour with a few of the firefighters. It was an amazing scene. It brings back memories of my mother who, during World War II, was with Bob Hope doing USO. Guys were handing Travolta their cellphones, asking him to speak to their girlfriends—it was a great relief from the oppression. I saw Jason Alexander being walked in by a cop who hadn't been on the scene and didn't know where he was going. I had my cart that time, so I said: 'Hop in.' We hooked up with a fire captain from Long Island who in turn brought us around in his vehicle. We had a grand tour of the site. We had him on the roof of 10 & 10. By coincidence, Kelsey Grammer was up there too with some other firefighters. We went off to the firehouse by the South Street Seaport, where we took group photos with the guys, and we met the son of a firefighter who had been lost. Jason was basically doing a comedy routine and some magic for the kid, cheering him up, spreading goodwill. We were down there a couple of hours, cruising around, and I kept asking him: 'You sure you don't need to be somewhere?' He said: 'No, this is where I should be.' The same was true for Evander Holyfield."

Before leaving his guide the prizefighter signed a white panel over the cracked windshield on the front of Kevin's electric cart, with the notation "Phil 4:13," invoking a line in one of the letters of Saint Paul that reads: "I can do all things through Christ which strengtheneth me."

Kevin was the right cicerone for anybody who didn't want, or couldn't get, an official view of the broken city. In his low monotone he illuminated a world of the ordinary, often with a smile or a mirthless little laugh, because nothing in this world of astonishments was all that much of a deal for him. Kevin was unstaggerable. Kevin was unembarrassable. In a place where visitors without uniforms or union cards cloaked their discomfiture in vestments of piety, reverence, whatever it took to feel appropriate, Kevin was out of line in every direction. As Donavin phrased it: "Kevin doesn't know where Kevin leaves off and where everyone else begins." For better or worse, he was endless. But some of his most exasperating attributes were, in fact, the means of his success, so that you couldn't have had half a Kevin, a half that constituted a tenacious and respectably productive volunteer. He became what he did by virtue of being impossible. Here is an illustration.

When he brought me into 120 Liberty Street, the smaller, slightly more ornate sister building to 114 that has its entrance at 125 Cedar, Kevin's goal was to share information about Red Cross assistance with its tenants. These were mostly artists like the painter Michael Cook who, unlike the co-op owners at 114, could afford to live in the neighborhood only because their apartments had been rent-controlled for years. I later learned that these tenants— who I used to see masked and suited up, trying their unprofessional best to do the cleaning that the EPA/DEP should have done instantly, impeccably, without any discussion—were being screwed by everybody, to a degree that one of them or, perhaps, all of them collectively ought to write a book about their trials and endurances. It's an important story. In fact the street itself, Cedar, like Liberty, deserves more attention. You could begin by saying: "One morning quiet little Cedar Street was shaken when a wheel from the left landing gear of a Boeing 767–200ER, embedded in an exterior column panel from the south face of One World Trade Center, flew over St. Nicholas Church and dived into the street with a clank, a shudder and a thud." But as soon as I set foot in this nice old building with its terra-cotta façade that bespoke nearly a century of witnessing New York, I could see that it was the wrong place for me or anyone else, and my exasperation with Kevin intensified with every fuckedout floor he took me to. "He's going to get us sick," I thought, "*I'll* be arrested, and we'll both die of lung disease—*for no reason at all,* because no one is *in* this godforsaken dump."

Blithely indifferent to the mold, the damp, the dust, the slumlike depression of the place, Kevin kept climbing up, calling down hallways, knocking on the doors of ghost dwellings, listening like a lunatic—*as if there would ever be an answer*—in order to share a piece of information with the dust. It is an understatement to say that he was in his element. He hadn't the slightest clue of the discomfort he was inflicting. After he instructed me to use the elevator and to meet him on a higher floor, I saw that I was faced with two choices: to bolt, or to shoot him and *then* bolt.

"Hello?" he was calling as the elevator opened. "Anyone here?"

"Yes, Kevin," I thought. "And I'm here to kill you."

Then a voice called out: "Who's there?"

It was one of the artists, Michael Mulhern, a painter who was methodically photographing his canvases before rolling them up for evacuation. Michael invited us in, he took the information from Kevin, he let me photograph his home and its view of the site below, he showed me a profile the *Times* had done with him that morning, and he gave me an account of how the South Tower fell into his home and his studio, unseating his life, contaminating his art.[14] Kevin's unwarranted liberties had, once again, proven to work: he had helped the documentary, helped Michael a bit, and he had even helped the building, for another piece of its story would now be told. Could one complain?

Kevin himself practically never complained, at least not to me, not on his own account: he was too busy for that. Only once did his temper blow, and that was at the Red Cross for keeping, for themselves, too many copies of the Twin Tower posters he had wanted to bring to the guys around the site. "I got little or no help, cooperation, or proper distribution from the Red Cross," he told me. "I had convinced the photographer, Everen Brown, to send the posters to the Red Cross here so they'd go to the people deserving them, not to Red Cross around the country. Then they pulled a fast one in the end and kept three thousand posters for themselves! I coerced them into giving me back three hundred and I took them to the Ten House to give to firefighters." But this was a rational explanation offered long after the fact. The day that I encountered him entangled with the Red Cross, Kevin was unswerving, flushed, shouting. Yes it was only a poster, a nice shot of the Twins, but from where he was calling there wasn't any *only* to a picture of the Twins.

If Kevin himself ever felt a sense of the horrific he never disclosed it: he was too busy for that too. If Kevin ever wanted to pack it in, take a powder, it never looked that way, unless you count falling asleep, midsentence, upon a pile of toxic junk in a cramped airless chamber that was not fit for a dog. When Kevin showed me the bench by the Hudson on which he used to bivouac, unshowered, during the first few weeks, he did so fondly. Reenacting the attitude with which he settled himself into the hollow of its hard wooden slats, he adjusted his assbackways cap, closed his eyes and said: "Quite comfortable." He meant it. His father and mother, Tex McCrary and Jinx Falkenburg, had been famous and successful, so that Kevin had grown up in modest luxury. But in a few hours here, with his toes bleeding from walking the pile in a girlfriend's shoes, his clothing and his lungs painted in dust, fumes in his nostrils, the smoke-sky thundering with all-night patrols of F-16s and helicopters, in total uncertainty about the fate of the city, the country, the world, Kevin slept sounder than ever before.

It isn't quite true to say that Kevin transcended obstacles and hardships. When one of the Catholic saints who is known as the Little Flower, Saint Thérèse de Lisieur, patroness of missions, said that if we aren't big enough to rise above our trials we should pass underneath them, she was undoubtedly speaking of Kevin. Kevin was the ultimate *under* man. He passed under blockades, obstinacies, suspicions, accusations, insults, and for nearly a year he passed under the radar. Kevin told me: "A liaison between the mayor's office and the group that's in St. Joe's Chapel said to me: 'What should we call you?' I used to have an affinity for the Gray Ghost, a character in the Civil War who, if he didn't win all of the battles, at least he escaped with his life. That's me down here: not always winning, but at least escaping with my life and liberty." After he'd left the site for over a year, he said to me: "I'm still delivering bread to a church that feeds the homeless. They don't know who I am. I just drop off boxes of bread several times a week. Remember: my mother was in the *Lone Ranger* movies. That's my style."

This style, and his being an *under* man, created the impression of not having adversaries, and that, more than anything, gave you the sense of something strange about Kevin. In a place where the appearance of opposition was so common—people were fighting fire, fighting fumes, fighting fatigue, fighting the pile, fighting the Hudson River, fighting Brother Death, fighting despair, fighting time, fighting terrorism—Kevin's low-keyed cheerfulness appeared to be missing something. It wasn't. Kevin could duck and dodge without thinking. He could invite himself anywhere. Approbation would fell someone else, not him.

Jim O'Connor, who worked for St. Joseph's Chapel as a kind of sacristan and who could pass neither underneath nor over the barricades until the end of September, was informed by local congregants—whose services were moved, temporarily, to a health club a little farther south at Rector Place—that there were people doing volunteer work at St. Joseph's. You can read all about it in the *Times*, they said. Sure enough, there was an article on Kevin and a guy named Flick (Perry Flicker), stationed at St. Joseph's, servicing the site.[15] Jim was unmanned by this. How did *they* manage *that*, when *he*, who belonged there, was being turned away? "At first," Jim told me, "before FEMA came along, it was just Kevin and Flick improvising. All these ferries were coming in with supplies, and there they were. I don't know how they did it. His father, Tex, had been evacuated but Kevin never left." Someone had offered Jim a clerical collar and shirt with which to facilitate unmolested passage to the chapel but, unlike Owen Burdick over at Trinity, Jim was just a little too nervous about the chance, God forbid, of being called onto the site to preside over remains, so he waited until he had cased out a system of his own. Once he was on the scene, Jim saw that Kevin had a hand in everything. "You've seen *Seinfeld,* right? Kevin is Kramer. No visible means of support, and turning up everywhere. Kevin seemed to know *everybody* wherever you went. I used to call him the Mayor of Gateway Plaza."

Jim and I were talking in the chapel after a total restoration necessitated by the volume of relief.

"You saw the big piano that's out there?" Jim said. "I wanted to move it down to Rector Place. I couldn't imagine how. I couldn't bring a truck in. So Kevin said: 'I know *exactly* what to do. Wait here.' He disappeared and came back with this electric golf cart."

"That's the one from the VIP Cruises next door," I said. "The owner, Mark Philipps, let him use it."

"He used to sleep there, too," Jim said. "So he drove it in, straight up to the door, we had three guys lifting and we loaded it onto this little golf cart. I'm watching the thing sag, I was *not* sure about it, I thought it was going to sink. But somehow it worked and he drove it out of here."

"Perfect example," I said, "of how he mastered the makeshift."

"He did," Jim said affectionately. "He was Kramer!"

I said to Kevin: "I'm surprised you didn't drive the cart directly into the chapel."

"I tried," he said, joking. "It wouldn't fit through the doors."

Stephan Mueller, the German-born journalist I quoted in chapter 2, told me that someone had called Kevin the Ground Zero Guru. "He knows *everything* that's happening down here," Stephan said. "Ground Zero—that's his passion. He feels he's doing the right thing—which he is. In a way, he's the quintessential New Yorker." Lightheartedly, Kevin once referred to people like himself—volunteers who sprang to action instantly—as Minutemen. He was disgusted when he saw them disrespected. He had seen what they could do. As the perimeter became more officialized, some of them were unceremoniously ejected, insulted, even handcuffed and driven off to jail. Kevin never tried to single himself out from them.

"There was an understanding at first," Kevin explained. "There was a need and we were filling it. Then, as we were meeting with FEMA, the NYPD or OEM, they started raising concerns about all the outsiders, the undesirables, the independents who didn't have affiliation or credentials, so we all saw the writing on the wall: hook up somehow or get booted out." Against the insinuation, which came from several sources, that to function independently was somehow transgressive, dangerous or dishonorable, Kevin countered with a modest defense: "Every now and again I'll talk to someone who was out there the first week or so, and they'll say: 'I remember that drink of water,' or: 'I remember that baloney sandwich.'"

As I saw it, there wasn't anyone else quite like Kevin, but I can speak only about the Kevin that I know, which is a quite narrow frame, for it's a view of a man who was born September 11 and who lived until roughly the age of one. Before and after that his existence is a blank. I knew he'd been taking care of his father after surgery, but did he have an apartment of his own? An income? Was he pursuing some profession? Was he truly unconcerned about the dust that he worked in, slept with and swallowed every day? To ask such questions was the same as not asking, so I gave up asking and I settled on this: when the Towers came down, the World Trade Center created an urban nightmare in which at least one new life was born. That year was

Kevin's time and, for all his faults, he used it to prove himself worthy of re-gard. The narrow frame in which I see him is as wide as a legend, a legend in a brokendown electric golf cart that was straining under the weight of bottled water, Gatorade, boots, or a piano while the flatbeds were straining under their loads of mangled steel. Each played a part.

For anything anybody would have to say against him, myself included—for to know him was to be driven crazy by him—I would always have a "Yes, but" for Kevin. The first of these yesbuts arose on the night Ray and I first encountered him. It was November, it was cold, it was late—around mid-night. As I was shooting the thick carpets of dust rising above us, Ray was attracted by the sight of stained glass. We wandered over. We were looking at the exterior of this small Catholic chapel. I was pretending, for Ray's sake, to take an interest, when Kevin materialized in the doorway. I thought he was the priest. I expected an eviction. But Kevin said: "Too bad you weren't here earlier."

"We were, but—"

"No, I mean *here*. I could have taken you in."

He was talking about the site, where he had walked a team of photogra-phers, including the BBC, into a ceremony (Putin was there) commemorat-ing the tragedy. *This is some hell of a nervy priest, or a privileged one,* I thought, *who can bring in photographers.* And why would this stranger have taken *me?* I was soon to learn the answer: it was important for him to get this big story told, one that he knew, from the first, was too big for him or, even, for the networks and newspapers empowered with influence. He also knew that it was too big for politics. Many if not most of the people for whom he created access worked for organizations—fundamentalist churches, the *New York Post*—that were not of his persuasion and would have hated his political points of view. When I say *from the first* I am thinking about the fact that when he led a band of people through that dark supermarket, he included disposable cameras among the supplies to be distributed. In the McCrary version of crisis management, invented and improvised that morning, pho-tography was an essential.

"The moment passes," Kevin told me, "and if you don't record it, you have to rely on the professional historian. Thank God people have documented this event. This story will be around for as long as the fall of Rome or the burning of the library at Alexandria. From the very first day guys were taken out in handcuffs. The police had their orders: no cameras. But I'd passed out at least twenty or thirty disposable cameras, and I could see that a lot of people had them on the site, or they knew where to get them. When celebrities showed up all these cameras would appear miraculously from every direction!"

The fact that Kevin's father had taken a team of photographers into Hiroshima after the bomb was a powerful influence.

"Thinking about what happened with my father," Kevin said, "when the film he arranged to be taken was destroyed because they thought it was too horrible to show, I was determined to document as much as I could, with a very discreet camera that I kept on my person, under my shirt. I had some unique pictures—shots of celebrities, city officials, the wreckage—but it wasn't as if I were selling them to the *Inquirer*—or to anyone. I would drop off a xerox at one of the firehouses with a note that if anybody wanted to have copies, they should give me a call."

Without any ado Kevin invited us into the chapel. Conventional traces of religion had all but disappeared. The altar was covered, there were no votive candles—I didn't even see a crucifix—and fourteen stations of the cross, double-hung on the west wall between Saint Anthony and the Sacred Heart, were obscured by a screen. Kevin gave us seats, it was warm, we were able to use the john, and I remembered that breather when, a short time later, the place was overrun by an annoying religious group that, when I came to find Kevin, didn't care to know about the part he had played, spoke of him dismissively, and resisted even letting me through the door to blow my nose. Officially Christianized by a group called Calvary Chapel, its hospitality had acquired a mean streak. Dismayed at seeing the history of the place co-opted—with smugness and arrogance—so soon!—"No, there was no relief here until Reverend So-and-so came from California and started it up"— I would firmly correct them, but it was plain that if you weren't *with* an organization—and, presumably, if you weren't with its Christ—then you hadn't done a thing and you probably didn't exist. When I told Kevin about it he shrugged it off: "What do they know? They come from out of town for ten days and they're gone." Even Jim O'Connor was made to feel less than welcome in his own place of employment, but he, like Kevin, displayed no bitterness and in fact he shared an amusing story about it.

"It wasn't a Catholic group," Jim told me, "and you know religious groups have their differences, their animosities, sometimes especially when they're closest to each other. Well, they wanted to remove the big statues, the Sacred Heart and the Saint Anthony. They said it was for their safety but I think it was a little more than that. 'They'll be fine,' I said. 'No, we should remove them,' they said, 'just so someone doesn't knock them over.' 'Listen,' I said, 'I was here on the 11th when the South Tower fell and this entire chapel felt as if it were *thrown* into the air and then dropped back down. If *that* didn't knock them over, I'm not worried about it.'"

As Ray and I enjoyed St. Joseph's hospitality, Kevin told us how, in the wake of the second collapse, he had collected a stream of dazed and dusted people into the Gateway apartment, which was on the ground floor and convenient for them to reach, to catch a breath of better air, to rinse themselves off. A pregnant woman especially appreciated the offer. Women wheeling strollers and baby carriages on the riverwalk were eager to take shelter with their children. There was a priest among them too. People were simply glad to be *in*. Jim later described the scene to me in a similar vein, although Jim's time there was in between the two collapses.

"When the South Tower fell that was one thing," Jim said. "Then came those waves of debris. A policewoman ran in and told us to leave the chapel, move west through the building. In the lobby you could see out the windows: it looked like a blender when it's making a malted milkshake. It had that brownish color and it was *churning*. Oddly, the air was better inside, even here in the chapel. You could hear it being pelted but none of the stained glass was broken. It was inches thick with dust directly out in the vestibule, but inside the chapel it wasn't bad: you could breathe. People were coming in for shelter. Someone in that first apartment was taking people in. Hard to exactly remember Kevin. There was a lot of confusion here. There was a woman with a baby that I wanted to get south, toward the Staten Island Ferries, which I figured had to be the safest bet, so we walked in that direction. It was not the clear blue day that people remember, not where I was walking. There were columns of dark smoke blowing south down the island that, I hate to say it, looked almost biblical.[16] We were over by the Holocaust Museum, next to the water, when I saw some movement at the North Tower. Then you could hear it again. This time we all knew what it meant. Another policewoman shouted: 'Face the other way! Cover yourselves! Get down!' We all turned, so I didn't see it fall."

My conversation with Jim was interrupted by a brief midday service in the chapel. When it ended and the priest disappeared, Jim took the chalice and walked it swiftly out of the room. I wasn't sure why he was moving so fast. Jim is a small quick man with a neatly trimmed beard and plenty of positive energy. Perhaps he walked that way all the time; perhaps he had a busy agenda and his affable reception to my queries had set it back; or perhaps it was his practice to remove the chalice hastily. Whatever the reason, the image of Jim rushing with the chalice in his hands was interchangeable, for me, with the image of Jim spiriting mother and child to safe harbor. For me, a man wholly without religion, it was one of many proofs from my days around the site that the decency with which people acted on the 11th and in its aftermath—what a Biblican might call the word made flesh—served to strengthen the iconography of their faith, showing that religious symbolism is, at least, well made and well disposed toward the acts of good men. Hundreds of times, in front of parishioners who had worked in the Twin Towers, Jim had carried the body and blood of his savior into the safety of the room down the hall. On the 11th he did it again, did it a little differently, but the eyes of this infidel cannot tell them apart.

When relief at the chapel developed beyond the days of Kevin and, by permission of St. Peter's, which runs St. Joseph's, it passed into the hands of two Protestant church groups, Kevin was not technically invited to stay on. I say *technically* because I saw Kevin approached for information about everything. On one typical day we were outside the chapel with a man from a group of Hispanic volunteers. He was talking about counseling for people at the site. In the midst of this discussion a van passed the barricades and drove a few yards into the esplanade, a one-lane road that runs adjacent the Hudson River and serves the World Financial Center from behind. The driver rolled down his window and called out: "Are you Kevin McCrary?"

"Yeah."

The man was delighted, as if he'd been tracking him for ages.

"Get in!"

Without asking why, Kevin climbed over a wall and the van drove him away. Not thirty seconds passed before a man came quickly out of the chapel. He was worried, harried: he *had* to get into a room, he *couldn't* without Kevin.

"Where'd he go?"

"He was kidnapped," I said. "That's the way it is with him."

"I need him to be here."

"So does everybody."

Using a cellphone I alerted him to the problem, for which he promised to return as soon as he could.

That first night in the chapel, as Kevin showed us the article in the *Times* about the work he had done there, inviting us to look through his packets of snapshots—smoky overheads from the night of 11th and the morning of the 12th—I was punchy from the cold and I was stuck on that earlier pronouncement of his: "I could have taken you in." I was so tantalized by the prospect it held, so disappointed to have missed it, that it clouded and distorted Kevin's speech, turning him into a ghost of the man who had said it. I wouldn't have dreamt of turning the camera on. If Kevin had related, word for word, a conversation he had had with Giuliani, or with the Buddha, or with the angel Gabriel it would not have made a difference. This is what he sounded like: "At first *I could have taken you in* we set up a station out front distributing food and supplies that *I could have taken you in* were pouring in from this armada of boats and ferries from everywhere and *I could have taken you in* we had people sleeping here, we laid mats down and cots and we made sandwiches and *I could have taken you in.*" We left with an agreement for an interview with Kevin and the scant possibility of taking a few shots from a Gateway roof that looked directly onto the site. As the eastern part of Gateway Plaza along South End Avenue was more severely pelted than the rest of the complex, so it was now completely closed. Security was tightening. People with press credentials had been arrested. Kevin would see about it. I was encouraged by the encounter—we were walking away, now, with a quite remarkable prospect—an overview of the site—but Ray was oppositional.

"I don't think we should have a thing to do with him."

"Why not?"

We were dragging through the streets, headed home.

"Because the guy's completely crazy. Once we get sucked in it's going to torture us. The way he came out, brought us in, showing us all that stuff? Something's not right. He was there in that space but I felt as if he were making it all up."

"We saw the article."

"I still don't trust it. I'd rather slit my throat. It's too weird."

"But it's a guy like that we need," I said. "Who *else* is going to help us? Is the Mayor going to work with us? Follow proper channels you'll be standing on Broadway, trying to take a shot over a fence. Is he crazy? Good for him. Look at *us*. We're crazy too."

A few weeks later, after he introduced us to Donavin in the narrow, chandeliered lobby of 114 where it stank of Trade dust and the blood of rancid meat from an adjoining pizza joint, Kevin went to 10 & 10 Fire to do some business. Then he stopped back to encourage us to stay as long as we liked—he had to run.

"But then how do we get out?" I said.

While Kevin was at the Ten House, Donavin had opened a door in the lobby with a crowbar, an ordinary moment that has symbolized, for me, the makeshift situation obtaining on Liberty Street. Beneath the nice old chandeliers of 114 there was urgency, expediency, worry, dust, and the stench of decayed chickens. We had also met Ray Sage, an electrician who had worked with Donavin there when they converted it to a residential space. "We really cowboy'd this building," Ray said. On the evening of the 12th Ray had bicycled from Brooklyn through the dust-slick streets just to survey the damage to the building in which he naturally took an interest. "My building," he called it. Donavin, who had cycled over from Brooklyn on the night of September 11 to get his wife a breast pump from their Pearl Street apartment, described the scene in a similar way. "It was snowing horribly," he told me, "coming down big time. Army in the streets. Big equipment. People everywhere. Gridwork from the exterior laying like kids' blocks. Next morning I was crawling over that stuff. And huge fires—not just smoke. But that night it sounded like a war. At the same time it was dead quiet except for weird sounds you couldn't pinpoint, sounds you never heard before. It was like a war where people are shooting but they're hiding." Ray remembered seeing the homeless in their customary storefront hangouts, their forms white with dust, sleeping as if they hadn't seen the attacks, and dusty pigeons walking around dazed and directionless. As he was leaving the neighborhood Ray was stopped, he was arrested, his bike was confiscated, he was charged with a federal crime and he was thrown into the jug. He was out on bail. A trial was pending. Apparently, Ray had been walking amongst the piles of Tower trash on the Liberty rooftop when he spotted a very small twist of metal—it fit in his backpack—which he was taking home to Brooklyn for a shrine on which to place a few candles. Instead, they placed a few candles on Ray. As a dedicated cyclist he didn't own a driver's license. He did not have a union card. Unidentified! A policewoman decided that the metal was a piece of a plane: *tampering with evidence.*

This story had given me pause.

"Just walk along Liberty," Kevin said. "No one'll bother you."

"And if they *do* bother us?"

"They won't."

"What about the checkpoints?"

"They don't *care* if you're *leaving.*"

As we approached the intersection of Liberty and Church, where a Burger King inhabited a three-story building from the 19th century, I saw two grapplers out of the corner of my eye. After a long acquaintance from afar they were huge, mythically huge to me now, bright yellow under the floods, terrific in their task. We ought to have kept moving but I told Ray we needed to unobtrusively turn around, a seemingly simple act but for men without passes and with a camera it was smart not to loiter. We loitered anyway. For just a minute. There it was, then, the site, directly in front of us. Good to take it in without a zoom in your eyes. One could hear it, smell it, feel the vibration of the work in one's bones, which is where it needed to be. Touch me today or twenty years hence you will feel that vibration. The film *Liberty Street* and this book are part of it. A block farther east, at the checkpoint on Broadway, I was grateful to Kevin that I was now, at last, on the inside looking out. I would never have dreamed, then, that a year and a half later I would still be walking Liberty Street, camera in my case, still loitering, still picking up on the vibration.

If Kevin can drop us off at Liberty Street and disappear, we can drop *him* off and delve into a footnote about that night in the lobby. It concerns the rotted meat. During one of the first extended conversations we had together, Donavin elucidated a law he had based on the behavior he encountered at Ground Zero.

"Eighty-seven and a half percent of the world is not very nice," Donavin said. "There's a lot of difficult people who like it that way and who keep it that way on purpose. Destructive, self-destructive, obsessed with control, they're impossible to deal with and not doing anyone any good. It's disappointing. If you can't get along down here, what's the point? I understand that you have to be cautious. You don't have to be an asshole. Some things are so restricted you can't even breathe. More important things are left lax. I'd like to reverse that. Eighty-seven point five percent: they're just making things worse. Twelve and a half percent are okay."

As Donavin tells it, the smell of rancid meat in the lobby of 114, which I remember because it persisted for half a year, was a gift to all the guys who were working at Liberty Street from the Department of Health, which exemplified the Eighty-seven Percent Rule. As to how this urban agency added its portion of grief to that troubled little building on that old resilient street, it was the first story Donavin ever told me and it was during that first visit to the building in November.

"Smells like flesh," I had said.

"It is," he said. "But it's not *that*—you can get *that* other places. This smell, here, is actual meat out of a freezer. The pizza guys next door. The power went off, the meat rotted—but let me tell you what happened—you won't believe it." He then told the story, still chafing over the rank imbecility of the affair. The anecdote was also Donavin's last story, for the next time I heard it, over a year later, he was wrapping his work on Liberty Street. Time hadn't cooled him.

"One day the guys from the Department of Health come in," he said. "They've got their badges and their clipboards and the guy says: 'We understand you've got meat in the freezers here, it's rotting and it has to be removed. It's unsafe.' So we all go to the basement, we open up these huge walk-in freezers, and everyone just about passes out from the stench. They all get suited up and they put on their respirators—there's six or so guys doing the work and there's three supervisors with their clipboards—and they start bagging it up. But the bags are really cheap and the meat is dripping out of them, it's getting on the floor and it's stinking the place up. This is the Department of Health—it's their *job* to do this—and they don't even have decent bags! Then they started up the stairs toward the lobby. I had just had it cleaned, professionally, for about four thousand dollars, every corner, every inch of all the walls, the floor, the ceiling, the molding around the elevators, the chandeliers—everything. So I said: 'Whoa! Stop right there! No *way* are you coming up the stairs with those bags. You cannot go out the front. You have to go to the back and take it out by Cedar Street.'

"So, the guy tells all of his men to stop in their tracks, not to take another step. They all stop. Totally. It was like a military operation. I have never seen anything like it, ever. *Completely* still, *completely* quiet. I thought: '*This* is really *something*.' And he says to me: 'Do you mean to tell me you are insisting that I not leave the building in this way? Because I have determined that taking the front door is the only safe way of removing this material.' So I said to him: 'Is that what you determined? How did you determine that?' And he says to me: 'That determination is from my boss. If you want to take it up with him, we can do that, but if we do, these bags don't move. We leave them right here, exactly where they are, *nobody* touches them until this is resolved.' I said: 'You mean to tell me you're going to leave these dead chickens dripping from bags right here all over my stairs? For how long?' And the guy says: 'We will have to work that out. Now: do you want to change the procedure, Sir?' That's what he says to me, exactly like that. 'Do you want to change the procedure, Sir?' This guy's boss, who was a very important man, had made up his mind: this was the proper way. It didn't matter that it didn't make sense. Everything comes down the ladder. At each rung someone protects himself from the wrath above and someone else is knocked off.

"*Well,* I wasn't going to leave all this dead rancid meat sitting in bags that are dripping all over the fucking steps, and when I saw these *automatons,* I said *okay, fine,* no way to reason with *this,* not even down here with all this DNA around us, so I told him to take it out, dragging the bags across the lobby, where it dripped *every*where—that chicken drip was *all over*—and they never cleaned it up, *any* of it. They didn't use Clorox, nothing—they just walked out, threw it into a New York City garbage truck and left the biggest mess you can imagine. If part of the biohazard was that you could spread it around the building, well, this was worse than ever. Chickens and cheese, holes in the bags, pouring *all over. They're* the Department of Health, and *they* dripped and left all that poison on the floor. What the hell kind of an organization is *that?*

"The place was a *total* mess. *We* had to clean it, but the stink never left it. It would go right up the stairwell. Everybody was smelling it and dying. *You* smelled it. I had to call the cleaners *again,* pay them *again* to use their scrubber machines—it was *still* there, that smell. We had to stand there inside of it *every* day—this was the *lobby,* this was the place we had to meet, discuss things, wait for people, deal with all the ten tons of shit going down. I mean, I had to get a crane off the site just to take down all those dumpsters full of papers and huge pieces of the Trades and office equipment and piles of shit up to your knees on the roof; we have to argue, apply, beg for passes, wait on line just to get *in* here; we're getting the fumes so bad I have to send my people home; the FBI is following me—*me*—they're behind me on the road, they're here in the building, O yeah you guys're doing a *great* job, *that'll* keep this country safe—and here the fucking Department of Health is spraying the lobby with fucking dead pizza meat!

"So. That's when I decided that *any* agency of *any* official kind—city, federal, doesn't matter—could be totally fucked up, completely useless, and everything that happened after that proved it true."

It was Kevin who pointed out the spotters to me. It was during days of shooting from the empty livingroom of his father's new apartment in Gateway Plaza. The old Gateway digs where his father had lived for years, in a corner

An FDNY spotter hoes for signs of flesh in Ground Zero earth spread in front of him by a grappler.

by the North Cove Marina with views of a playground and traffic on the Hudson, were insufficient now. The twenty-ninth floor and even closer to the site, with a crow's nest view from its east-facing windows, is exactly where Tex McCrary wanted to be. He hadn't moved furniture in yet—as it happened, old Tex's living there was not to be—but he had come to the empty apartment to sit for an interview with the *New York Post* and after that he talked to me. Handholding the camera with the mic attached to it, I squatted on the floor and I listened to a life that approximated a century, a life in which he had walked through the ruins of Hiroshima; worked as an editor at the *New York Daily Mirror* and the *American Mercury;* promoted Eisenhower's first presidential race ("I Like Ike" was Tex's phrase); collaborated with LeFrak, the developer, on originating Battery Park City; brainstormed with Yamasaki, the Port Authority's Guy Tozzoli, and Governor Rockefeller as they stewarded the gleam of a bold notion into a city of steel and glass; worked for Nixon, worked for Reagan; hatched a plot to make the *Intrepid* a museum on the Hudson; and together with Kevin's mother, Jinx Falkenburg—actress, model, World War II pinup girl (she was the first Miss Rheingold)—had joined Bob Hope's USO tour to Berlin and had hosted a string of successful talk shows, on radio and television, that made Tex and Jinx a pair of household names during the postwar years in which I was growing up in Queens.

After evacuating to Jersey, Tex, like many evacuees on the 11th, had found himself depending upon the kindness of strangers. When the man who had taken him into his home presented his business card, Tex was delighted that his host was a mortician. "I have a funny feeling you'll be back," the man told him. Tex loved that remark. On the business card, Tex jotted another line from the mortician: "Not ready for you *yet* . . . "

Even under the cold harsh light of a shadeless lamp that his son had requisitioned from a nearby dumpster ("No *way* it's going to work," I thought, but of course it did, without even a change of bulb), Tex looked brighteyed, handsome, vital, a 91 that had a lot more to do before ferrying again over the Hudson—or the Styx—to reune with that mortician in Jersey. He was impeccably dressed, a smart scarf neatly draped over his suit jacket and tie, his hands settled comfortably on the handle of his cane. The man who, at the birth of television, sitting in front of a big broadcast camera, had talked to hundreds of guests—and to America—with ease, was of course completely relaxed with the lens of my little Sony. Recent operations had rasped out his voice, but he delivered every answer with the authority of a man who had made things happen. The force of a debris cloud had knocked him into the street but in a larger sense the 11th hadn't knocked him over at all. Or so it seemed. Tex was optimistic, excitedly so. When Kevin rolled out a wall-size enlargement of a picture he had taken on the site, Tex said that he planned to hang it up in that room, facing, on the opposite wall, another big enlargement, a picture of the site before the Twin Towers were built. Between the past and the present, for Tex there was the future and it was all fulminating out that window. "It's Easter morning," he said about the potential for the neighborhood. "I want to be a part of it."

After talking to Tex twice I could see that it would not be much of a breeze being his son. This can be said of most fathers, but Tex had done too much for a father. For men who never want for big bold ideas, sometimes a son is incidental, like an old idea that won't recede from consciousness and can't be given a fresh face. After a conversation with Tex in the Edison Hotel on Fifty-third Street, Kevin and I were taking the elevator. "Your Dad's amazing," I said. "But it's got to be a fairly tough deal being his son."

"*Tell* me about it," Kevin said.

It would be nice to say of Kevin that when he walked into the rank snowy air of the 11th, he walked out of his famous father's shadow forever. But I believe he was looking for his father everywhere, at least looking for his approval, which, in the case of any father, is tantamount to proof of one's existence. He was aware of the quotations in his behavior that harked back to the lives of both his parents. Kevin's Ground Zero in Lower Manhattan took its name from his father's Ground Zero in Hiroshima, and the McCrarys brought photographers into both of them. When Kevin stood with John Travolta as the men called their girlfriends for John to say hi—no, really, it's really *him*—or toured around the site with Kevin Costner, who had flown to New York privately with his wife just to see what could be seen, Kevin was, in Churchill's phrase, doing them the honors of war, for he respected the fact that stars who are allegedly out of touch had come to the site in order to touch more than most people would dream. In the case of celebrities who stopped to socialize it wasn't a USO tour but it was, in a sense, a way of entertaining the troops.

Still, nothing could answer the search for fatherly confirmation, not even among Kevin's beloved firefighters, men who, regardless of age, were fathers to multitudes, even to the women who were turned on to see them and who volunteered as more than water girls. The way Kevin documented his volunteer efforts with photographs that often included a pose of himself, and the way he would exhibit his photographs to everybody, especially to strangers, was sometimes seen as self-promotion. It was the opposite. Every time he took his pictures out—Kevin with Robert De Niro, Kevin with Ted Koppel, Kevin with firefighters, Kevin with politicians, Kevin in the smoky ruins, Kevin everywhere—he was asking you to check the proof, to verify the evidence. In other words, asking you to tell him who he was. When I prodded Tex to acknowledge his son's achievement, there was a dutiful tip of the hat, undoubtedly heartfelt, but then Tex was off to the races again. It was foolish of me. If Tex had told his son what a wonderful chap he was every day for six months, Kevin wouldn't have gotten it; or, if he had, it wouldn't have made a difference. It was too late for that. That father didn't breathe who had the lasting benediction Kevin required. He was beyond confirmation.

As I might be making this all up, treat this Kevin as a postulate—Proposition K—a K that helped humanize Ground Zero for me. Without Kevin and his father (as without David and Donavin), there might have been too much dust and steel for me. I, who barely knew him, was determined to confirm the unconfirmable for K, even if only to say: "Kevin exists. He did things. He showed a will and a heart."

Kevin had arranged for me to shoot in the empty space once my interview with Tex had concluded, so as soon as the door closed on his father I opened a window, let the noise pour in, set the Sony on the ledge, and I shot the site at the height of its December activities. Over the next couple of days other witnesses, invited there by Kevin, came and went. At street level one could taste this event, but to encompass its scale you needed a view from higher ground, and no one wasn't impressed to see the site from these windows, or from the roof at Liberty Street, not excepting men who had worked there for months.

A minister from out of town told me he had only just arrived at Ground Zero when he was called onto the pile to preside over remains. His vocation was ill served by a cozy sense of self and a ridiculous business card that played on the recipient a smooth optical trick with the name of Jesus—just the memento I've always wanted, especially at the ruins of the World Trade Center—but he was a decent man who had driven down from Canada to make a contribution and I was contented to let him make it off camera. The fact is, though, national tragedies don't make men less foolish, and I will always remember that a parson who had just said a prayer over a corpse that had rotted for three months turned his back to the busy site and stood there beaming over a lame Jesus trick.

A crew dispatched to the city by a very high-profile religious organization shot a little of what they called B-roll, background footage for a television piece about Christian volunteers. I was only half expecting them to jettison the notion of B-roll as applied to what was smoking in their lens. When a member of the crew introduced herself and sat down between the two approaches, B-roll professionalism and A-roll obsession, we didn't talk—I wouldn't have talked to Madonna, or *the* Madonna—but I could smell her perfume and it was too reminiscent of another universe so I was glad that a few good shots seemed to suffice and they departed in no time.

In a bizarre circumstance only Kevin could have concocted I had to conduct an interview with a pair of German girls with the entire sprawl of the sight in between us, for Kevin called me from his bicycle in the middle of Cortlandt Street on the east side of the site and he handed his walkie-talkie to them for an on-camera chat. Kevin was procuring me the European reaction, never mind that I was trying to shoot the New York reaction. I held the walkie-talkie up to the microphone, the Germans talked awhile in their adorable accents, and with my one free hand I continued to shoot the site. It was always thus with Kevin. You had to be charmed by it. Even as a promise was being fulfilled there was still the Kevin factor, the threat of some disruption, the chance that your focus, your hardhat, your pass, your entire workday could be dispersed in the service of other forces. Democracy!

At one point Kevin put his own cameras down and he patiently guided me, as I moved the lens around, in picking out spotters in the minutely detailed, densely populated tapestry of the site. It took awhile for me to find the crew of cops and firefighters. They were standing on a cross-section of beams looking down from a perspective that I couldn't say for certain was the pile, the pit, or somewhere in between. Impacted with debris, partially buried, it looked like a portion of old bridge that had been lost in a flood long ago. In fact I believe it was an underground passage—a subterranean tunnel turned "bridge"—for the PATH train. Now and then grapplers would stop, the atmosphere changed, some of the spotters slid slowly down a steep muddy slope, a few of them carrying spades, and they would examine the patch of ground under suspicion, urban prospectors in brown overalls and black coats with yellow stripes all gathered in a circle and hunched over— for what prize?

The sight of these spotters was not an especially graphic one. No, but it shook me. I didn't know this at first. At the end of the night, before I left the building, I telephoned a friend and tried to tell her about the spotters. I couldn't speak. Tears, for me, are not a literary subject but to render this Minuteman I need to talk tears without attaching any importance to my own. Think of them, then, not as sorrow but as water. Walking across town I could not hold them back. On the divider between downtown and uptown West Street, I couldn't see well enough to cross. Wiping them away was not helpful. A policewoman ignored me: for cops in that neighborhood, faces full of tears were commonplace. I sat in the center of the street, soaking two handkerchiefs. Five minutes, ten. It wasn't like crying, it was like being ill when you think it's under control and then it pours out again. A part of me observed it with wonder. Well: didn't I say I wanted to see what there was to cry about? I walked to the Starbucks opposite Battery Park, I ordered a coffee and I sat against the back wall crying. I cried through the coffee and another ten minutes. They played Sinatra's "One for My Baby," a song, easy and sad, one of the few, that seemed apt for Ground Zero, that most musicless work-space for which not much of anything was apt, but the tears paid no mind to Sinatra. I had been crying over an hour. Perhaps, I thought, like people who can't stop the hiccups, I would never stop crying. Strange life ahead. I would have to carry a sign:

CRYING BECAUSE OF THE SPOTTERS
AT GZ FORGIVE ME

At the approach to the Midtown Tunnel where vehicles were spot-checked in such a perfunctory fashion you were moved to say, aloud: "It's simply not se-curity," the way you would say: "It's simply not funny," I wondered whether the tears would arouse their suspicion. The cry driving home added another ninety minutes to this lachrymary adventure. When I walked through the door it continued. In bed, too. I went to sleep thinking I would have to make that sign. I'd do it in the morning.

At one point earlier, in the streets around the site, I had called Kevin and left him an underwater message: "Thanks for showing me the spotters." I wished he could have shown everybody. With my camera there to see them too, he probably felt that he had.

It isn't every day that one's illustrious father is suddenly evacuated out of his apartment in an emergency of catastrophic proportions. If Kevin did not lit-erally fill his father's shoes—as I have said, he accidentally wore a woman's shoes during his first long stretch around the site—he certainly filled his fa-ther's apartment. I ought to say *Tex's apartment* because, in my hearing at least, Tex was always Tex to Kevin, rarely "my father," suggesting that Kevin had long since conceded the primacy of the public over the private persona. What else can you do with a guy who, in recollecting the war, talks about Jimmy and assumes you will know it's General James Douglas MacArthur?

It is impossible to describe Tex's apartment after Tex had been away, and Kevin had been to play, for over two months. It was not that it had been thor-oughly Kevinized, for it had never been de-Tex'd. There was simply twice the evidence of living than it could hold, so that to move anywhere you had to disrupt both worlds, and the cohabitation created amusing juxtapositions. Beneath old glossies of Tex with his presidents, there were Kevin's maga-zines, fliers and paperbacks about alternative ways to health or religions of the East. Adjacent a stack of file boxes labeled **COLIN POWELL** (one of Tex's last presidential hopefuls, along with John McCain), there was a cabinet of Kevin's own research, including a stash of papers about black ops and other rogue deals behind federal doors and smokescreens. All of it intermingled with that dusty third world of Ground Zero as Kevin had brought it home with him. He had taken volunteers from out of town to sleep there but there were so many mountains of sheer *stuff* that it appeared as if everybody had emptied a suitcase. Realizing I'd left a sweater there, I resolved that I would never see it again, for either Kevin would have given it away—"There was this guy up from Georgia, he was freezing in this thin little jacket, so"—or else it was so dead lost under mounds of McCrary debris, in which Kevin's cat, Bink, roamed contentedly, that the expedition would have cost more than the sweater was worth. Hardhats, reflector vests, safety goggles, badges, boots, news clippings, cameras, odd clothing (some of it from dumpsters), computer printouts, drawings, maps, fliers, posters and photographs were spread over every inch of space, most of it identifiably Tex's space, so that you lifted up an object found around the site and beneath it was a memento from Bob Hope or a framed gold record dedicated to Tex and Jinx. When I asked whether the worlds of Father Republicanism and Son Progressivism ever collided head-on, Kevin, in his understated tone, said: "What's that old saying? Let sleeping dogs lie."

But Kevin didn't exactly do that with Tex. Long after the site was clean, I drove to Jinx's house in Mill Neck, Long Island for a last conversation with old Tex about the 11th. Tex was not well, Jinx was not well either (she died shortly after Tex), and she greeted me in the kitchen to say she wasn't prepared for this. It was Easter Sunday. Kevin's older brother Paddy was there. It was a day for the family. Tex, when I arrived, was sound asleep. "Let's do this another time," I said, inclining toward the door. "No," Kevin said. "He'll be up, he'll be fine." He ushered me in. Tex, at first drowsy, became quickly energized and we had a good talk. As I was backing out the drive, Kevin said: "You know that foreman from Tully I told you about? He might be ready to talk to you now. If you're interested, I'll see about it." Seventeen months since the attacks and Kevin was still the volunteer, still putting people together, still working.

I've talked to more than enough people, I thought.

"Sure," I said. "Call me, let me know."

I had learned that it was necessary to set your own limits around Kevin and it was equally necessary to renounce them. For each time I had said to myself, in doing something with Kevin: "This is insane," there were twice as many times I would say it without him, for it was totally insane for there to be a Ground Zero *at all* in Lower Manhattan—or anywhere else in the year 2001. It was crazy enough for the father to have walked the streets of Hiroshima where the trees, as he said, were stripped of foliage like gallows and the whole city stank like a barbeque pit. That the son should have his own Ground Zero outside Tex's apartment was not an act of God, it was madmen again doing more mad things and getting away with it. By comparison, Kevin's insanity seemed as sound as Kierkegaard, and his unspoken progressivism seemed as subversive as a helping hand held out in the dust.

Had you passed by Kevin on one of the benches of the promenade along the Hudson River in the summer of 2002, where he was idling with overstuffed shopping bags, a newspaper open on his lap, a bag of popcorn for snacking and for feeding his squirrel kinsmen who followed him like a superstar ("They all know me," he'd say), the image could have suggested either a cleancut bagman nesting under the sun or a choreful Downtowner taking a break to read the *Times*. In fact, Kevin's bags held a variety of World Trade relics and Ground Zero artifacts claimed off rooftops and streets: a blownout Scott pack; a shiny **B** plaque from an elevator bank in the basement of one of the Trades; a track for one of the windows with pebbles of glass in its groove; official papers with seared edges and burnholes; a small piece of one of the jets; transparencies of Windows on the World that were blown out of the restaurant and which, if you held them up to the light facing south, toward the New York Harbor, enabled you to gaze through the windows in the slides at the view, from above, that you were seeing from the ground. By putting a chunk of glass that was just the right thickness into the grove of the window track (he had an assortment of sizes from which to choose), Kevin enabled me to look out the window in a more literal way. After all, it was glass from one of the Twins, it rested in one of its tracks, and you could still see through it. It had come down in the world—I wasn't about to take my mother to see it—but it didn't seem wrong to take one last look.

Kevin showed me everything, including a lot of smaller bits he was carrying in halves of half-gallon soda bottles he had turned into a handy plastic container. I had seen a ship in a bottle: here was a building in a bottle, a hijacked jet in a bottle. Some of the items he pulled out perfunctorily and only identified with a phrase; others he displayed with archeological scrutiny and pride. At a glance it resembled a pile of garbage because it was. Strictly speaking he *was* a bagman. A phrase that I used in a previous chapter, *the Twin Towers turned to trash,* frequently came to mind in Lower Manhattan, not because of all those *ts* tumbling along in a rash of alliteration, but because it held true, true for both the small scale and the grand. Bags, bottles, pockets full of trash—what else would you expect from that great City of Trash?

None of Kevin's garbage had been cleaned. After enough of the bad dust accumulated he would gather it into a little plastic bag, only of course it wasn't a Ziploc or a Glad, it was a bag that, like the 7-Up canister, like all of Kevin's utilities, had been used for something else. As for why he took the dust away with him—was he being respectful toward it? was he doing it as a safety?—I have sometimes suspected he was taking it home to draw it into a hypodermic needle and shoot himself up with it. Why not? He had taken it every other way.

Kevin's *New York Times* was not what it seemed, either. It was the 9/11 anniversary issue, its pages crowded with names and photographs of the victims. He took a rubber band off a packet of business cards, all found objects, and he shuffled them around, matching them to the names of the deceased. "Here's another one that didn't make it out," he'd say. "That's the last business card anybody'll have from him."[17] Respecting or, at least, guessing at some mute appeal in them, he sorted and arranged multiple cards from one floor or one company. "So, out of four people . . . five people in one office . . . we know at least one didn't survive." Skaters were gliding past us. Young moms with infant strollers. Teams of Oriental tourists. Kids playing in Spanish. Summer lovebirds. Tugboats, ferries. We were in sight of Ellis Island and Bartholdi's green copper–skinned *Liberté Éclairant Le Monde,* a statue that was lighting the world better than liberty was. Bad time for liberty, lovely day in Lower Manhattan. Kevin, his sights set on another beautiful day, was doing what few of us cared to do: he was holding—and holding onto—September 11, turning its pieces in his white-dusted fingers, associating the names and the faces with debris from the killing ground and the irredeemable fact of our mortality. Around us, Downtown was doing the right thing: it was actively forgetting; and Kevin was doing the right thing too: without solemnity, without gravitas, he was actively remembering. Studying, verifying, annotating the lists in the Kevin McCrary Book of the Dead.

❖

Let's return, for a moment, to the Hunchback gamboling on the Liberty rooftop. When Kevin climbed down from the chiller, he picked up one of the articles he'd tossed down and showed it to us: a rainwrecked cardboard box from the post office. "I've come to get the mail," he said, as good a job description as any. Kevin explained that he had clanked those dusty metal pieces around to keep them from blowing off and crowning a passerby. This was quintessential Kevin. Two giants of the world had collapsed outside his windows, killing about three thousand people, one of whom might have been his father. Or him. The neighborhood is ruined. Life there will never be the same—if there's a life there at all for him after this is over. And yet here he was, picking up the detritus of September, repositioning pieces of the Towers in a place practically no one would go. One could say that he was kicking up dust that he and I were then forced to inhale. One could call him a meddler on a roof that wasn't his. One could argue that, in tossing around those remnants of September, he was tossing his life away. But I saw something else: I saw a light shining. I was looking at rarity. Was it as much Ground Zero as the fathers and the brothers who were called to claim a body, or the thousands of unidentified bits of flesh and bone, or the World Trade garage converted into a catacomb, or the kneeboots trudging through a green toxic swamp? I only know that before he descended the ladder, Kevin saw an aluminum box that appeared to be attached to the roof of the chiller. The lid was up. Kevin tried to close it. It was bent out of shape a little and it was resisting him. He pressed down harder but he couldn't get it to close. For God's sake, it wasn't *his* box. Or was it? I continue to think about it, continue to marvel at that moment. In a place where everything and everyone was broken, Kevin McCrary was doing his best to put bits of it back together, only because he wanted to make things better. Not by far. By just a little. He tried to get that lid down, get it to close the way it should.

7
THE NAUSEA

It was during the drive back to Long Island after my second or third excursion around the site that I was nauseated from glancing at construction along the FDR Drive. This sensation was not severe and it did not last long but it was discomfiting enough to wonder about. There was work under the Brooklyn Bridge. The north outer roadway of the Williamsburg Bridge was having a major restoration. It was the sight of either or both of these projects that first occasioned the nausea. I mentioned it to Ray but we did not discuss it much until it constituted a syndrome.

"Funny," I said as we headed up the Drive. "This happened a few times, now again, same thing. The sight of any construction away from the site makes me sick."

"Probably that stench," Ray said. "Makes *me* sick, too. Seems to worsen in the car." He had begun sniffing himself. "Maybe it's on my coat. Or maybe that's something else. Maybe it's me. Is it me? It could be me."

"Nothing to do with the odor," I said. "This is *only* in response to construction—even a hint or a sign of it—that *isn't* the site. I saw that work up there along the bridge and it made me queasy."

"You're talking about a mental thing?"

"No. Well, yes, but it's entirely physical too."

After many of these spells during the fall and early winter of 2001, including a few on the Long Island Expressway, which is never not crippled with repair, Ray floated the notion that a mechanism of memory was reproducing the nausea I felt at Ground Zero, a viable explanation were it not for one fact: I wasn't nauseated there. When, with respect to the evil odor, I used the phrase *sickening every breath*, I did not mean nausea but a repulsion to one's own course of breathing. And this syndrome of nausea was certainly not a memory. It was, however, entirely integrated, as if my mind and my body were nauseated equally. When you need to throw up, *you* don't want to, the body does, unless the nausea persists for long enough to torture you. In these cases, *I* was queasy, all of me, whatever there was of Peter Josyph. I had never felt anything quite like it. After a month I began to avert my gaze whenever it looked like construction up ahead, but construction is hard to avert, especially if you don't want to be driving off the road, so it happened at least once each time I drove the car. I briefly postulated that it might have had something to do with looking too long through the lens of the camera, but then it shouldn't have occurred as I drove *into* Manhattan, or driving on days off. In fact, the nausea afflicted me everywhere *excepting* the site itself.

"Happened again."

"The nausea? What *did* it?"

"I saw a crane back there. It wasn't even moving. The work was shut down. Nauseated right away."

The fact that a solitary vehicle, one that wasn't operating, could stimulate the nausea is why I said that even a hint of construction could do it. The queasiness never endured for more than a minute or two, but that was long enough, given that it resulted from the simple act of seeing, although a case could be made that no seeing is ever simple. When I say that even a sign of construction made me sick, here is what I mean.

A great book about Manhattan, Nathan Silver's *Lost New York* (New York: Weathervane, 1967), features photographs and discussions of interesting buildings that are demolished. The most remarkable section of this book contains heartrending photographs of Pennsylvania Station in the act of being destroyed. Compared with the shack that's there today, that grand old station, backward though it was—what Frank Lloyd Wright called museum architecture—projected a kind of grandeur even in photographs. It was a blow to the soul of the city when they tore it down and dumped it into a swamp in the Jersey Meadowlands, and it's a mournful thing to meditate pictures of the process.

One evening Ray and I were smoking Don Diegos at a bench on Fulton Street. We were opposite a bookstore, a Downtown branch of the famous Strand, one of the great readers' institutions in New York. To say *a branch of the famous Strand* is a kind of contradiction, for the Strand, which is farther uptown on Broadway, is a one-of-a-kind store with its own quirky mystique, but in an essentially bookless neighborhood any sort of Strand is remark-able. We had passed it dozens of times too early, too late, too exhausted. Tonight I was too tired to do anything else—driving home was unthink-able—so we went to investigate. In the New York section I happened upon a book of unpublished photographs by Peter Moore called *The Destruction of Penn Station* (New York: D.A.P., 2001). I thought of the pictures in *Lost New York* and I recalled a short story I published in 1996, "Wallace Halder Takes a Train," in which my character sits on a suitcase in the new Penn Station.

He remembered the jealous thrill he felt when he first saw photographs of the old Penn Station with its heaven of crystal domes and vast vaulted patterns of artful skylit glass and steel ranging over the platforms, and its majestic General Waiting Room, the proper grand welcome of an authentic work of architecture, retrograde surely yeah but potent nevertheless, filled with spaces to take a traveler's breath away, making him do great things, even a flapsole dogdown loser could fly up into historic deeds yearning to be recorded with the lives of princes and poets, and those pictures in Halder's memory now counted among the saddest. "For fifty-three years they had a building," he said aloud. "Mom, Dad, whoever was alive then, they had it. Now this."

The Moore book, one could say, was up Halder's alley; mine, too, and I was eager to see more of that awesome demolition. But looking at a picture of a bulldozer at work nauseated me instantly. I shut the book and dropped it on the table. The sight of the demolition—the sight of *the photograph* of the demolition—had had the same effect as my seeing a worksite, only this was a little worse, owing, I suspect, to the fatigue in which it found me. Now I was uncomfortable with moving around the store. I felt faint. I took a few deep breaths. I took a few short steps. I had been feeling old and depleted. Now I felt debilitated, swooning over a page like a character out of Poe.

From the first, I had detected in my nausea components of alienation from the everyday sights that were making me feel sick. If I dug down and dragged this nonverbal phenomenon into the light of the intellect and put a name to it, I could boil it down to one word: contempt. This simple awareness formed into the best explanation I can offer. The explanation is vague. The sensation was not.

In a short space of time Ground Zero established itself as the quintessential construction site: the ideal, the Platonic form of construction. Nothing was being built—what was deconstructed on the 11th was disimpacted, disentangled, and redistributed to people in lands afar—but all the powers of construction were active there, on a scale and a schedule that were unprecedented, even in the testimony of seasoned professionals. No one had seen anything quite like it. I was seeing it a lot because seeing was my task.

As a result, Ground Zero both defined and exemplified construction for me. But I wonder whether exemplifying something that well can rob a definition of its uses in the world, especially if it is both at its most fundamental and at its most extreme for the person perceiving it. After a first of this kind can there ever be another? I could stand to see construction at Ground Zero, only there, because nothing else physically qualified. Nothing else was real. And I couldn't bear the sight of something that ought not to exist and, to my mind, did not—and yet I was forced to look at it. What was making me sick about the sight, even the signs, of other work was that work's very existence. It *couldn't* be, so why was it pretending? It made me sick for it to pretend, made me sick to see something that wasn't there. I said that I wanted to stand in the vicinity of the impossible. When I had done so sufficiently, the site became the *only* thing possible.

In Jean Paul Sartre's novel *La Nausée*, or *Nausea*, the book's narrator, Antoine Roquentin, is made sick from looking at things that are, to his mind, too reified, too submerged in their own thingness for him to stomach. In a splendid café scene, Roquentin looks at a glass of beer and says: "Enough." Later he chastises a pair of suspenders for not achieving the color to which they aspire. As I remembered it, Roquentin's nausea was something like my own in that the sensation was physical and yet more than that. I started taking the novel around, looking for clues in it, but Roquentin's nausea was too esoteric, too incandescent to help me out.

At the conclusion of Sartre's novel, Roquentin appears to be getting better. I too am recovering—or so I say, perhaps prematurely. In August of 2002, as I was driving on the Long Island Expressway, the sight of a truck transporting a grappler sickened me. That fall, walking through the JetBlue terminal at JFK, I could not look to my left because I knew they were doing construction there. And tonight, an hour ago, I turned away from television as soon as I saw a crane. So perhaps I am not recovered at all. Sickness over dumptrucks. Contempt for lesser construction. Trying not to see men at work—men *elsewhere* at work. It was a strange enough business that the urge to write it down became the initial impulse for writing at all about the site, something I had never intended to do.

When he was a young man in Italy, J. Carter Brown, future director of the National Gallery of Art in Washington, D.C., was given this advice by the critic Bernard Berenson: "You should look and look and look until you are made blind by looking, and then you will have an illumination." Berenson was talking about art, not ruins, although appreciation of ruins is an integral part of comprehending cultures of the past, and schools of aesthetics have been formed around the representation and cultivation of ruins. One could say that, by necessity, this is part of the aesthetic behind my film. As for the promise of illumination, I would love to share it with you after the looking and the looking I have done at Ground Zero, but so far the most I can say is that a nausea comes to me in the world of the ordinary, and I cannot escape the feeling that these normal men in normal trucks and normal hardhats are deluding themselves daily, and that their machines are really toys, and that all their undertaking is child's play because in Lower Manhattan the real thing happened once and forever.

In the rain on a Liberty rooftop, a schoolboy discovers
a piece of the plane that entered the North Tower.

THE MUD PEOPLE

One morning, sitting at the bar in O'Hara's, I was leafing through an un-glued copy, the bar copy, of *One Nation*, the *Life* picture book of September 11. It was only eleven-thirty but either Donavin and I were both ready for Irish brew or neither of us was ready for anything else on Liberty Street. "It's beer-thirty," Donavin said as we crossed Cedar Street from the loading bay in back of 114.

O'Hara's had started to fill after the North Tower was hit, and after the second strike it was swarming with people, mostly men and women of busi-ness, but O'Hara's had been smart enough to close before the South Tower collapsed. Mike, the bartender, was in the stairwell of the building, which also houses apartments, when the South Tower fell and he recalls being not so much afraid as totally certain, as were several of the survivors I have met, that he was a dead man—"O I was sure of it—this building was shaking like an earthquake"—and being grateful he was going to die fast and untortured when the collapse brought down the little building over his head. Mike had brought over the book after I'd told him I had seen in it a chilling exterior of the devastated bar, and that I had seen another picture, taken during one of Kevin McCrary's early runs through the ash of the redzone, in which the en-tire place appears to have been modeled in white clay.[18] Kevin recalls seeing a note that was fingered into the dust on a menu there: "Thanks for the beers—FDNY," although whoever jimmied and cleaned out the bar's locked registers weren't as open about identifying themselves.

This disassembled copy of *One Nation* was fortuitous. I had intended to bring along my own copy that morning, as I wanted to show Donavin the second of the 767s disappearing, in two pages of video frames, into the face of the South Tower.[19] "Like butter," is how Gautam Patel described to me its appearance from the roof of his building at Park Row, where he was looking past the ugly black slab of the Millennium Hotel toward the Twins wrapped in fire and gray smoke. When, in March of 2002, Gautam arranged for me to go up there and shoot what was visible of the site—just a slice of the north end—and his remarkable neighborhood, of which the view is interesting in every direction—Municipal Building, Brooklyn Bridge, bored Justice with a sword and a scale, guy in a cherrypicker cleaning the glass of gaslamps, gold weathervaned spire of St. Paul's above a street full of tourists (who linger over fence-hung memorials more than the site itself), the fanlighted windows, the glimpses of half-curtained life, white roofs of city buses that stopped at the Beekman Starbucks to pick up stray evacuees on the 11th, pigeons pecking lunch out of a Broadway puddle by the Rockefeller Clock, the droopneck Bishop's Crook lampposts with garlanded scrollwork, the stonecut pilasters and balustrades, the quoined corners, and in the severe Dutch angles of my lens the competing façades that were stacked like rival decades or centuries— I heard the noise of shoveling on a rooftop below. It was two guys—working, of course, without protective gear—finally cleaning up, with hoses and shovels and brooms, bits of Gautam's two favorite buildings.

Gautam loved and still loves the Twin Towers. When he came to the States from India, the Twins were waiting for him as he walked up into Manhattan out of the PATH train from Jersey. They were his first astonishments, and as Gautam still collects images of the Twins, I printed out a frame I had taken, absently, early in 2001 when I was shooting a little drama on the FDR Drive, an image of the Twins that included the Woolworth Building and resembled the perspective from Gautam's corner. "Our healing doesn't feel yet," he said. "We love our great monuments." But for Gautam the Towers signified more than architecture, tourism, big business or bullshit about the American dream. They were his Statue of Liberty. They were his city. They were his job. They were his customers. They were his two lucky stars. They were his morning, his night. "I love to see every day," he told me. Now he gestured with a smooth lateral motion of his index finger to demonstrate the stroke of demolition to which he was witness. "Like you put a finger in the butter," he said.

It certainly seems that way in the video frames. The jet, which was doing 542 mph, appears to be welcomed into the building with no disruption, as if Yamasaki expected it to happen every morning and designed the sleek surface of his tower as a port. In fact it was swallowed up in one-fifth of a second. When you study the tape in extreme slow motion, a frame at a time, you see that the jet, which looks too small, too innocuous to be the fierce rainmaker it was, crosses Liberty Street in roughly the same number of frames as it takes for its absorption into the building and for its emergence again as fire, debris, and a drippage of JPA jet fuel that blotches the white face of the building like ink.

"When that second plane hit," Donavin said, "it was the hugest thing I've ever seen, and time totally stopped. I felt something against my face. I thought something had shot out of the North Tower to Tower Two. I don't remember *anything* after that."

Evan Fairbanks, a photographer who shot this video sequence and who kept his camera working until the South Tower fell rather too close to his lens, was in the studio of Trinity Television with the archbishop of Wales, Rowan Williams, now the archbishop of Canterbury, when word came through that the North Tower was burning.[20] From a study of the tape I have gathered that, after a few minutes of footage on the pedestrian bridge that takes you over Church Street from the little ambulatory back of the Trinity churchyard, he came out at 74 Trinity Place and walked north on Church toward the Towers. He was shooting in front of the Burger King at the corner of Church and Liberty when the final few seconds of United Flight 175 entered the top of his video frame just before it entered the building. This is where Donavin was standing when it happened, so there couldn't have been more than a few yards between them.

I wanted to meet Fairbanks but I could never find him. The images in his video, which I have seen on a big screen at the New-York Historical Society and have studied more closely in a copy made for me by Kevin McCrary, tell you as much about the man holding the camera as they do about the attacks. The camera and the cameraman walk, run, swerve, veer, duck, but they never stop investigating until the first collapse. The Fairbanks footage is compellingly detailed, silent, dangerous. It is also as close as I can come to seeing what Donavin saw that morning, and as close as he himself can come to seeing what he saw. As Fairbanks slowly walks west on Liberty Street, the camera catches a moment of worried life at 114, a moment in which Donavin might be visible in the frame if you could zoom into the image. When Kevin showed the footage to some of the guys at Liberty Street later in 2002, they were exhilarated to see that a camera had recorded these events from their perspective, a perspective they had presumed to be confined to their remembrance. The verification had a liberating effect but it freed up fear, too, making their personal nightmares a little more real than they had a right to be. Both Donavin and Curtis, one of the supers at 114, were still reeling from the tape the following day.

Late that afternoon, when we were alone at 114, out on the sidewalk, under the bridge of the workers' scaffold, standing by the graffiti'd wooden doors which, for more than a year, replaced the glass and steel that was ruined on the 11th, Curtis recounted his morning for me in a way that I had never heard. Newly terrorized, he was demonstrative, animated, coaxing me to follow as he showed me where he stood, where he ran, how he carried himself. Nothing that was told on the windswept shores of Troy could have interested me more than Curtis's sidewalk story. If I had been able to shoot, it would have comprised one of the most dynamic sequences in my film, but I couldn't allow myself to disrupt this performance by drawing out the camera, for Curtis was not at all comfortable in front of it.

"Believe me, Peter, I tell you no lies," is how he started in his emphatic Belizean accent. "I never in my *life* before seen no buildin comin down, but I *knew* there couldn't be nothin else make that sound. I'm sit-tin in my chair, I hear that sound, the floor in the buildin start shakin, the glass here, the chandeliers, the elevator doors—everything. You see over here, top of where the doors used to be? That's the magnets, to shut the doors in tight. Nothin ever make those doors shake like that. I go to the door the basement, *just* in time to open it, it push me flyin down the stairs. I get right back up again like nothin at all happen, come back up the stairs, but the door won't open. I kick it three times, try to force it, it won't budge."

"From the force of the cloud against it?"

"Yeah. I can't get out. I look outside the window here, couldn't see nothin. *Completely* dark. So I go back down the basement, take off my shirt, pour some water, clean some the dust off my face. Then I come up again, try goin up the stairs, see about the people in the buildin, but the door goin upstairs locked. So I go back down and out the back the buildin on Cedar Street, it's like, unbelievable. Dust all over, white, like winter."

"Quiet?"

"Except a siren goin off somewhere. People hurt—one girl, her face all bleedin. The guys that I know in the deli, over by Church Street? One guy tells me he's lookin for the other guy, his friend, where'm I goin? I say *I'm get-tin out of here,* I had enough. I even had to bump some people out the way, tryin to talk to me, they see me all dirty, or stand there hangin round, they want to look up, but you best get out my way, I was *bring it on, Brother,* I wasn't goina stop for *nothin,* I was mad, believe me, Peter, I was already so fuckin mad I wasn't stoppin for *nobody.* When I get to Brooklyn Bridge, that's when I see the second Tower goin down. I think of all the firemen, a lot of people die, because I see them all passin me before on Liberty Street. That's when I started on my long journey uptown. I walked all the way to 114th Street. Took me about two hours. When I get to my home I look in my wallet, I find one number from the buildin, Mark Wainger, so I call it, *and he picks up the phone.* I say: 'Mister Mark! What are you *doin* there?' He says: 'Curtis—where are *you?*' I said: 'I'm at my home.' Mister Mark says: 'So am I. I'm not gonna leave.' Later on the cops, they had to take him out."

Curtis, who showed me how he was cleaning the left glass panel of the doors at 114, a posture that placed his back to the World Trade Center when the North Tower was hit, methodically listed everybody there that day in the building—"There was Mister Mark, there was David, there was the woman from Weight Watchers"—as if it grounded him to get it all straight, now, the way it grounded him that morning. The list included a little girl. He was concerned for her safety. Then he got a call that David's children weren't accounted for. "So I go over by Deutsche Bank, try to find the kids. If you get the tape I'll show you *exactly* where I was. I was standin on the street, right below, lookin up, when the second plane flew over my head into the buildin."

"Did you hear it?"

"It was loud. Then I see it passin over, goin right into the buildin."

"Completely?"

"Just before he goes into the buildin, it turn to the side, like this." Curtis slanted his hand to the left by forty-five degrees. "Like you chop down a tree with an axe."

"No explosion though?"

"No explosion, till the nose comin out the other side, like you see on the tape, then you hear the explosion. When all the glass and shit start comin down, that's when I run into Deutsche Bank, stand by the door, a lady she starts yellin at me to close it, no *way* I'm gonna be trapped in that buildin. When I was runnin into the buildin I see a big fat guy fallin down, but I couldn't help the guy, I jumped *over* him, I was too . . . I seen people fallin out the buildin, parts of bodies on the street . . . I tell you no lies, Peter, I never want to see nothin like that ever again in my life, trust me Peter, trust me Peter."

It was roughly then, when Curtis returned to 114, meeting up with Donavin and David, that Fairbanks started to walk west on Liberty Street, so Curtis too may have been there in the lobby when Fairbanks shot it. Owing to the angle of Fairbanks's lens at the moment of impact, a few seconds before 9:03, the United jet looks as if it were passing over 114, although its 156-foot wingspan flew more directly (one supposes) over 90 West Street a block west of the Deutsche Bank and over Curtis's head as it made its last maneuver.

I see Curtis's hand turning . . . Gautam's finger advancing . . . reenactments by men who came to New York for something else. Balanced at the edge of the Liberty rooftop, looking out over the site into the past, Curtis once told me: "Yeah, it was a hard tragedy, that day. I don't have nothin like that in my country."

I said: "We never had anything like it here either, Curtis."

As a journalist in India, Gautam had witnessed many "critical situations," as he called them, including assassination of a government minister, and he reflexively reverted to the mode of journalist to take photographs of both Towers burning. "I am used to for these things," he said. "I scare, who's going to report?" This is why he was on the roof, shaking in his shoes, when the South Tower fell, and why he was smothered by the cloud when it stormed over Park Row. Still, distrustful of similes, I bought a 16-ounce slab of butter, let it stand on the counter for a day, and stuck my finger into it. Gautam's phrase, *like butter,* seemed appropriate to Fairbanks's images. No mess, no resistance: easy, easy. But I don't believe Curtis would have used the same analogy for what it looked like from down below on Liberty Street.

Gautam's and Curtis's descriptions of the second strike were verified, for me, by Chris York, a business professor and consultant who witnessed the events from the forty-eighth floor of his building just two blocks south at Rector Place. Like Evan Fairbanks, he was training his video camera on the North Tower burning. Despite the roar of the plane, which he placed about 150 feet above him, Chris couldn't imagine another attack—"What is a jetliner doing flying up West Street?"—and so even as the huge form, appearing in his peripheral vision, compelled him to lower the camera a moment, he thought of it as an act of reckless tourism, a pilot who was flying alarmingly low in order to get a more sensational view of the scene. Then it accelerated, climbed, banked to the right and, as Chris phrased it, "it was literally *absorbed* into the building like a pencil into butter. I saw the plane melt into the South Tower." Chris then added something that I had heard from no one else. "In retrospect, it was almost as if he might have been chickening out in the last second."

As Curtis had showed me how the plane had banked to the left, I turned my back to Chris and I banked my right hand to the right. "Like this, is that correct—to the right?" Chris was certain of this: he had seen it bank to the right. But not one of the tapes I have seen of the final approach—at least eight or ten—supports this description, and the gash in the South Tower that you see quite clearly in Chris's own video footage slants diagonally, like an *accent aigu,* opening the building from upper right to lower left.

"I remember it," Donavin said. "I couldn't stop looking at it, trying to figure it out."

"On Chris's tape?"

"No, on the street. I was searching for David's kids, but every time I looked up I was totally, totally baffled by that gash. I just couldn't make sense of it, the shape that plane had made going in, the imprint. What the hell *is* that? It mesmerized me. At one point I thought it sort of looked like a duck."

The night after speaking to Chris I happened upon a picture that clearly demonstrated the plane banking left. In fact it came in at an angle of 38 degrees, nose tilted a little down and to the left. So I faxed him the image, asking whether perhaps he might have misremembered the motion. Chris, who had been a lawyer for four years with the Strategic Air Command at a B-58 base, and had seen a lot of runway as an officer-of-the-day during the Viet Nam War, responded with the same professional clarity he displayed in our initial conversation.

"I've been reviewing my memory banks," he said, "and it seems clear that as it passed me it was right over West Street and it accelerated for sure and went up. And in order, indeed, to hit the Tower, it did have to bank right—that is, turn right—and so dip its right wing. Otherwise it would have missed and perhaps hit a glancing blow and gone right into the North Tower, since it was proceeding straight up West Street. But it's true: it could easily, at the last split second, have turned back toward the left in order to impact the building the way it did. So I think that I could probably testify to that effect. Straight in, accelerate, go up, slightly to the right, and then at the last second adjust back toward dipping the left wing. Sort of a jerky kind of adjustment. Boy, it's tough, though. We're splittin hairs."

I am told that this maneuver—the rudder turning one direction, the wing dipping the other—can straighten a plane that is turning too far too fast. The dip of that wing might have been accidental, or it might have been an inexperienced pilot, in the heat of his last moment, remembering the words of his flight instructor. But as Chris has suggested, it is possible that, despite the killer's clear intention, Flight 175 might have missed the South Tower on one side or the other, or it might have struck it a lesser blow, one that would not have been fatal. When I told this to my friend Rick Wallach, an aviation enthusiast and a pilot, he said: "Or, it might've torn the wing off and gone cartwheeling into Lower Manhattan with a tank full of fuel, and it might've done even uglier damage."

I discussed these issues with William Langewiesche, who began piloting planes at the age of fourteen and whose *Inside the Sky* is a thoughtful exploration into the meaning of flight. "My understanding is a more simple thing," he said. "If the guy almost missed, he would probably have clipped his left wing on the east side of the South Tower. By hooking a little bit of a left turn there, he smacked it." About Chris York's description of the bank in one direction, the dip in the other, he said: "I have no idea what the profile was previous to the impact." It was not fundamental to what Langewiesche was writing about in *American Ground: Unbuilding the World Trade Center*, which he discusses toward the end of this book. "Without knowing," Langewiesche said, "I would be *a little* cautious of that description. Just a little cautious."

I, for one, cannot stop thinking about the entry of that plane. If it was *like butter*, for how long were its passengers still seated and alive in some semblance of the jet that left Logan? Did anybody imagine they could climb out alive? One worker saw the wing cut through his office. Were there people who saw the hijackers, saw other passengers, before they died together? One website plays in slow motion and in closeup the videographic record of the strike. After studying it for hours I went to sleep one night with the site still up on my computer. When I stumbled back down, blearyeyed, the next morning, the first thing I saw was the 767 plowing into the South Tower. But even with the computer off, it's the same: South Tower at midnight, South Tower at dawn, and the questions it raises are as strong in me as ever. *Like butter*. Why is the phrase so troubling? One reason is that it gives a grade of shame to U.S. preparedness. Do you want to kill thousands in the most powerful nation on the earth? *Like butter* means: *it was easy*. Even when they know, for sure, we are coming, this man Bush, he goes to clear brush and play with his dog on a Texas ranch. Is the building up to code? Is the country up to code? We will show them up to code—*like butter*.

The previous day, September 10, Donavin the Wheel Lover's truck did what nothing with wheels should ever do to Donavin: it failed him, having died on the Brooklyn Bridge, from which he pushed it off himself and got a hand—applause, not assistance—from a cop who had never seen *anybody* do that. "The solenoid switch for the fuel pump was fried," Donavin told me. "If I'd've known it was that and not the pump, I'd've fixed it myself, gone to Liberty, finished the job, and then I wouldn't've been there on the 11th."

Even before the hour of hell, the 11th was a morning rare and strange for this Pennsylvania Mennonite, for he had deprived himself of his vehicle, which he takes everywhere. It had accumulated too many tickets on Liberty Street and, after yesterday's fiasco, he was not in a mood for more grief. Donavin walked to work at 114 from his apartment on Pearl Street to pave the way for a delivery from his woodshop in Greenpoint. Although he was born in Lancaster, it is a measure of his New Yorkness that Donavin still wondered, even after the South Tower was wounded, how the hell he was going to get his furniture into the building. The goddamned delivery was overdue enough. What was *this* now, to fuck things further? Furniture: he was fixed on furniture, *his* furniture. When Curtis said: "This is messed *up*, y'all," an expression and an attitude that Donavin reenacted for me at least a dozen times, this concise understatement worked over Donavin like a kind of invocation, and somehow served to better drive the message home, the message being: *this is not just another day—it's not even close.* Still, what is the point of doing beautiful work, and setting up for the installation, if the sky is going to open and a fireball is going to shoot the morning all to pieces?

This impulse in Donavin to push past even the most daunting obstacles is central to his character, and is partly why he operates well in New York, that most profoundly pushful and resistant of cities, and why he was frustrated but seldom, if ever, intimidated at Ground Zero. I think, too, that Donavin showed a dependency on routine—even if it is newly formulated for that day, or that hour—and a refusal to abide its interference, which is also characteristically New York and which contributed to the city's inability to scope out the scale of the unfolding catastrophe. Whatever else they are, disasters in New York are just more pains in the ass, more ways to drag the entire motherfuckerous day into a New York ditch. No way, pal: up *yours*. Where's my coffee?

This question of where the coffee was leads to interesting answers, whether or not you see them as symbolic of the daily dependencies that were, in some cases, slow to fall away on the morning of the 11th. When he first walked across Maiden Lane toward Liberty Street, Donavin could see that the North Tower was burning. There was paper everywhere drifting down over the fortress of the Federal Reserve Bank and over the old smaller buildings ahead of him on Maiden Lane, so named because Dutch women used to wash laundry in a stream there, a quaint attribution one can easily believe when you contemplate the streamlike curve between Broadway and Nassau Street. As badly as he needed to get to work that morning—the furniture was long overdue—he had lagged behind a little more to play with his new son. "He was a month old and so cute in the morning I couldn't leave," he told me. "It overrode the hole in my stomach from being late with the furniture." He had heard a phone message about something crashing into the North Tower, but "I assumed a plane just clipped it," Donavin said, "until I saw the paper trail. It was like a tremendous flatbed of Hammerhill bond had been dumped out of the sky."

He was nonetheless annoyed that the coffee he had bought from a vendor on the street was disappointing, so he stopped into the small seatless Starbucks in the galleria at Platt and William streets, where he poured something better for himself because the baristas were too upset to serve him. As he continued along Maiden Lane he held out his hand to receive a thin strip of tin, of which there were thousands flittering down, but only when he held it, seeing the holes at either end and thinking about its distinctive size, did he recognize a slat of venetian blind from one of the Twins. Like the slats we discovered on the Liberty rooftop and in one of the lightshafts, the piece of blind was seared black from the explosion. And even then, before the second strike, Donavin saw shoes. "Shoes *all over*."

"On Maiden?"

"No, but as soon as I got to Broadway. And Church. Greenwich Street was covered with shoes. There were *piles* of them over there. There must have been *two hundred* shoes on one block. People saw the impact, all that stuff flyin, they kicked off or ran out of their shoes."

"Mostly women's shoes?"

"Men's too. At one point, for half a second, I was looking, thinking—because some of them were really expensive shoes, really nice—I thought: 'Hmmm . . . those *might* look good . . .'"

An hour later, returning to his wife Erika (Buddy) and baby Brett (Little Man), Donavin was hustling up the east side of Broadway to get to Maiden Lane again. He could have continued along Liberty Street after it crossed Broadway, but he wanted to keep an eye on the Towers while he went, and the fifty-four stories of One Liberty Plaza would have obstructed the view from there. As there were crowds moving south, fleeing the opposite way, the Broadway sidewalk was slow, painfully slow for a man who is worried about his family and who trusts, passionately, in the virtue of speed. For Donavin, the properties of speed are as dependable, as absolute as an element in the periodic table. "When you slow down is always, *always* when there's trouble," he would say. "Newton's Law. An object in motion *stays* in

TOUCHING PEOPLE

motion, and that's me. I use objects to go even faster. I learned that from racing. You can use even a huge rock field to get traction." Facing a block of obstructive Broadway, Donavin, a natural *traceur* who has mastered parkour without ever hearing the word, climbed onto the poles of the long bridge-scaffold that rose over the sidewalk and monkied above the heads of pedestrian traffic. "Most people assume that an obstacle's a hindrance. You have to smile at obstacles. You look around, you know where you are, you don't waste energy, you use a little fluency, you reach your goal ahead of schedule."

We were walking down Broadway late one afternoon when he pointed up and said: "My monkey bars," referring to the scaffold, still in place a year later, by which he had invested his commitment to Newton's Law. As Donavin passed over the dense population to cover the block to Maiden Lane a little faster, the white cup with the green Starbucks circle enclosing a black and white mermaid, the cup containing the coffee he had poured on William Street, was clenched in his teeth.

David Stanke, too, kept at least as much comfort of routine as could fit in a cup of coffee. He was just across the street from the World Trade Center, in the Dey Street Starbucks, when he was shaken by the tremor of American Flight 11 tearing into the North Tower. "I felt the shock wave, the pressure," he told me. "I heard the glass rattle," something I thought about whenever I sat there with him. Although the Dey Street window did not afford a view of the North Tower, David saw it in the face of a woman in the street who ejaculated an oath and struck a horrified pose that reminded him of science-fiction. The firebreathing jaws of Godzilla were appearing over the Tokyo skyline. "When someone looks up that high in horror, you know something's happening up top. Some of my memories of the day have been dim. This is distinct. She had been walking along with that going-to-work trudge, she looked up, and I saw *her* world shatter. I knew it was big. I reacted faster than everyone else. They were standing still or still sitting as I ran out the door. The fireball didn't last long before it was smoke, but I ran out in time to see the receding explosion. The woman simply said: 'Terrorists.' I rolled my eyes at her as if to say *of course.*"

After assessing the level of danger from the Dey Street sidewalk, David retreated to Broadway to seek safer vantage from which to observe and calculate. "The top could have tipped," he said. "You saw the full width of the building in flames, the fire coming out both ends and there was fire on the South Tower too. I wanted to put some distance and another building between us. My thinking went from: 'O my God—entire floors of people gone,' to: 'No one above the impact will ever get down,' to: 'Is the top going to fall into the streets?' That's when I ran. I looked at the time. My wife was mid-town. Hannah was at PS 89. Hopefully, at 8:46, the rest of the kids were in daycare. But I had to be sure of that."

Once he resolved on returning to Liberty Street, David ducked back into the Starbucks to pick up his case and . . . well, why not, his iced Americano. It was in his hand as he hurried across the tree-lined perimeter of the Austin Tobin Plaza, a detail that I find fascinating: David heading home, taking a cut across the plaza between the Tuesday Farmers' Market and the east side of World Trade Four, *with his coffee in his hand.* "Whenever I leave here," he said, "if I'm done with my coffee I throw it out; if I'm not, I take it with me. It's a short sprint from here to home. That morning I barely even noticed it. As it turned out, I didn't need the extra caffeine for the rest of the day."

David's short walk under the Trades with a cup of iced Starbucks interested me enough that on the morning of September 11, 2002, I placed an aerial photograph of the World Trade Center on a small round table in the Park Row Starbucks, which is opposite Gautam's store on Beekman Street, and together we sketched the course of David's walk.

"You didn't go *around* Building Four."

"No."

"That would take you out of your way."

"Right. That was one of the problems we always had with that building: you couldn't walk to 114 from the plaza without going around either side of Four."

World Trade Four, which housed the New York Board of Trade, offices of the Deutsche Bank and a ground-floor restaurant, was an ugly black nine-story building that David had never liked, but he passed through it often enough to take it as a way of life. After it was gone—on the 11th its entire west side was squashed down so that it looked like a ramp: "It was like you could ride a motorcycle up it," Donavin said—David came to appreciate the way it helped surround the Twin Towers like the small dependencies that encompass and complete the geography of a cathedral. "Only in this case," David said, "the outerbuildings didn't protect it."

"But why did you cross the street at all? The North Tower was burning. Crossing over brought you *closer* to the destruction."

"It was a natural way to walk. I may even have hugged the wall of Four out of a sense of protection from debris. But I don't remember." Another time he said: "I was a little nervous about cutting through that corner—it was so close—but I wanted to get home to find out about the kids, so I just took off."

"Were the market people running?'

"I only remember passing the trucks. I have no sense of people on that walk. It wasn't crowded. No stampede. But my attention was pretty focused on getting home, so that walk is kind of a blank. Are you trying to catch me in another inconsistency?"

David was recalling that at one point he'd told me he was walking together with Donavin when the second of the hijacked jets hit home, whereas Donavin was sure that he was alone and, based on David's earlier recollection, so was I. When I brought the two together to discuss it, it was ironed out in favor of the men on different streets. The slip pleased me, though, because it hinted at the camaraderie David had expressed when he spoke about Donavin's departure for Pearl Street in order to help his own family. "When we separated," he said to Donavin, "I felt the way you do when you're camping in the woods and you're used to being with someone, then suddenly you're alone and you realize how much it helped having them there."

David recalled the moment of second impact clearly. He was returning from the initial search for his children, flying to Liberty Street without delay, which is what the plane was doing, and so he remembers not looking at the explosion and that he did not take cover from the debris, dodging behind a post only once to let a wave of people pass. "Before the South Tower was hit, it was an emergency. Now it had accelerated drastically. Every second counted. From the first hit, the scope of life lost was beyond my comprehension. I knew it was too big to think about. I didn't need to stand there and look. I knew enough. I didn't know it was a plane, I only knew that the attack had continued. I thought: 'O my God,' and I saw a panicked mass of people running at me at full speed."

By uniting himself with Donavin for this first reconnoiter, David had put them together for the second impact, which is how, for the course of the slip, he preferred to remember it. He brought Donavin into the picture about ten minutes sooner because he needed him to be there. Who can blame him? It is a moment of desolation nearly too deep to bear. A man knows that his four small children are under the burning of one of the world's tallest buildings. He goes home looking for the youngest: not there. He gets a call: bad news, all three of them are out with their nanny in the street. He looks for them: not there. He goes to the daycare center over on South End Avenue where he hopes to find them waiting. Not there either. As he heads back home another building, *closer,* blows like a bomb. New York is under attack. He is standing in a war, and his kids might be more in the heat of it than he is.

"I hadn't calculated the terror in the street," David said. "I saw the terror in the sky and I wasn't thinking about blast radius or falling of debris. Assuming the kids were in daycare, and that Hannah was at school, I was standing at the window with a photographic impulse: 'Let's capture this.' When I got the call from Sarah that the kids were in trouble down in front of the Deutsche Bank—the nanny, Tricia, couldn't get them home—everything, *everything* went away, and from that point onward I never looked up again. *I've got to find the kids now.* I looked along Liberty Street but I didn't see them there and I didn't see much, mostly litter. I would find out later that just two blocks over it was hell. A lot of debris coming down, and unmentionables. I cut south and over to West Street to get to the daycare. After the second blast, the emotion, *I've got to find them,* was so intensified that I might have passed out from hyperventilation. Your legs feel weak and the body doesn't move as fast as the mind wants it to move, and so it almost falls."

Donavin recalled David's condition sympathetically.

"David was a little crazed—understandably, with all his kids out there," he said. "There were thousands of people on both sides of the sidewalk. David took one side and I took the other and we looked through the crowd, mostly moving in the opposite direction. We wondered how a fireproofed building with all that double drywall could be that much on fire. I couldn't believe paper and whatever else was up there could have that much fire in it. Stuff falling down. Fires everywhere. People running for boats. But it was still a perfect day when we walked down Greenwich and across West Street trying to find David's kids. I am *so* glad I was busy looking for them. There were all these little explosions. I think subconsciously I knew what they were but I didn't want to deal with it."

"Donavin kept me connected to reality," David said. "He was also good at working the system. He doesn't take an answer as the final word. Donavin is: 'How can I work *around* that answer?'"

"When we couldn't find the kids," Donavin said, "we headed back, thinking that they might have made it home, but when the cops wouldn't let us through I gave David tactics to buffalo the cops. We decoyed each other. 'How're we going to do this?' 'This is how. When I'm talking to this guy, you go over there and . . .' So that's how we got across the Westside Highway and basically back to the building, by creating these diversions. The cops were hindering us but, of course, at the same time buildings were coming down so they were right: we needed to get the hell out of there. The fires were really bad at this point. I know structure, I know the ratings on steel beams, I know the coatings on them, and I know that my family is three and a half blocks down Maiden so I needed to get them out of there. That's when David and I split."

When David once said that he was sorry not to have helped people out before crowding onto a ferry to Staten Island, where he reunited with three of his children (the fourth, Hannah, was in New Jersey), I said: "Are you kidding? You dealt with every father's most primal nightmares—*all* of them at once. Bombs, fire, war, panic, confusion, catastrophe—and *where the hell are the kids?* I would say that's enough for one day."

"I'm not blaming myself, I'm respecting others," David said. "It pains me to think about this woman from the Port Authority running in and pulling people out, directing them. To think of doing anything *right below*—and this is after they were burning for an hour."

When I asked him about walking down Greenwich Street before the first collapse, David said: "It was a big area now, the whole south end of the island in which to locate the kids, a needle in a haystack. Then I remember a day of sunlight and shadows becoming overcast, dusty. I thought: Sodom and Gomorrah. 'Don't look back—don't take that second—there's nothing to see that'll help you—run!'" It doesn't surprise me that, when he ran down Greenwich Street, David, a six-foot-five marathon runner, was dismayed at how poorly his lungs appeared to be working or that, sitting in an office while an artificial night was rising up out of the building he used to see from his livingroom, he heard a stranger say: "Buddy, you'd better start breathing."

This persistence of mine in addressing the same issue more than once, even half a dozen times—whether to unpack a lost observation, to clarify an issue or to secure a better soundtrack—could easily have driven any number of my subjects into feeling like the killer on *Columbo*. In the light of something David once told me: "I used to be hungry for every story, trying to get them all straight. Now I don't like to think about the way things were," I was grateful he had spoken to me at all. And yet even now I could sit down with David and say: "What happened to you that morning?" If this is a way of saying *take me back there with you*, it will, of course, take a trick of time, not a turn of phrase, for me to be properly answered.

About that walk to Liberty Street from the Dey Street Starbucks, David said: "My recollection is *not* of an emergency such as people have described it." David had forgotten all about his cup of coffee until a week or so later when, standing in the soot and the trash of his apartment, gazing into the jumble that had once been town to him, he found the cup sitting on the windowsill, plastered and partly drained of its liquid, exactly where he'd left it when his wife called to tell him that the kids were at risk and he was thrown back into the streets. "I was surprised when I saw it," he said. "It was sitting there with all that shattered glass and debris. It hadn't been knocked off the sill."

The *One Nation* cover I was holding in my hands was merely a folder for the O'Hara's bar copy of the book, of which the unbound pages had been shuffled out of order. As I was looking for the Fairbanks frames to show to Donavin, I happened upon an AP photograph, taken by Gulnara Samollova, of men and women cloaked and masked in World Trade cement (pp. 66–67). I said to Donavin: "This is what you mean when you say they were Abominable Snowmen."

"No way," Donavin said. "Totally not even close. I'm talking about nothing at all discernible of the human form."

"So, these are more polite—these are George Segal sculptures?"

"O these are normal, these people are pristine, nothing at all to what I saw on Maiden Lane. The people I was dragging into that building you couldn't tell they were people. No resemblance. Covered, *caked* in gray shit. *Mounds* of it." Mud People, he called them. "No gender, no nothing. As I was walking down to Pearl it was *The Night of the Living Dead*. Like they were magnets and it was iron ore stalactiting off of them. And walking around directionless, *lingering,* some of them, zombies, not wanting to leave, not knowing *what* to do, where to go."

"Stunned?"

"Totally, totally stunned. Still carrying their briefcases. I think it came down Maiden Lane, that cloud, stronger than anywhere. It shot through that column, that curve in the street, *so* fast. The ionic shock when it hit the glass at 59—*boom.*"

Number 59 Maiden Lane, an office tower at William Street—the Home Insurance Building—is opposite the Federal Reserve Bank and diagonally across from where Jeremy Irons blows up a subway station in *Die Hard 2* in order to bulldoze a way into the gold of the Reserve, which is a quarter of the gold in this country. Donavin, who stood with his son Collin to watch them film that faux disaster, was sprinting and, literally, *flying* down the street September 11 in the hope of short-seconding a real one. When, after the *Die*

Hard shoot, he and his son took some broken tiles from this station that was built to be exploded in the eye of an Arriflex, it would have seemed impossible that one day the Twin Towers were going to come get him, hurling against his legs and his back, assaulting his ears with the shrapneling of trucks and shop windows, or that shards of *Die Hard* would be sharing the same space with a twist of aluminum siding he collected on Cedar Street and later dumped, ceremonially, into the Newtown Creek because his friends said it was too damn spooky to have the World Trade Center in his shop.

"The cloud was first," Donavin said, "then the shock. When I jumped into the building I felt the oscillation in the glass. That's why they thought the glass was going to cave in and were telling everybody to stand away. I was less concerned about the glass. I was lying on the floor, flopping around like a fish, just grateful to be out of that fucking cloud."

Donavin had leaped over a fountain that, on later inspection, showed itself to be too broad for anybody to jump unless he had walked out of a Marvel comic book.

"You had to climb the wall to the plaza first," I said, "so that would halt your momentum. Traversing that pond from a standing position—you'd have to have flown."

"Humans *can* fly when a building's falling on them," he said. "I wanted to get into something before it hit me. I cut the corner of that fountain as close as I could because I didn't want to get killed. It wasn't a good day to die for me. But when I think about it, at the end of that day, September 11, I could honestly say that I did the right thing. I tried to save some people and not just leave them out in the street, banging on the glass with their briefcases. People in the building were screaming at me, swearing—'You stupid son of a bitch!'—because they didn't want me to open the door, I shouldn't try to let people in. I thought they were going to lynch me. I didn't care. One guy, completely covered in dust, had his face pressed flat against the glass. So I propped the door open with my foot while I called people to come to my voice and reached around for them. I was afraid they'd lock the door behind me. They would have. They were crazed, terrified. A lot of them had just come down to the lobby, heading for work, no *idea* what had happened, that a building had just fallen into the street. It was night out there. Brutal. Black ash. They looked out and they thought: 'What's *this*? I was just upstairs, beautiful day, how'd it get to be *nighttime*?' I opened the door full out in order to calculate the seconds before it closed. When I yelled out: 'Come to my voice!' the powder was such amazing insulation that I couldn't even hear myself. It was like yelling underwater or on the moon, the sound was so completely absorbed. And it was so long. I was listening to the silence. I got at least four or five people in. I would push the door open, rush out, rush back, or I would hold it with my foot and feel around with the other leg, calling to people.

"After I started home, I took this one girl—she was torn up, a mess, her arm was bleeding, bruises—to the Western Union office over on Pearl just to get her off the streets. I told them I had to look after my wife and my boy, so they took her. At first I was over the pizza place, but the pizza guys were saying: 'No no no no, you can't bring a wounded bleeding person—get her the hell out of here!'"

"We ought to go back with the camera, say: 'You were the guys who wouldn't even—'"

"Well, it was hard enough for *anybody* to know what to do without taking care of someone else, in that condition, all torn up like that. Who am I to talk? But I think I at least passed the test, trying to help as best I could before I went for my own family."

One day when Donavin was griping about the mournful dents his Chevy Suburban had suffered from all the traffic on Liberty Street—"Look at my poor truck, they've destroyed it, and look at this, as if it hasn't suffered enough"— I asked him whether he'd needed to ram into things as he tore out of Manhattan on the 11th. "Not much," he said. "Just a bunch of forklifts plowing through the South Street Seaport—and people."

He had already told me, in free honest moments, that it was interesting to have to work the obstacles in his path. It was a skill he had honed in racing cars, motorcycles, snowmobiles, snowboards, dune buggies—anything that moved. "I kind of enjoyed it, actually, bumping them out of the way." Farther uptown he was one second shy of broadsiding a taxi in order to keep his truck rolling, for no one—not the slomo hack, not his slomo passenger, not a guy loading Coke onto a handtruck—showed the slightest sign of catastrophe. "*Completely* different world. Maybe one-eighth of the people looking up toward the smoke. Otherwise, it was a time warp. No panic, no fear. Normal life. I was ready to shove the taxi. I needed to move."

But I had forgotten about the people. "Who were the people?"

"They *all* wanted to climb into my truck. When Buddy and I were pulling out with Little Man in the back seat, she *knew* I'd be wanting to take all these

TOUCHING PEOPLE

people with us, so she said to me: '*There is not one chance in this world that you are going to let one single person in this van.*'"

"Brett had had enough dust for the day," I said. "He didn't need to meet the Mud People."

"Exactly."

"Plus a few seconds more you'd've been under the second collapse."

"*No* seconds. As I was dealing with the car seat I heard that same sound, same rumbling, like the Jolly Green Giant running down Broadway. 'Forget it—just get *in*.'"

"So, good thing she said it."

"Totally right. When we got to the truck on Maiden, I kept poking through the dust with my key, feeling around, trying to find the hole, but I couldn't fucking find it, so I had to wipe the door with my ass—Brett was in my other arm—to get the key in. When I opened the door all this stuff from the roof just came pouring inside, whoosh! all over the seats, everywhere. It was like a duststorm. I realized I should have cleared it away before I opened the door—it was piled like six, eight inches high on the roof, the whole truck, and it all went rushing in. I cleaned it fast as I could, then I heard that sound—which I *knew, no doubt*—I got us all in and I took off skidding and sliding around in the snow. I had to hit four-wheel or I wouldn't've moved. I took *one* look back and saw it coming. It was *moving*. I took *off*. As we were trying to pull away, people were *throwing* themselves onto the truck, begging me, imploring me to take them, but by then I was ready to say: 'You're just going to have to fucking *die*, because I've got to get the fuck *out* of here.'"

When I read the above to Donavin he was silent for a moment. "Hearing you read that," he said, "I could be *right* back there on that day. And it tells me a lot about myself. You really got it down perfectly." September 11 then consumed him the way it always did whenever we talked about it. So much for "I don't remember *anything* after that." It had taken me a year but I was learning that everybody remembered everything, or practically. There is an almost mystical cast to remembering trauma. Trauma is real magic—presto, you're different—and we are right to invoke that magic as if it mattered. This time we were sitting in the vast galleria of the World Financial Center just north of the Winter Garden. Again, Starbucks in our hands; again, Starbucks the starting point. With nearly a dozen of them between the Battery and

Chambers Street, including one on Broadway below Trinity Church where the King's Arms, the first coffeehouse in New York, used to stand, you could write an entire book taking Starbucks Coffee, its outlets, its patrons, its workers, its brew, as an approach to September 11, only what you might think of as too narrow a focus would probably prove too broad. David, whose Dey Street Starbucks was closed for half a year, warmly reunited with some of its workers when it reopened for business. Six to nine months after the event I was seeing reunions of customers with people who had made coffee for them that morning, after which—who was living, who was dead? "We only lost two," one young barista said. "At first, a security guard locked the exit doors and we couldn't get out, but then . . ." Connections, in some cases, were strong enough between patrons and workers that I was not able to tell in which category the two who were lost had belonged.

"The timing of jumping off of that scaffold," Donavin said, "with the Starbucks cup in my teeth and my feet touching down on Maiden Lane, with the Tower coming down . . . was practically one step. At first I was skipping. It was a real boyish singsongy 'La-la la-la-la.' I was happy. It was such a relief to be out of the crowd. For the past half hour, first with David, then here, I'd been fighting all these people. Now I was alone. There was *no one.* Everybody was rushing along up and down Broadway, the cops were standing there with their arms out, directing people, blocking things off. So it was three little skips saying: 'I'm away from you people!' I was doing a little dance, spinning around with my arms out. Then *Dsssh Dsssh Dsssh Dsssh Dsssh!* You felt it through the ground—all your senses felt it. Something was *definitely* wrong. And *the hand,* the huge dark hand reaching down. Unbelievable how much stuff was flying. Glass shattering. When the building was coming down you could tell it was major, you heard the jackhammering sound and the echoes, but it was muffled, too. At first I just stood there."

"You didn't run?"

"No, I just stood for a few half seconds. I watched it for a while until it was halfway down the building. The cloud was square, it was right where the Tower was, and it looked exactly like the Towers. You couldn't tell what was what. But there were sections shooting radically out of the sides of the building, north, south, so I figured *if it's goin that way it'll be comin here too.* Once I heard people moaning, screaming, hurt, that's when I started to run. Then stuff started hitting me, hitting people who were running, too—I could hear the *thumps*—so it was *fuck this shit.* That's when I took off. Speed was on my side."

He did not mean *speed* as merely a property of motion, or as *running faster than them.* He meant it as an entity to which many years of critical study and assiduous pursuit were dedicated, something he had served well enough for him to be served by it now.

"You said that after you dived into the revolving doors at 59, people were coming down, expecting to go to work."

"There must've been forty or fifty of them," he said, "out of the elevators, standing in the lobby."

"But isn't it an office building?"

"Maybe they were on their way to appointments."

"No sense of coming down to run away?"

"None. But I didn't look a single one of them in the eye. Then I did look at this one guy who was giving out masks, and one guy in the back, by William Street, when I said: 'You're not gonna fuckin lock me *out*, are you?' Over on Maiden there was no one else to be taking in, so I figured my job was done. I remember moving my hands along the sneezeguards of the Jubilee, the food place over by John and William streets, where a girl was filing her nails, talking on the phone with *no conception* of what was happening. She was chatting with her mother about how she was getting home. 'Guess I can't take the train so I'll probably have to take a bus,' blah blah. It was the difference between life-and-death panic and total unconcern. I interrupted her. 'Do you sell dust masks here?' She didn't get it, no connection to things at all, so I suggested to the owner that he bring some wet towels around. He did. At the back doors on William, these wooden doors, I was trying to loosen these cremone-type bolts to open'm up but no one paid any fucking attention to me, people were stepping all over me, then ten people slamming on it knocked it totally down and practically crushed me. I thought: 'You people are gonna fuckin *kill* yourselves. I can't stop *that*.' That's when I got out of there. I can't forget this Spanish delivery guy, he was standing around Fletcher and Pearl, middle of the street. He had taken his shirt off and was tearing it into pieces, giving them out. It was great. I remember him."

When I once thanked Donavin for doing me a kindness, he said: "That's the first time I've helped anyone in my life." I picked one counterexample: the morning of the 11th. "I didn't help those people," he said. "I just dragged them."

"Where exactly did you meet the wounded woman?"

"Platt Street, close to Pearl. I'd made a few attempts to get home, but there were so many people floundering around—they didn't know *what* they were doing—so I'd lead them in somewhere, take a wet something, brush off their little faces. It wasn't easy. Everybody was closing their doors. This girl's friend asked me: 'Can you *please* help us?' O my God this woman was really hurt. I started to carry her but she said it wasn't necessary. 'Can you just walk with us?' But this girl, she could barely walk, I was holding her up. She was bleeding on her cheek and her ear, her shoulder, her arm, her leg, too—her pants were torn. I found out later she went to the hospital for three weeks. Her friend was injured too but I didn't notice it then. It was snowing horribly. It was so hard to breathe it took me two tries to get out of 59. It was coming down big-time. I didn't even notice my Suburban. But it was the only car on the street. There were no other cars. Everybody had gotten out of there."

When Donavin made tracks with his family in the truck, which he renamed a UEV—Urban Escape Vehicle—Water Street was jammed up for miles. So was South Street. So he drove up north in the southbound lane, jumping the curb and driving on the sidewalk whenever emergency vehicles were racing downtown. As he zigzagged a route up to the Williamsburg Bridge he collided with an ambulance that darted across his path with its siren off. It hit him in the front on the passenger side but it didn't stop. Neither did Donavin. "Speed was on my side." But the speedster took time enough to negotiate safety and comfort for others, time that could have enveloped the whole family in a gray hand of death.

9

Kevin McCrary used to wonder whether the height of the Twin Towers exceeded the distance from the plaza to Tex's apartment in Battery Park City. He was curious to know how he and his father would fare if the Twins fell over. He contemplated this and other bad scenarios after the North Tower was bombed in 1993 but he had always pondered the question. There wasn't anything morbid or obsessive about it. Catastrophic speculations arise naturally at the feet of such vertical boldaciousness. We all fear the sky falling in one way or another. Some long for it. Under threats of Islamist fascism or homegrown offensives such as we saw in Oklahoma City, once-idle imaginings can feel like preparedness, and hysterical symptoms can start to look like self-preservation. The fact that those buildings couldn't have held together enough to topple down on people like trees didn't dispel either the image or the anxiety. If the world were to allow for the felling of those giants, to say that they couldn't fall down flat was a quibble that was easily ignored.

However they would fall, we now understand it wasn't easy to have predicted where *out of reach* or *safely out of harm's way* would be. Look at the dockworkers in India concerned about contaminants in the World Trade steel they were offloading from freighters. According to the Basel Convention a nation is responsible for the safety of its exports, but that didn't affect the scrapped steel from the Trade Center because the United States hasn't cared to sign the Basel Convention. So, guys in India worried about their health and they complained about the pieces of Lower Manhattan coming to get them on the *Brozna*, the *Shen Quan Hai* and the *Pindos*.[21] And if *they* did not feel safe, shouldn't we allow for restless concerns on Liberty Street?

One day in the 1990s, floating the same postulate as Kevin had, Donavin and his older son Collin paced off, step by step, the height of the tallest Twin, starting at its base and measuring down Maiden Lane the 1,368 feet until they reached their apartment on Pearl Street. "We were right on the border,"

Donavin told me. "It was close. We might've just made it, we might not've." On the 11th that apartment, with month-old Little Man in residence, saw the Trades moving in—not as steel, as ash—as the family moved out. But I like to envision that pace-off with Collin, that midday outing between a father and a son down that old bending street that used to debouch onto Broadway with the best Broadway view of both Towers. Charles Dickens, who walked Lower Manhattan and wrote about the perilous nature of life on Wall Street in his book *American Notes,* could have used such a curious walk to launch a new novel into serial publication in *Master Humphrey's Clock* and *Harper's Weekly.* "The question as to whether, when they walked thus together under the shadow of the Tower, the gentleman and the boy who could only have been his son might, perchance, have been perceived, from either rooftop or window, to be satisfying more than a mere flush of eccentrical whim with which to entertain the day, will be answered soon enough." Was it folly, was it paranoia? In a neighborhood coerced into *eating* those buildings, no one can be faulted for having paced off their measure, especially as the people who put them up were partially bluffing about their safety.[22] It is, at least, taking your curiosity into your own hands—and feet.

I had done something similar in that same neighborhood when I climbed up the stairs, fifty-plus floors, to the top of the Woolworth Building, where construction guys invited me onto an unprotected balcony to share the view with them. In those days the Twins were a prime part of the view, but that is not why I had walked up to the top. I had had a crazy notion about wanting to know more of what the height of the building meant, meant really, in the day when it was built. Could I feel in my legs what they saw in their eyes? Climbing the dome of St. Peter's in Fellini's *La Dolce Vita,* a woman asks the protagonist, Marcello, how high it is. "O very very high," he says. When the climb doesn't ever seem to end, that elemental *high* means something. To the mass of evacuees moving at one floor per minute down the World Trade stairwells, of which both buildings were short one set, *high* could have meant you would die that day, as it could have for firefighters moving the other way with up to a hundred pounds of gear and commitment to a job in which bad luck can burn you alive.[23]

And so here is a question. If a carpenter and his son showed sufficient curiosity to take that rulered walk through the Austin Tobin Plaza, across Broadway and on down Maiden Lane in even lighthearted anxiety over the fate of those extra-terrestrials, didn't they deserve some measure of prevention from the mightiest force of government on the globe? Donavin & Son,

Donavin Gratz's Ground Zero pass.

in that singular occupation, measuring off the distance between life and sudden death while the rest of Downtown rushed about its daily business, is one of the many images that prompted me to wonder, as I photographed the site, whether the safety of the American citizenry was ever on the Bush agenda.

That pace-off was not the only time Donavin turned one of the Towers, those potential bonecrushers, into a yardstick. For the carpenter in Donavin, the Twins were the handiest of instruments for testing the trueness of buildings in Lower Manhattan. Whatever it was to anyone else, the World Trade Center was a straightedge to him and he could carry it anywhere conveniently. Donavin positioned, visually, a corner of the building under inspection so that its vertical line was left with only a narrow space between it and a Tower. This was, in effect, the introduction of the straightedge. "It's a natural plumb bob," he said. "Perfectly vertical, perfectly plumb, so no matter how you look at it, it's going to show if something else is straight." By shifting his head to one side, Donavin moved the lines of both buildings until they touched and their edges crossed or blended. Then he would separate them slightly. In the light between the two, any imperfection in the vertical line of the building being tested showed itself beside the straightedge of the Tower. If it listed, if it bowed, you would see it.

"As a carpenter, that's how you test your framing work," Donavin said, "to tell when a stud is out, to tell when a doorway's out. You get used to it after a while."

Casually, impulsively, Donavin was taking the tallest structures in the city and matching them up against buildings with which they shared a sightline.

"It's a disorder," he told me. "I'd have to take a quick glance at the Trades just to check on every building."

Like an accountant I know who reaches his hand around, without looking, to do sums on his calculator during a conversation with you, sums that have nothing to do with your taxes or anything else, Donavin would sometimes close one eye when he was talking at a window and he'd shift his head slowly in structural judgment. I was too late for the Trades but he was using other buildings that had passed the Trade test and were trustworthy now to take their place. It served no professional purpose but it was a professional act, for it flowed from what he did and it was interesting and instructive to test the work of brother builders from these older generations. Walking the streets around Ground Zero while the flatbeds were carrying off his old straightedge, we would pause, now and then, to pick up the Chase Manhattan Bank, or One Liberty Plaza, and together we would hold it against a building from the '20s or the '30s, or something older, in order to take its measure. The plumb police were pleased.

"These old tall buildings are totally perfect," Donavin said. "I've never found a leaner. The Trade Towers were great for that, though—the biggest straight line there is. They were so easy to find, so tall and perfectly straight that I used them all the time, ten times a day, every day. I would sight *every* building as I was walking Downtown. That was my favorite thing to do. They were the best straightedge. September 11, I lost my benchmark."

MISTER MARK STAYS FOR BREAKFAST

I can't remember who described Mark Wainger to me in the following way: "Mark's the sort of guy who would stand at a broken window after a terror attack, or up on the rooftop, raising his hands over his head, shouting after the terrorists: 'Hey! I'm still here! Is that the best you can do?'"

Mark is the resident of 114 to whom Curtis, the super, was referring when he said that after he walked uptown on the 11th, he telephoned Liberty Street and spoke to Mister Mark who, surprisingly, was still at home. To hear Mister Mark tell it, he stayed at Liberty Street through the morning of the 11th and the remainder of the day—he didn't leave till five o'clock—because it appeared reasonable to do so. Once the Twins had done collapsing on him there wasn't any compelling cause to vacate the premises. I, for my part, would not have stopped running till I had reached the other side of the earth, and I don't mean Brooklyn or Jersey.

During my first fall walkaround in the Liberty Street apartments, blown-out windows were leaning against walls; the evacuation speaker still aimed over the site from Mark's guestroom window; elevator maintenance, distribution of passes, the logistics of garbage disposal and the freeing up of dumpsters were hot issues; and shifts of unbelievably youthful out-of-state Christians were asking Donavin how best to serve New York. I watched one team disposing of piles and pails of trash by passing along, in three-man relays, one slab of drywall, one boulder of concrete, one twisted fixture at a time so that a man on a windowsill could take aim and toss them carefully into a dumpster on Cedar Street. When the cops made them stop, Donavin took it in stride. "We don't do it then," he'd say. "There'll be different cops there tomorrow and they'll say something different." It was during this walkaround that Donavin referred me to framed family photographs of Mark, who lived with his wife and two children on the sixth floor of 114, a flight below David.

"You should see Mark's video," Donavin said.

"From that morning?"

"From that morning."

"From just before?"

"From just before *and* after. The South Tower fell, then he started shooting again. *In*-credible."

One could see by the snapshots that Mister Mark's resistance and resolve hadn't fomented out of imposing physical features: he is of medium height, bone thin, and with his gray-flecked beard and wireframed spectacles he looks like a bright, self-motivated, socially ambiguous software designer from MIT, which he is. He is successful in business but he never looks like business. The one time I saw him in a suit, dressed for a meeting at the World Financial Center, he didn't look uncomfortable but the suit was wasted on him. In the company he cofounded in 1985 the programming staff wore jeans and T-shirts, even when meeting with men in suits who always met with other men in suits. In the eyes of Mark's clientele the T-shirts signified the quirky, informal, seemingly hibernative cast of computer genius, and Mark accumulated hundreds of them, including some from what he calls "a commie T-shirt commune in Minnesota." Mark's face was made for sandals but he wears, almost exclusively, New Balance sneakers. When he leaped out of bed that Tuesday morning Mark slipped into his sneakers without socks, so that after the first collapse the mesh tops of his sneakers drew debris between his toes.

"There's this grit grinding away the whole time I'm walking around," Mark told me, "and you're thinking this is building, and bones, and people. You're surrounded by it. There's nothing you can do."

If Mark was lucky in business he was lucky in life, too, which is a hard thing to say about a man who buys a home across the street from a landmark in one of the safest parts of town until one day the landmark hammers a hole in his building and scatters itself across his luxury co-op, teaching Mark and everyone else a lesson that none of us wants to hear: the safe spaces aren't safe, and no height is too high for falling. But Mark at least *looked* lucky when Donavin also pointed out the perilous missile—a condenser for an air-conditioning unit (it looks like a radiator)—that crashed through the window of Mark's library, a smallish room in the northeast corner of his apartment. If Mark had sought protection from the collapse by heading east across the house instead of south, it would have brained him.

When I spoke to Mark for the first time we were up on the roof in the early days when Liberty Street, with its clear view of the site and, from the south side of the roof, the end of the island, was new to me. Places up there were bombinating, and pungent whiffs of rot raised glances between friends who didn't often look at each other. The landings and steps of fire escapes were heaped with trash and on the floor of a lightshaft I could see, with the aid of the zoom, the hand of a doll, a putty knife, colorful curtains, a booklet of step-by-step instructions for SUPER AIRPLANE POWER, packs of cigarettes, seared swaths of insulation, and an isolated photograph of a child and a black dog in an autumn field. The site was noisy that day with a drilling that sounded mechanically hysterical. I shot the site and the neighborhood and I examined, stupidly, a hunk of South Tower that had not been removed yet. Made of shining silver-alloy Alcoa that was approved by Yamasaki for its deftness at playing with the sun, it was a twisted part of what was known as the curtain wall and it had landed under a wooden water tower that was draped, no one knew by whom, with multicolored Tibetan prayer flags. Laying hands on the siding and sounding it for energy neither engaged nor improved my intelligence. You can't stage-manage your own enlightenment. Anyway, hadn't I asked for *a naked contact with reality*? Here it was. The one thought that I did have—*this piece of the Twin Towers doesn't belong here at all*—was more stultifying than stimulating and probably untrue, grounded, as it was, in a contradiction in terms—*curtain wall*—and in the presumption that this mass of allegedly lightweight aluminum did belong up in the clouds a hundred stories over my head.

Under his jacket Mark was wearing a T-shirt that read: *Another Brilyunt Mind Distroyed by the New Jersey Edukashun Sistum*. After eliciting a summary account of Mark's ordeal, I asked him whether he planned on returning to Liberty Street or whether he'd thought about abandoning the city. "This was our home for close to three years," Mark said. "And ... ah ..." He laughed a little. "No expletive-deleted terrorists are going to scare us away."

More out of courtesy toward the concerns of my camera than to project a clean image, Mark had substituted *expletive-deleted* for an exclamatory adjective. As this is New York, the adjective in mind had to be *fucking*. "Fucking terrorists." This was thoughtful of Mark, but I would have preferred his uncensored expression. I was also wary of passing along that *fucking* as fact, so I later asked him about it. Mark's first response was to wonder whether, if he had said what he was thinking, he would have been rude enough to say *motherfucking terrorists*. He tended toward *fucking*. "But then I thought back to our interview on the roof," he said, "and it was just a short jump from that viewpoint to 9/11 itself, and then I realized *motherfucking* was too weak."

Mark's final decision as to what he had wanted to say extended to four unprintable adjectives. "You might find that surprising," he said, "from someone who doesn't curse. But that's because, with two kids at home, I have given up the habit to set a good example."

The habit returned quickly on the 11th. When the video he shot on his Hi-8 Sony cuts abruptly from the livingroom antics of his children, Lucy and Alex—taken another day, in another world—to the black-smoked wounds of Tower Two and its contents dancing in the air, the first thing you hear on the soundtrack, along with the faintly mechanical noise of the zoom switch working and a siren in the streets, is Mark saying, soberly: "Holy fuckin shit. That's the World Trade Center."

When Mark was growing up during the '60s, the kids in his neighborhood were brought up religious, and some of them were told they'd be struck with lightning bolts if they cursed out loud. "Being the son of an agnostic Presbyterian mom and an agnostic Jewish dad," Mark said, "I had no such fears." Mark cursed for the religionists, proving his immunity to lightning. If God was trying, at last, to get him on the 11th God just barely missed, twice, and Mark is still capable of formulating curses. "So, yes," he said about the deletion during our rooftop conversation, "they were motherfucking, cocksucking, scumbag asshole terrorists."

As Mark likes to work alone and at night, he went to bed at five o'clock that morning and he slept through the explosion in Tower One. The second event, which was diagonally across the street, practically over his head, woke him with a BA-BOOM and by shaking his waterbed at 9:02:59 a.m. Mark supposes that the alarms and the sirens had jostled his sleep before that, a case of a nightmare reaching into a dream, taking hold of a man, and leading him out of a bed of easeful water into a vision of hellfire.

When Mark stood up, David was a few blocks away on Albany Street trying to locate his children; Curtis was a block away in front of the Deutsche Bank, scampering for cover; Donavin was at the corner of Church and Liberty streets, thinking about his furniture and marveling at the explosion; Kevin and Tex McCrary were at the notional end of Liberty Street in Battery Park City, which is built over earth that was displaced by the Towers and was soon to be showered by them. A friend of mine, Rich, who was on the fifth floor of a Dey Street building, just across from David's Starbucks, said that the second strike, unlike the first, was such a powerful blast that it felt as if his building were going to fall. Three divers that I met—Brendan, Adam, and Hector (I have quoted Hector to you)—were *in* the water doing repairs beneath the World Financial Center when they were called to come quickly to the surface at West Street, where they were greeted by the explosion of Tower Two with fireballs made of people, chunks of debris on burning cars, seats and other pieces of the plane with blood and bodies in the street. The trailer they abandoned became a kind of HQ for firefighters on whom the Twin Towers subsequently collapsed. I was thirty-five miles away, protected and oblivious. Working with Mark's video, watching it frame by frame, synchronizing it with his commentary, has helped me to see what was happening in Manhattan while I was walking around in my kitchen, thinking about my privileges and pleasures as if they were problems.

The blast that rocked the waterbed had also rocked the building, so Mark knew that something was drastically wrong. He went to the windows. "As soon as I saw it," he said, "I could tell it was going to be a bad day. I grabbed the video camera. That was the first thing I thought: to shoot some video. It's a pretty horrific, awesome sight. You're seeing some real tragedy and you feel helpless about it. There's nothing you can do ninety stories up. I'm sure the firefighters felt the same way. So part of it was just bearing witness, and hoping for the best."

Mark's television was dead. Phone calls filled him in, but he had assumed these were acts of terrorism. His wife and his children were elsewhere, out of harm's way, and he himself did not sense any danger—the worst he imagined was that the top of a Tower could topple—so why not stay? "I felt perfectly fine in my livingroom. You feel safe at home. It's almost like watching it on a big-screen TV. It could be an Arnold Schwarzenegger film, except it's real this time."

Mark stood at the closed windows and shot up at the building and some of the action on the street. His brief closeups of the burning mangled façade of the South Tower are compelling. When Donavin, watching it with David, said slowly in almost a whisper: "It was *so hot*," it wasn't a trite conversational truism. In the video you can feel the temperature through your eyes. Down on Liberty and Church streets there aren't many people. "It was strangely deserted for 9:15 on a weekday," Mark said. "Normally, at that time of day, hustle and bustle, traffic jams, cars honking, thousands of people in the streets. Now it was eerily quiet." Small fires are scattered along the sidewalks of Cortlandt Street. A patrol car runs over a hump of flaming debris. Lying between the gutter and the Church Street sidewalk is a beam from one of the Towers. Papers are flying in airdrafts, fire is falling, passing vehicles are stirring up thick flakes of dirty gray snow. At the northeast corner of Cortlandt and Church streets an abandoned car sits on the sidewalk. It appears to have crashed into the wall of the department store, Century 21, adding to the sense of a horror movie in which panicked cars careen out of control. Around the corner of Church and Liberty, the trucks and pavilions of the greenmarket are empty. It was for produce here that Kevin was going to shop when he heard the first explosion across the street. Before the Twins went up, the Washington Market along West Street had served the larger purpose of supplying daily produce to stores and restaurants the way the Fulton Fish Market, a few blocks east, supplied fish until deserting to the Bronx. "For a while they were packing up their fruits and vegetables," Mark said. "But at some point they realized it wasn't a safe place, so they all got out."

One streetside fruitseller, Mohammed, who worked Liberty Street and who liked to give David's daughter Hannah a free banana, told me that he knew it was time to get out of there when he saw all the businessmen departing. "When businessmen running," he said, "time for *me* to run." But Mohammed had forgotten his Koran. He ran back for it. The South Tower fell. Mohammed fled for cover into the Edison Garage. His leg was injured— he was limping when we met at his temporary stand on Nassau Street in front of Chase Manhattan Plaza, where nervy security guards loved to wave their hands frantically, saying: "No video! We own the whole block!" If Mohammed had dashed for cover into St. Nicholas, the small Greek Orthodox church by the garage (by small I mean thirty-five feet high), he would have been pulverized. The last I heard only a beam the size of an arm had been recovered, along with pages of New Testament, a bell clapper, a twist of candelabrum, chunks of altar. I didn't ask Mohammed whether he felt that the Koran had nearly gotten him killed or whether he felt it had saved his life. I wanted to talk more but he vanished into an unknown midtown location.

"You realized this was a momentous occasion that needed to be witnessed," Mark said. "The World Trade Center's on fire, so you train your camera on it. It didn't dawn on me that the footage was important. Without TV I couldn't know how close cameras were. But I basically figured this'd be on the news. I shot the Towers, I shot the street—there's only so much you can shoot. Watching the Towers burn you felt helpless and it doesn't really change: you keep seeing black smoke. Even across the street, the fire was so high that you couldn't see much in the small viewfinder, so I didn't know *what* I was shooting until I watched it on a TV and saw all the detail. I was on autopilot. It was what my body was doing while my mind was thinking: 'O my God—what *is* this? What can we *do?*'"

The phone rang. You hear it on Mark's tape. Mark turned off the camera and talked awhile at the window. As he went to hang up the phone he heard a sound of metallic rain. Then, an interesting detail: "I sort of glimpsed, out of the corner of my eye, a big part of the building sort of tumbling." This reminds me of Jim O'Connor's account of looking up from the Holocaust Memorial: "I saw some movement at the North Tower." Or Donavin's: "Something started to move, and that's when I realized: *run.*" In seeing these slight shifts of a building these three men witnessed a great turning of civilization.

Meanwhile down in the Austin Tobin Plaza, where a stage erected for lunchtime performances was burning from debris, Muzak was playing, so that the shift in civilization even had a tune to it. What was the song? No one was able to tell me, and I have never read a word about it. But I can make a guess. In a remarkable piece of footage that I saw on television, shot a moment before the South Tower fell, one can hear, in the background, an insipid instrumental of Billy Joel's "She's Always a Woman to Me." Clearly, if you can't stage-manage your own satori, you can't stage-manage your own catastrophe, either. There is enough bad music for the worst of situations that you don't have to wait for television.

It was then that Mark's windows were broken in, the weighty condenser crashed into his library, and Mark went down to the floor.

"Every sense was being bombarded," he said. "That's what made it a one-of-a-kind type of thing. It was the noise of it, it was being hit by pieces of rubble, it was the dust that was in your eyes, your nose, your mouth that you could taste and choke on. My mouth was filled up with it. I couldn't breathe. I couldn't see past my nose. I was crawling over broken glass along the floor around a couch to avoid getting hit by anything else. I knew I had been whacked in a couple of places because it hurt. As soon as I could see again and spit out the dust I thought: 'O, well, let's go see.' And as long as I was going to see, I thought I'd grab the camera."

On the tape of this sequence at the window one can hear Mark saying: "What in God's name have they done. What in God's name have they done." More arresting is the piercing crunch of his sneakers over the glass and other debris on the floor. There isn't much sound of the site through the blownout windows. It's as if the world were gone for a while. Remember

Donavin's phrase: "I was listening to the silence." But when you listen carefully you hear, faintly, a scattering of voices, maybe a shout or two, among the first calls from what is now Ground Zero, voices of people who may have been smothered in half an hour.

"I didn't know what had happened," Mark said. "It was still inconceivable that the whole building had fallen down. Because it was so dusty I couldn't see very far but there was clearly more debris than from just the top of the building. So I was confused. It had been bad before. Now it was *really* bad."

On the tape, as Mark trains his camera out the disintegrated window, at first down to slaughtered trucks and three-column panels stripped of Alcoa's curtain wall, half buried in dust—panning left, right, tilting up and down, trying to find an image—he says: "That's Liberty Street. I can't fuckin focus. There's nothin to focus on."

These befuddled comments, mumbled into the camera by an isolated New Yorker who cannot find the world that used to stand across the street, constitute a rare recorded instance of a consciousness working in a moment of cataclysm. Mark has said that he was in a state of shock for much of the day, but Mark is not shouting, he's not sobbing, he's not frantic. It's just Mark looking out at Liberty Street, getting his bearings in the new neighborhood.

Between the two collapses Mark spoke on the telephone with his younger brother David, who lives in New Jersey. The call came through almost directly after the tape on Mark's camera ran out. Parts of the conversation are in my movie because the answering machine recorded two minutes of it. When Mark moved his family into temporary quarters at number 80 Chambers Street, he plugged in the machine. It had erased itself—the conversation was gone. But even here Mark had made a smart move. Before unplugging it he recorded all its messages onto his camera, thus preserving an intimate moment out of the interval of time in which there was one Twin Tower and Mark was choking on the other.

It's an interesting document, this midmorning chat between brothers on opposite sides of the Hudson River. A passage of ten seconds had separated them more than geography, more than the complexities of sibling rivalry, although you wouldn't easily know it from the tape. Reassurances from Mark that his family is safe. A brief report on his injuries. You get a sense of hypoxia: Mark is breathing a lot of dust and smoke. The centerpiece of the tape is this duet for two voices, a classic in the art of understatement:

DAVID: "Evidently the South Tower has collapsed."

MARK: "Holy shit."

DAVID: "Yes."

MARK: "Yeah."

DAVID: "Yes."

MARK: "Yeah. I saw somethin comin at us and then boom, the windows blew out."

DAVID: "Yup. Yes."

Later, as a concession to his wife, who felt that he was too cavalier about his safety, Mark kept to the Cedar Street side of their apartment while the North Tower collapsed. Odd to say about an event of such immensity, it was a close repetition of effects: the now familiar shuddering rumble, the blasts of debris, the artificial night. Just another 250,000 tons of building vacating the air, rearranging their molecules. "After that," Mark said, "there was nothing more to worry about, nothing else to fall down." He summarized the rest of his day with this sentence, a strange one to hear: "I was there for another seven hours after the buildings fell." Strange because it presupposes an understanding of *after the buildings fell*. Even now I am tempted to say: "What do you mean *after the buildings fell*?"

A call from an absent neighbor on the floor below Mark sent him off through the building, looking for a girl and her sitter. It was during this search that Mark discovered the damage beneath him. He said: "I had to tell them they now had a new picture window where a steel girder had knocked out two feet of concrete and brick and put a ten- to fifteen-foot square hole in our building. There were bricks from the front of the building halfway back in their livingroom. I was one floor up from that. So I'm glad it didn't hit any higher."

I had once asked Donavin to do a Sherlock Holmes for me on a low purple table, called a playboy, that he had built for that fifth-floor apartment. It had been struck by the beam and had flown, legless, out of the front room, through an adjoining hallway and into another space, careering off walls as it traveled. In his workshop in Brooklyn, where the table, which was ceded back to him, was waiting to be repaired, Donavin elucidated the marks of its adventure. His speech was all carpenter: what it meant that it was gashed here or there, that the legs were knocked off, that the purple had turned pale. The man who had built it appreciated the power that had maimed it. "It was *hammered,*" he said. "This thing was *flyin.*" Then we traced its trajectory through the fifth-floor apartment. When I showed this sequence of the film to a friend of mine, he surprised me by saying: "I don't know about all that table stuff. After all, it's just an inanimate object." But it was exactly the sort of thing that interested me. Take a table, take something I can see, can comprehend, and read it for me aloud, making the table tell me about that morning. How can a piece of furniture that travels half a block as a result of being slammed, like a hockey puck, by a section of South Tower be regarded as inanimate? It was no more inanimate than the brick that Donavin found in the wall of that apartment. I was there when he absently happened to reach into a hole and draw it out. "It's a fuckin brick," he said, examining it, marveling again at the forces let loose on Liberty Street. "It shot right through the fuckin wall!" As a man who studied the strength and resistance of building materials, Donavin could calculate the impact at work, bracketing its tragic dimensions, delighting in the contemplation of what had been achieved. Carefully, he returned the brick to its place within the wall. That brick, like the cracks and dents in the playboy, like the hole in the building, like the AC condenser, like the crunch of Mark's sneakers, told me as much about Mark's morning as anything else. In that neighborhood nothing was inanimate.

In accounts of that morning the word *surreal* is often used to evoke the disorientation of a world that is altered so drastically so soon. For Mark, as for others, what contributed to a sense of the absurd was the stark juxtaposition of disaster and normalcy.

Mark said: "World Trade Four was squashed by the South Tower, pretty much covered by those outside girders. The flagpoles were still up in the plaza: I could see the flags flying. And piles of this gray dust all over the aluminum superstructure of the Towers. Ninety West was really burning, there was nothing but black smoke pouring across my field of vision, so I was holding a wet cloth over my face. When it was too hard to breathe I'd retreat to one of the back rooms, take some calls, and when it seemed to get better I'd go to the front to see if I could see anything else. It was quiet for the first hour or two until a giant bulldozer came down Church Street, clearing a path for the Fire Department. Then it turned down Liberty Street, where we typically had a row of cars parked on our side of the street. The bulldozer started crunching into those parked cars and shoving them onto the sidewalk."

That winter there were still piles of cars on Liberty Street and I shot them for my film, but those were wrecked cars that were hauled out of the site.

When he finally evacuated, Mark was not able to exit on Liberty Street.

"The front door was knocked off its hinges," he said, "and the rubble, which had flown all the way into Church Street, was at least eight to ten feet high in front of the door, and the main debris pile was roughly up to the sixth floor. Which is why the Fire Department commandeered our apartment— without telling us. When we came back five or six days later we found them lounging in the front rooms. But we were the least looted of any apartment in the building, and we think it's because the Fire Department was there round the clock. The theory was, they'd be there to warn people with walkie-talkies if something on the pile started to shake or topple over. But we never saw them do that the whole time they were there. It looked more like an R & R spot for them. In those early days, who could blame them?"

After the two collapses Mark encountered at least three search parties as they made their way to each room in the building.

"I tried to keep them from breaking in our stairwell doors," he said, "but of course they busted them open. I told them everybody's fine and they were okay with that. The first two firefighters who came in at ten-thirty or eleven were both crying. It was a terrible scene for them. Many of their comrades had been in the Towers, so they were all shook up. I was certainly in shock. Part of it was just from wandering in the apartment: 'O boy, look at this.' And from all that debris that had crawled into my sneakers, and what it meant. But my refrigerator was full. I had a choice of beverages. I stopped and had some granola and yogurt for breakfast because it was noon or one p.m. and I was hungry. Absurdly, life goes on even in the midst of major disaster. That was one of the strange things. Here all your possessions in the place you've called your home for the past three years are totally trashed, and yet the lights are on till four o'clock, my computers are working, I'm getting emails, the phone's fine, lots of people are calling—the little incidentals of life are there for you, just like they were on September 10."

I first watched Mark's footage standing beside him in the lobby at 114. He ran it for me on the LCD monitor of the camera on which it was shot. As with the documentary 9/11, directed by the Naudet Brothers and James Hanlon, which I saw, surrounded with guys from the site, in the Miami Sub space to which Kevin had brought food and television, or the uncollected, unseen 9/11 videos that Kevin showed us at 114, it reminded me of the night when I saw the great John Cassavettes film *Husbands* in an uptown Broadway theater. When the course of the film brought John Cassavettes, Peter Falk and Ben Gazzara into a scene in front of the theater in which I was sitting, I had to resist turning around to look for them at the door.

Watching it with Mark again in easier circumstances was informative, revelatory, but the Mark watching the tape couldn't compete with the Mark who had shot it; or, to put it another way, the action of and in the tape itself was more Mark than anything Mark could say to me. Mark knew that. There was no self-importance about anything he said. He did not understand why I was writing a chapter about him or featuring his morning in a sequence of my film. It was a different affair when I managed, after months of failed attempts, to maneuver David and Donavin into a room for long enough to watch Mark's tape together, first at full speed, then in superslow motion. Their expressions and comments, even without Mark's video, could have comprised a short film in itself. The morning rewrote itself all over their faces and they were falling under its transporting influence again, as if the film were saying: *This is where you were—this is where you might've died—don't you remember?* When I pointed out a brief shot of a man with a fire extinguisher who is using it against some of the fire falling on Cortlandt Street, David rewound the tape in order to find it. "Well, he had the right idea," David said. "He just didn't have the right equipment. No one did." During the "after" sequence, both David and Donavin observed that a lamppost at the corner or Church and Liberty streets is still standing—and lit. It reminded me of something that Donavin had said when the Con Ed guys repowered Liberty Street and the pole of a barbershop close to 114 suddenly whirred into action. The red-and-white striped cylinder had disintegrated— there was only the bent chassis of the motor with a spindle attached to it— but Donavin was smitten. "It takes a lickin and keeps on tickin," he said. "And it took one hell of a lickin. I get this sense of . . . rebirth? I feel totally rejuvenated watching that stupid fucking thing spin around."

In slow motion every article of debris becomes a subject for study: is it furniture, a piece of a plane, a person, part of the building? I have watched Mark's tape many times this way, so that the forms are familiar although I still haven't a clue to what they are. I can at least say, by now, that there don't appear to be people in the air. Mark is glad for this. The thought of jumpers could wipe out anybody. While he was watching the tape, Donavin recalled

TOUCHING PEOPLE

seeing "little puffs of white" that morning. As usual on this subject he declined to elaborate. The motion of debris into, out of, and back again into the picture frame justifies terms like *dancing* or *flying*, for that stuff is doing a lot more than falling. It is hard, though, to estimate the size of what you see. That little black blotch—how little is it really? You strain to see a person in the building, if only for the illusion of scale. And, irrationally, you want to connect: if you can find them, see them, you are with them there forever. These few brief minutes of extenuated time: if this is what is given to me, if I can observe it in detail—well then, I will observe it. If before they go to bed people are dropping to their knees tonight to pray, I can slow down a Tuesday of suicide and murder and sit with it tonight one frame, one fraction of a second at a time.

As we were looking at the sequence of life in the streets, David interrupted Donavin and said, hurriedly: "Look at that—there's people going *in*." It was a man on the sidewalk in front of Building Four walking northward, alone, at a normal pace, in the direction of the Church Street entrance to the complex. "Look at these guys," David said, but he meant one person. The man does seem curiously oblivious. "And this is right before it came down," Donavin said. The sense of *this is the world in which nobody knows yet,* a world in which the buildings that were about to fall *couldn't,* is even more potent when you look at footage taken in Mark's apartment in the days before the 11th. Night. Celebration. Mark and his brother, both families, grandparents, in-laws. Gifts, food, jokes. Good life on Liberty Street. In the background glimpses of the World Trade Center seen as lights from its windows. Those windows were real then, at the time they were shot, and they were innocuous then, but now they constitute an unsettling vision and are charged with the power of the 11th, a power that was there from the time the Trade Center was built. Shining forever in Mark's tape, so close to Mark's home, the windows are ghosts, seemingly innocent, unbearably dangerous. They don't know it and never will.

11

DARK SCIENCE

The more I looked upon the aftermath, the more September 11 in New York asserted itself as a war of one battle (and so not a war at all), one of the swiftest and strangest in history. Has it ever happened that the enemy is dead, its bodies all dispersed, before most of its casualties are inflicted? Rarer still to see landmarks delegated and deputized to consummate the slaughter, for which a comprehensive statistic will never be determined. The buildings even assisted each other, for the collapse of Tower One was hastened slightly by the fanning of its flames when the South Tower stormed out of the sky.

We were walking down West Street, toward Battery Park, after a January session on the Liberty rooftop, when I postulated to Ray that September 11 generated an urban black hole, a nexus of negative energy that would suck down and disappear everything in the vicinity: David and his family, Kevin, Tex, the Cedar Street painters, Mark, Donavin, all of us included. Terrorism had brought a Bermuda Triangle to Lower Manhattan. If cataclysmic events can so dismantle and demoralize an individual psyche that recovery, however convincing its appearance, is destined to remain an illusion, perhaps there are mortal blows to cities such that rehabilitation and rehabitation are not paths that are truly open to them. Soulful beatitudes were showered upon the site and they continued to make their way to Lower Manhattan from every quarter, but the departed death-crusaders were prevailing, so that to follow Plato's definition of *being* as *power* was to see that they were very much alive in the neighborhood. So-called survivors, along with everybody living and working around the site, would one day double the list of casualties.

This was not a notion I would have expressed publicly, for such a way of talking is often only a way of walking, less legitimate thinking than an ambulant daydream, the sort of worksong, or barking at the moon, by which you mitigate repetition, waiting, depression, cold and fatigue. But this perception or misperception had some staying power. Months later, when I broached it to Donavin, he gave me a long look that betokened either thoughtfulness or shock at the depth of my stupidity, I couldn't determine which. We were driving away from the site up the Westside Highway past the newly restored Winter Garden, where debris from the North Tower had crashed through the panes of its huge glass atrium, and where David's oldest daughter, Hannah, who was five, and her nanny, Bing, who was still in her teens, saw the jumpers—seeing even one was too many—as they made their cautious way around the buildings, courting the Hudson River in case they needed to dive in. When a chief of security at World Financial told me, with justifiable pride, about achieving a hundred percent evacuation that morning, she recounted candidly how she lost it for a moment when she saw one of the jumpers crash down through an awning. It was a good thing she lost it. Her husband, who worked nearby, saw her condition and walked her out of there just ahead of the first collapse. As she spoke to me in World Financial Three I could see through the windows a workman, alone, scaling the steep slope on the dome of World Financial Two, and two men with paintbrushes were rising on a scaffold behind the Winter Garden. This stark juxtaposition of remembrance and renewal gave me an eerie sensation I had felt quite often hearing stories around the site: that it hadn't happened yet; or, more precisely, that it hadn't not happened yet.

"That's an interesting theory," Donavin said in the truck about my dark observation. "Maybe that's why I'm broke all the time."

I would never have floated this speculation to David, concerning whom the notion of negative energy was, to me, inseparable from the toxicity of the area and the health of his family. Hannah's school, for instance—PS 89— had allegedly been cleaned, but *clean*, like *safe*, was perhaps the most lying word in the city at that time and an easy way to prove it was to take the short walk between the school and the activity at Pier 25. The fault did not reside in removal of the debris but in not removing the kids until the debris was all gone—and in lying about the safety of leaving them there. This was an issue he worried over, but David had exhibited an inexhaustible talent for rising above it. Within his persona is the capacity to rise, or of seeming to rise, above everything, including the most mortifying concerns at Ground Zero. Of course some of what he said to me was pure denialism. When, with regard to Hannah's school, he would talk about the frequency with which they ought to hose down the playground, I needed to tune out, thinking: "This is sheer madness, this talk of *hosing down*. Get those kids out of there!" I understood, though, that neither he nor I could climb all the trees at once, and we could not simultaneously chronicle life there, keep ourselves together, support one another, *and* argue. Besides, it was frustratingly clear that the entire United States was in denial about the 11th, and it would have been absurd for me to vent that frustration with anybody on Liberty Street.

Although David would not have thought of himself as a writer he was writing like a writer and his letters, articles, and op-eds published in the *New York Times*, the *Wall Street Journal*, the *Daily News*, the *New York Post*, *Time*, *Slate*, and the *Downtown Express* about restoring or re-creating the neighborhood were models of quiet cautionary pleading and advice. You could not but marvel at his composure, a truly impressive balancing act. In the days before I met him he was a little less composed. "Early on it was really bad at night and I was jumpy," he said. "Once I got over the shock and the fear, the waking up in panic, there was an overwhelming tiredness. I'd stand up on the roof and practically cry for the longest time taking in what had happened." The phrase *practically cry* might seem a bit of a dodge, but in fact it works well for what Lower Manhattan was doing for over a year: if it wasn't crying, it was practically crying. David methodically but casually photographed the site whenever he came to Liberty Street, and the one time he tried to characterize its early influence he kept all the components in proportion. "Whether it was based on fear and the instinct for survival," he said, "or whether it was based on the fact that there were three thousand displaced souls out there, there was a darkness hanging over us and it was positional. It wasn't as if you went to New Jersey and it vanished, but if you walked around the site, or in this place, you could *feel* it, and it was a really horrible feeling."

Then one early August afternoon when reconstruction was under way, David addressed the site, calmly, in terms that conformed to my own peripatetic ruminations; terms that I was, in a way, glad to hear from him because I was sure that at some point he must have fallen prey to them.

"It's like a dark fantasy from a novel," he said of the site, in the redesigning of which he had tried to play a role, or at least assert a residential voice, since he first set foot in the wreckage of his home. "Don't look into it. If you do, you will not be able to look away. And the more you look, the deeper it will suck you in, till you aren't controlling yourself, *it's* controlling *you,* and you don't know how lost you are. We have to rebuild our house and it pulls us there for that, but there's a part of me that wishes I had no connection with it and they could just bury it over and start building."

In some ways, many of which were bureaucratic, Liberty Street was buried over long before the site itself. When I spoke with an architect who was hoping to be consulted in redesigning the neighborhood, he addressed the two interests that needed to be served: the business community and the families of victims. When I mentioned the Downtowners who were living across the street he acknowledged their importance but later, off camera, he expressed his belief that the Deutsche Bank, a block west on Liberty, would surely be demolished and perhaps, along with it, the stretch of Liberty Street that included 114. And, as I have said, when the first few conjectures for re-constituting the neighborhood were shown to the public, they appropriated the blocks on which 114 and the Deutsche Bank reside. Imagine waking up to the *Times* one morning to see that your home, which has been turned into a dump, is now an architectural fantasy and knowing it is more than impo-lite urban planners with their brains up their ass, it is a great monster force of redevelopment that is sacrificing you, your life, your house, and your his-tory to a drafting concept. "It's astonishing," the painter Michael Cook told me, "that they would have the nerve, after everything that's happened, to simply erase our block off the map, along with twenty-five years in which we've pioneered our residential spaces here, as if we didn't exist."

This level of disregard not of residential concerns but of residential exis-tence only extenuated the treatment Liberty Street had come to expect. Passes had been hard to get—even for Donavin, who wasted hours, days, just try-ing to get to work—and having a pass did not protect you from perfunctory, sometimes hostile dismissals from functionaries who showed little respect toward the few who, of all the thousands of people coming and going at Ground Zero, were entitled, obligated—and, perhaps, cursed—to call it home. I had seen union workers shaking their heads at David as he passed the checkpoints, as if David were a jerk for still pretending to live there; as if David were a jerk for not respecting the new rule of 9/11 entitlements. After a rally to garner support for residential rights at which David gave a good closing speech, a journalist approached him: "Are there any family of vic-tims here?" *Time* magazine's first anniversary issue, "9/11 One Year Later," featured two two-page photographs of "Liberty Street," the first on Septem-ber 11, 2001, the second on July 2, 2002 (pp. 24–27). The trouble is that they are both pictures of Cortlandt Street. Dennis Smith, a retired firefighter, wrote a fine book called *Report from Ground Zero,* but a sentence in it erases David's block. "The three buildings on Liberty Street between West and Church streets are completely burned-out hulks, but they are still stand-ing."[24] Of course Smith knew the Ten House on Liberty Street, so he must have meant to say "The three *big* buildings on Liberty Street," or "The three

Liberty Street between Church and Greenwich streets, with 114 Liberty in the center. Behind the missing panel in the middle of the building is David Stanke's livingroom. Mark Wainger lives one flight below. Beneath that, on the 5th floor, a section of South Tower tore out the façade. The building to the right is 120 Liberty Street (125 Cedar), where the painter Michael Cook lived. The dark form on the right is the black-veiled Deutsche Bank (Bankers Trust). Barely discernable at the bottom right of the frame is part of the 10 & 10 Fire House.

buildings on Liberty Street between West and Greenwich." Smith's book was written in the white heat of the moment—in this instance, literally—and this is too small a fault even to mention . . . except that insignificant errors can typify a situation, and mine is perhaps the only book that *has* to mention it. Defending Liberty Street . . .

A few hours prior to the first anniversary, to which residents weren't invited, David and I observed the day by smoking a quiet cigar on the sidewalk at 114. David was reminiscing about the runs he used to take, in the evening, through the streets of Lower Manhattan, over the Brooklyn Bridge and back, ending in the refreshing spray of the fountain in the plaza around Fritz Koenig's big bronze *Sphere* (which is now in Battery Park, with some of its wounds intact). I heard a similar tone of fondness from Donavin, who loved to recall skateboarding the World Trade complex with his older son Collin. They skated the inside of the fountain (when it was dry), the South Bridge on Liberty Street, and the World Financial Center where they would lie on their backs with their faces under water from a fountain behind World Financial Three. Donavin liked to lie down and show me. "Like this. It was cool. You would tilt back and dunk and you'd be looking up at the buildings."

"You mean World Financial, not the North Tower."

"North Tower."

"Wasn't it blocked?"

"You could see the very top, like Windows on the World. Those were big-ass buildings—*if you remember.*"

David's remembrance of the Twins was more reflective than reflexive. "Sometimes a building that doesn't strike you as attractive in itself fits into the city because it makes a difference," he said. "It's a contrast to the things around it and that's what makes it work in the skyline. That was part of their magic once I got a feel for them: how they stood over us and were reflections of the sky and were *in* the sky. Amidst all the diverse architecture of Downtown, you saw these two shimmering, textured buildings that were reflections of the weather, of how the clouds hung on them, and of how they played with the light. Their unique texture—what they were made out of—was important to what was beautiful about them." Yamasaki, who obsessed over the tone and the texture of the curtain wall, would have been pleased. "I sure knew they were there," David said. "I didn't take them for granted in any way." David expressed an attachment to the entire complex. "Probably fifty percent of the time I stepped out of my front door," he said, "I went into the World Trade Center. To take the subway, run an errand, go to a shop, take my kids to run around. It was home. It was town, the way Ann Arbor was town when I went to school there, except that this was a covered town and with the kids that was important. In the winter I didn't even have to put their coats on. 'Let's go run around in the Trade Center a bit.' Like you say, it was our front yard. The plaza was a big cement place, a little cold, a little hard but with an impressive fountain in the center, the Twin Towers on the side, and these low black buildings surrounding it like a fort. Because of that, a lot of people didn't come in. So I could go there with the kids, find a corner, and have a huge amount of space where they could throw balls, run around, and I didn't need to worry: it was our own protected play area, quiet and intimate. And yet there *were* people around, it *was* part of the energy of New York. Tourists on the weekends. Businesspeople on breaks. I loved watching people coming in and out of the doors going to work or on their way home at night, or in the summer when it was packed with people listening to music, grabbing an extra half hour of lunch. Every aspect of it was a strong part of our life."

Amidst the rubble next door Michael Cook, suited up in his white hooded Tyvek gear with a respirator around his neck, had told me something similar. "It was cold steel but it was our home, our neighborhood, our reality," Michael said, "so there was still that warmth to us. You could sit among a group of friends, enjoy the fountain, hear interesting music, listen to the birds, and feel a sense of urban nature. And we enjoyed the vitality of it, even just looking out our windows. Rainy mornings millions of people would pour out of the exits and pop up their umbrellas. Great scenes!"

David's and Michael's memories of life on Liberty Street were significant contrasts to all the people who saw the Twins more exclusively as monumental blunders or as great gray machines of capitalism. But my observance with David was shattered and dispersed by three detectives who, while declining to identify themselves in any way, ordered us to move.

"I live here," David said simply.

"He was here on the 11th," I said. "I bought him a cigar just to celebrate surviving the last year."

"This is our own way of commemorating," David said.

None of this mattered. The president was coming. Three of the Stanke children had to be rushed past meat that had fallen into the street after the second jetliner had exploded above their heads, but David was not permitted to finish smoking one cigar. It wasn't that they didn't believe he lived there— they never asked for identification—it was that they didn't care. It didn't matter, either, when he told them that his presence there, and mine, had been cleared with the police in advance. As ever, *clearance* was in the eyes of the beholder. We departed without complaint but I was nonetheless dismayed that, after the year he had seen, David was being chased, once again, out of his own street. If it didn't matter to them that David lived there, it didn't matter to me that the president was coming. After all, we are talking about the duration of less than half a cigar. "But all in all," Bush had said in December of 2001, "it's been a fabulous year for Laura and me."[25] One cannot begrudge a president his presidential pleasures, but a year ago Bush sat comfortably under the gaze of his minders and handlers while a neighborhood that he was sworn to protect became a charnel house. A man with any presidential character would have said: "If there's a guy like David Stanke in

that mess, fuck it, let him finish his cigar: I'll wait." During a spring ceremony we had been told that if we didn't step away from the Liberty windows
we'd be picked off by SWAT teams. This threat was mollified by a pair of
more patient and understanding officers who, it turns out, had been there in
the building when the site was at its worst and who, after clearing things
up—keeping us from getting shot—asked if they could take a picture or
two. But as Donavin and David and Mark and Kevin were there, the SWAT
teams might have done liberty (if not Liberty Street) a favor by picking them
off all at once, completing an Ashcroftian circle in which victims of the attacks become targets in the cause of security.

Yes, I might have disagreed with David, but in some situations even huge
disagreements are trivial. During the talks we had together on the streets of
the neighborhood, on the Liberty rooftop, in the disorder of his home or in a
nearby Starbucks, I never dilated upon views to which I knew he would be opposed. I was there to draw him out, to commiserate, occasionally to entertain
but never to make tension for a life that was troubled enough. Troubled
enough: a good phrase. When the weight of the new century crashed down
on the 11th, there were people upon whom it fell directly. Some died, some
were living. That was what this film had boiled down to for me: some of the
living, and where they lived now, and what it looked like and sounded like to
be there. To my mind, troubled enough. On Bob Dylan's first album, a track
called "Song for Woody" contains this line: *I'm out here a thousand miles from
my home.* Wherever you lived, Ground Zero was a thousand miles from
there. It was especially tough for people like David who were living across
the street from a place that was so far away, that sank so far down into
nowhere and, in so many ways, seemed fated to take Liberty Street with it.

Big Frank, who could not see the site without seeing and being lifted by his
cross, would, I am sure, disagree with my dark pseudoscience of the urban
black hole. As a tribute to Big Frank I wanted to find an impressive angle on
the rusty brown cross he had showed me in the rain and of which he had
spoken to me so proudly, so I shot it one day behind a curtain of dust and
steam after they moved it to the east side of the site. The next time we met
was at the half anniversary organized by Kevin in the Miami Sub space so
that the guys could take breaks and have a look at 9/11, which was broadcast
that night. Communications from telephone and radio receivers that were

audible in the documentary mingled with those of firefighters, cops, and union workers who were there to see the film, so that in watching my own footage it is hard to tell them apart. Big Frank, whose employment at the site had terminated, looked tired, and perhaps he was just that, tired, but I did not sense the same vitality in him and I wondered whether working on the site had not perhaps done as much for him as finding the cross there. I also suspected that, like everyone else I'd gotten to know, he was both getting along just fine and he wasn't. If it was nonsense that everybody would tumble into a black hole, surely there was some kind of a black hole in everybody.

An East Indian named Nian, who runs a cigar store the size of a closet adjacent the entry to 114, and who burned both his hands on a shaft of hot steel as he was passing Liberty Park between the first and second collapses (he was in his little store when the South Tower fell), phrased it interestingly. "There is no smile after 9/11," he said as we stood in the dark shop, which was essentially as it was well over a year ago. His stock of pipes, fine cigars and expensive lighters had been taken but cans of soda in the refrigerator dared you, through the glass, to wonder whether the dust could have penetrated airtight containers and whether the soda was still there because the people who would have bought it didn't live to cross the street. On the floor where the battered aluminum gate rattles down I found a piece of Tower glass, one of the largest I had seen. "For work you have to have the smile," Nian said. "The people need to see it, so you put on a smile, I always had a smile and I will have the smile again but this is not the real smile, real smile is gone."

"Who knows, though," I said. "Maybe, with the future, as the neighborhood returns, the real smile will return."

"Not the real smile," he said. "The Twin Towers came down. No more Towers. No more smile. Everything is lost."

That he would clean up his proud little hole-in-the-wall shop and put his business back to order didn't matter enough to him. That the Towers had been destroyed would be the dominating principle for all the rest of his life. What I found so apposite about what he said was the dimension of decisiveness layered over the feeling. Nian was not predicting his emotional future: he was resolving it. At a distance of over a year this could appear to be a sign of chronic depression, pure and simple. Of course it was depression, but it wasn't pure, wasn't simple, and I was encouraged by the hint that he, Nian, might be policing himself to do, really do, in a more than superficial way, something that was often disingenuously proclaimed in signs scrawled and printed everywhere: **NEVER FORGET.** In recounting the episodes and the emotional atmospheres of his youth, Churchill said: "It was a good thing to have a little despair." I would apply this to the men at Ground Zero, especially to those who were witness to the 11th. Whose upbringing, education, training, occupation, or day-to-day life had prepared them for the horror that had broken upon the city? Given the situation a little despair made sense, showing that an easy denialism hadn't moved too fast too soon to anesthetize and patch over the wounded psyche. I am not sure that we need to *get over* everything. I wonder whether we really *get over* anything. How witnesses to the 11th are expected to *get over it* while obeying the injunction to **NEVER FORGET** has not been adequately explained. I am sure that a portion of what I saw was a projection of my own troubled mind, but whenever I said to someone: "People are doing well down there, but on the deepest level they are really fucked up," it was my way of saying they were a normal bunch of guys in a critically abnormal situation, and the work that might have been saving them was still upsetting to them, and to a degree that was not easy to gauge by their performance. When I say that Big Frank looked tired, and more than tired, I do not mean to be easy with the truth of anybody for the sake of making a point, especially with strangers I encountered in the margins of a disaster. But in those margins I saw a world that was worthy of great novels, and if a chronicle such as this were to be used by a novelist of the future as a tertiary source for his tale, a source that yielded a couple of index cards or maybe a spark of inspiration—"Use Big Frank type crossfinder maybe combine w/ATV Mike see Ch 2 both bearded, large, determined, maybe have X see him later, out of place in newer, cleaner world, etc"—I would feel as if it had served a higher purpose. All characters in memoirs, including the few that aspire not to lie, are fictions of a sort by the necessities of the form; but so too are the characters in our minds, for any reminiscence is a complex act of imagination. Gautam, David, Donavin, Big Frank—to see them as anything less than troubled characters would, for me, belittle the intensity of what they encountered.

"When Tower One plummeted into the roof of Building Six," Big Frank had told me, "it compromised eight floors and two sublevels, compacting it."

The word *compromised* has stayed with me as a perfectly valid technical term stretching the far limits of understatement.

"From the debris we recovered three bodies," Frank said. "As the latter part of the night turned into morning we were removing the third body from the subterranean levels. I looked up and, with daybreak hitting the glass of the atrium, I saw four beautifully structured crosses, reminding me of Calvary.

I fell to my knees and cried for fifteen or twenty minutes. I was tired. We had just removed three bodies. Once you've seen this place you wish you had the power to lift it all up and bring everybody home, but it's impossible. The cross inspired me in recovering those who were less fortunate. Afterwards, I worked alongside the machines and we recovered around forty-five bodies."

I imagine Big Frank was also affected by the film, *9/11*, which appeared to resonate emotionally in everyone. The faces that I saw through the lens that night while unobtrusively cradling the camera in my arms could have filled a sketchbook that would occupy a portrait painter, or any artist interested in grouped faces of men with a lot on their minds, for the rest of their careers. On my little video viewer all the faces were beautiful, including those of Donavin and Kevin, who at one point were sitting so that their heads were as close as kid brothers at a Saturday matinee.

Big Frank had told me that his attachment to the site was not financial, and that he had started on a volunteer basis until he was hired on. "It's not a problem," he said tonight about the end of his employment, sipping a cup of coffee in the heatless space that had once served sandwiches to people who were there now as dust. "Monday morning I'll come down, get in line, try to find some work with another company." When I told him how the shot I had taken showed the cross holding its own at Ground Zero, he repeated the phrase with a quiet, affirmative nod: "It holds its own."

On another level, however, the cross appeared to me to inhabit a world apart, as if those beams, once they had fused into that ancient symbology, had been rendered out of place, out of date, even out of touch with the site from which they were raised and over which they presided. If I were a genuflector I would sooner have genuflected before ATV Mike's muddy Gator, or Kevin McCrary's electric golf cart, for which he carried a long extension cord to charge it in obscure boxes of current along Broadway and everywhere he went and which he drove—day, night, snow, rain—as far as Canal Street and all over the site with gallons of water, trays of hot food, cartons of Taiwanese safety boots, and rolls of his everpresent Twin Tower posters, all so crammed into the little bed on the back that you couldn't contemplate that crippled cart moving at all. Why Kevin wasn't killed crawling up Broadway at 5 mph against 65–70 mph traffic . . . why *I* wasn't killed when he parked me in the snow, without flashers, in one of the traffic lanes and disappeared interminably . . . or how he managed to run that thing for as long as he did, against every configuration of law and security, losing it at one point to G-men who covered over the name of the owner, then finding it again none the worse for the filching, are to me as much miracles as the cruciform joining of steel beams. For me, nothing was being kicked upstairs from that cross, and nothing was filtering down into the pit from it either, despite the fact that merely the sight of Big Frank, and the quiet confirmation of his faith that appeared in his face whenever he spoke about the cross, contradicted this heathen point of view. In fact, it was Big Frank himself who represented Big Frank's cross to me.

I did not tell him this, but the pictures I'd just taken—Big Frank's face as he smoked cigarettes, focusing on the footage of the Naudet Brothers (the Duane Street firehouse, the firefighters' expressions at the crashing of the jumpers, the North Tower lobby as the South Tower fell), meant more to me than even the most dramatic shots of Frank's great cross. When I described Big Frank to another worker at Ground Zero as "the guy who found the cross," I was told, with a little laugh: "Listen, there were crosses all *over* in those days," a reaction that bothered me not because it wasn't true but because it ignored, even mocked, a larger truth. Although terrorism made that monumental mess and although it was simply the odds, among countless fallen beams, for some symbolic order to punctuate the jumble of the pile, it was Big Frank climbing through the burning admixture of World Trade Center One and World Trade Center Six searching for the dead, and Big Frank dropping to his knees on the ash, that created a monument which is standing there today.

I felt equally abstracted from the flags on the site. The giant American flag attached to the black protective netting that was stretched over the north face of the Deutsche Bank reminded me of decals you see stuck to objects or billboards that weren't designed to receive them. For me, neither the cross nor the flag made much sense at all out of the ruins beneath them, and they said little more than: "I am large, I am here, I am revered." On the other hand, whenever I saw the cross I tended to see Big Frank, and whenever I saw the two small flags on the Liberty rooftop I tended to see David, who bought them for the building; or Kevin, who respectfully rolled them up after one official occasion for which they were hung from Liberty windows (the occasion on which we might have been "picked off"); or Donavin, who secured them to the edge of the roof and sporadically—"I've gotta go fix my flags"—fussed with their ropes and poles and reached out over the ledge to free them from positions of repose. "That looks pretty good—what d'you think?" So perhaps it's foolish for me to say that those flags never made me think of America, and that they only made me think of a few guys. David,

Kevin, and Donavin are America. And perhaps it's equally foolish to say that Big Frank's cross never once put me in mind of the caretaker around whom he modeled the life of his spirit. The kind portly worker who made me stuff my pockets with fruit, and who handed me two twenties in the rain without missing the finer shapes on the passing volunteers, might not have been apostolic enough for the Holy See but he was apostolic enough for a beaten and twisted infidel with a broken video camera and a missing front tooth.

Veering over the ledge of the Liberty rooftop, Donavin said: "I can kind of feel it from here, going over, what it's like. I can almost imagine it, but—"

"This is not 110 stories."

"I know. That's what I'm trying to do, feel it from that height, but I guess that's stupid, huh?"

"You don't need to conduct the experiment."

"No, but from here it doesn't seem so impossible, going over. If you landed on a truck or . . . maybe you could roll, break the fall . . . not die necessarily."

"You'd better not do it when the camera's off."

"I know I need to stop, but I *can't*, I keep putting myself up there."

A month or so later I took Donavin to the Bolivar Arellano Gallery. Bolivar, a photographer whom I quoted in chapter 4, survived that morning with only a gash in one of his legs. After that he dedicated his gallery on East Ninth Street to helping the families of firefighters. "The firemen . . . who gave their lives . . . are not getting paid to be killed," Bolivar told me, choking up. "They go to war with just their hands. They deserve all the honors a human being can give. They have families. Now they are widows. Now they are orphans." Families were thanking him for taking what would become *the last picture:* a husband, a father, a brother as he walked toward the buildings. In Bolivar's walkdown gallery he had stood up and shown me the posture in which he bent over, holding his two cameras, protecting a firefighter who was kneeling in front of him when the South Tower fell. "I look up and I say *O my God I'm dead.* I took one picture and I said *that's it, I hope somebody finds the camera because everything is coming down on me.* I saw a man kneeling. I said *well, I'm sure I'm going to die so I'm going to try to save his life.* So I jump on top of his body and I protect his body with mine. I was waiting for the debris to come on my back. The building is close. I am prepared to die.

TOUCHING PEOPLE

The only thing I'm going to say to him is to tell my family that I love them, but the moment I open my mouth everything comes down and the dust goes inside my mouth. I was angry. I thought: *Goddamnit—I'm going to die and my family's never going to hear my last message.*" But Bolivar survived, along with his cameras, to have the North Tower fall on him as well. Now he had a mission: exhibiting photographs from twenty-two photographers, all of the pictures donated for charity.

The roughest of these shots were hanging behind the gallery desk in the rear of the small space: a dead woman lying in the gutter, a severed hand with bloody tendons protruding, grisly reminders of how protected my camera was from the morning of the event, reminders of how protected we all were. But Donavin didn't get that far. He didn't get far at all. After looking, in total silence, at the Towers as they burned, the jumpers, the site as it smoked through the days and the nights, he dropped bills into a jar by the door and left the gallery. He had spent roughly three or four minutes inside. Standing on the sidewalk he looked out of sorts, not ill but not well.

"Sorry," he said. "Guess I saw more that day than I've wanted to admit. I'm gonna go see Little Man." He got into his car and drove to Pearl Street to be with his son.

It wasn't until nineteen months after the 11th that Donavin finally told me what was in those picks of dumpsters that were craned off the roof at 114. It was over the telephone. It was Donavin's birthday. He was calling from Lancaster, Pennsylvania. He was half lit, as he put it. His tenure at Liberty Street had ended. The previous day he and David had gotten together and arranged to part company amicably. I was worried about their friendship and had spoken to them both during the days before the meeting. "Am I going to have to make separate films for each of you?" I could not bear to see these men— men who, perhaps, could never be great friends but who were joined in this unique urban adventure—break apart under conditions of enmity. Donavin tonight was in a mellow mood. He was looking to buy a house in Pennsylvania. He had strung his guitar with a fine set of strings I had given him at Liberty Street over a year ago. As he played a few chords for me I told him I had seen a great picture of Liberty Street in *Above Hallowed Ground* (pp. 114 – 115). "I think it's taken through a busted window in Century 21," I said. "You're looking through the shattered glass, it sights along Liberty, you can see every window blasted out at 114, you can see the big gouge in the façade, you can see 120 all messed up too, the sign for Pronto Pizza's above the planks on the sidewalk bridge and you can see this long crane, it's practically right in front of the building."

"The yellow one?" Donavin said. "That's Kenny. He's the guy who worked all day on my roof. He was subbed out for Tully, I think, and he took some time away from hauling beams off the pile. He was there for six hours. I had all this cash and I offered him like fifteen hundred a pick but he wouldn't take a dime. I leaped right up on the crane—you don't do that, of course—I mean, the thing was *movin*—but I climbed up, I knocked on his door and I said: 'Look, Dude, I've been pacing on my roof for two days and I don't know how the shit I'm gonna get all them buckets off.' Because as soon as they found fingers, and shoes with feet in them, they had to put everything in buckets, get it down so they could sort it all through. 'Well you found the right guy,' Kenny said. 'You put that money away. I won't take any of it. You shouldn't let anyone else take your money either. Everything ought to be done here, for you, free of charge.' He hauled the dumpster up there, we had six guys working, stackin buckets into the dumpster, and he took it down to the street, fifteen, twenty times. Just did it to help out. That was the best thing to happen. I was going nuts, I couldn't think of *anything*—how the *fuck* was I going to get this off my roof! 'Don't you let anyone take your money,' Kenny said. 'This is for all the good people down here.'"

One day at 114 Liberty Street I put on a respirator and long protective gloves and I cleaned all the art in David's home. The art was being moved out to storage because, a year and a half after the attacks, the EPA was sending the DEP to abate the building, in its way, so everything had to go that could not be left to the DEP's discretion. As nothing much, including the health of Lower Manhattan, should be left to its discretion it was decided that, although I knew nothing about hazardous materials, that was more than the EPA and the DEP would know of art. Most of the pictures had been cleaned previously so it wasn't a tough job to wipe off, or pretend to be wiping off, whatever dust had accumulated. I say pretend because, despite the Department of Health's guidelines for happy home cleaning in Lower Manhattan, you can't abate anything with wet paper towels or wet mops and sponges and, anyway, the dust began visibly reaccumulating before David and I had carted the art out of the building. That dust would, of course, reenter the building after the DEP allegedly abated it, but the odds went against their doing a proper job so the thin deposits of dust on the pictures hardly mattered. Left to my own devices—if, say, I inherited the art along with the space in which it belonged—I would probably have braced a good guess about abatement with an aesthetic certainty and, excepting work by David's mother-in-law, Dora Foo Lee, which included a fine impressionistic take on the Twins, I would have played it safe and deposited most of the art in the dumpster on Cedar Street. But I had learned that with the issue of toxicity it was not much help to be too consistently logical—or cautious. If you wanted to act like that there was simply no place for you around Ground Zero. And in fact I was happy to put the camera down for a day, to play my insignificant part in the cleanup and, however inefficiently, apply a little hands-on effort in a field that I know. And to be doing it for David who, when he heard that I had lost the space in which I had painted, day and night, for over a decade, offered me a room in his evacuated home.

There must have been roughly a hundred pictures to be cleaned. The quality of the art didn't matter to me at all. Even undistinguished pictures have a right to shake off the poison. I worked seriously without shortchanging any of them and, excepting lunch, I took no break and I never touched the camera. It was chiefly the camaraderie that David appreciated and it pushed him with his own housecleaning. At one point I thought, as I pressed wet toweling into the tight space between a stretcher bar and the back of a canvas: "I too am cleaning up after the mess bin Laden made out of the Trades. What does it mean for one to be sharing this strange fate?"

One thing it meant, that day, is that David took me to lunch in the Garden Café over on South End Avenue a few doors down from the Sloan's supermarket in which Kevin went to dole out supplies on the 11th. That Tuesday morning, glass in front of the restaurant was broken in by people who sought water and protection from the cloud of the South Tower. Kevin—who, like Donavin, had an uncanny eye for seeing signs of the 11th—once lifted up the carpeting where it meets the doorjamb and he held up pieces of glass: "Still some 9/11 here." James Creedon, a paramedic whose accounts of that morning are among the best observed and most thoughtful I have heard, led a chain of sufferers here, where they paused and took water before pressing on to the river a block away. James, a bright young progressive who, as I have said, lost four men from his squad in the first collapse, walked with me one winter's day to find some of the places in his story, including the scene around St. Joseph's Chapel, of which he saw quite a lot when he returned to Ground Zero after treatment for injuries. We ran into Kevin and the two of them reminisced about the days in which Kevin was unofficially stationed there. James remembered the operation fondly.

"This was a very important spot for a lot of people," he said to Kevin. "There was a lot of staging here for EMS, a lot of the food and supplies were lined up over here, and this was one of the major chapels for Ground Zero workers. We spent hours and hours here. Hearing stories. People were crying. When they heard that someone had been found, this is where they came. I remember spending days here, eight hours, sixteen, not going home, working with people here from around the world."

It was interesting to watch them. They were matching up details perfectly. In those early days they were bumping against each other anonymously. Neither remembered the other, only the work they had done. About Kevin's solicitude for steady supplies of footwear, James said: "With subterranean fires burning up that material, people went through boots like crazy." Now, months later, they were learning each other's names, exchanging gifts of confirmation, filling in pieces of a picture that had passed too quickly. This sort of interplay intensified when Donavin and I took James up to the roof at 114, where James was able to point out precisely where he was standing when the South Tower fell (he was standing under it). I whip-panned the camera back and forth between the two but they were outpacing me because they were outpacing each other, and Donavin, who held his son, Little Man, throughout the conversation at the edge of the rooftop, said: "It's really good to talk to somebody else who has actually experienced this thing. I'm sure there's a ton of people who have stories like we do, but *I* have met very very few."

James said: "It's hard to talk about it."

Donavin said: "It's hard to talk about it. With Peter I have, but—"

"When I say the black hand," James said, "you're like: 'Yeah, the black hand.' When you say that blackness and the ghostly looks, I'm like: 'Yeah, of course I know what you're talking about.'"

When Kevin and James walked down South End Avenue, James was excited to see the Garden Café. "That's it. That's the place." On a previous walkaround we had missed this block and, not knowing the name, James had not been able to find it. Now James had something he wanted to say to Hanif and Ray, two of its employees. He told them how deeply he and others appreciated the refreshment they had taken, and how sorry he was to learn that after the first emergencies every drop of alcohol from the bar had been looted. It was like the disappointment that Donavin expressed about the looting he encountered, by men in uniform, when he first returned to 114. "I understand excitement over a treasure hunt," Donavin told me. "'O let's go see what we can find.' But this was a disaster. This was people's homes. It wasn't right. It's not good karma, either. When I said: 'What the hell are you people doing here?' they said: 'Well who are *you* and what are *you* doing here?' I said: 'I work for these people, I built all these kitchens and libraries and—' 'O, you *made* these cabinets?' Then they wanted to talk to me about *the furniture* . . . "

Looking through the glass in front of shelves of cakes and pastry, James said: "In an emergency, you don't rush into a place like this and say: 'Boy, what I really need is strawberry shortcake.' When you're choking and your eyes are burning the one thing everybody's looking for is water, water, water. No one could help people without it. So we were glad to have it here. In a situation like that you can't be guided by rules of ownership. You know it's not yours, someone else is paying for it, but you have to deal with that another time. Looting a bar is something else."

It was typical of James to be explaining the broken window, thanking a place for its water, and separating EMS procedures from the larceny of lowlifes even in a place where he couldn't have spent more than a few minutes. James, who is going to medical school, appears to have the makings of a very good physician, for it is habitual with him never to shortchange anybody.

During my lunch at the Garden Café with David Stanke, whose temporary quarters, at the moment, were down the block on Albany Street, he left his sandwich and went to meet his oldest daughter, Hannah. This is the girl whose nanny, Bing, had taken her from PS 89 that Tuesday morning. When they walked behind the Towers, Bing had told Hannah that they might need to dive into the river, but that is because Bing, who was an expert swimmer in the Philippines, meant that she would dive in confidently, holding Hannah safely. Hannah, who was five at the time, thought she'd be managing the Hudson on her own, and that is what she remembered: Bing told her that she might have to swim the Hudson River. This would have to traumatize a girl of five. At the age of fifty-three it would have traumatized me.

I had played with Hannah. Occasionally she talked about the 11th. Not much. Once, at Liberty Street, when she was moving things around on the kitchen counter, she said of a chipped cup: "It didn't hit the World Trade Center—it's not that. It was cracked already." Up on the roof in David's arms, gazing at the site, which was a little too sensational and stimulating for her, Hannah turned away and buried her face in David's shoulder, then she talked about the fire she had seen. I cheered her with a lie that there would be nice new big beautiful buildings going up. Her Aunt April told me that for months Hannah used to draw pictures of that morning, including stick figures representing the jumpers: graphic depictions, gruesome in the way that stick figures can be, of people bleeding and their bodies falling apart. This afternoon I didn't want to draw her out about it. I gave her some french fries and I wanted to have a discussion about the Bob the Builder vehicles at Pier 25 down the block from her school.

"Did you see the big machines that were working next to your school? The big big cranes lifting up all the stuff?"

"I was in kindergarten then," Hannah said. "I'm in first grade now."

"Did you see the big machines? Sometimes they're noisy."

"I saw the plane go right into the building," she said. "I saw it from my school."

I didn't think I'd been talking about the 11th.

"Wow. You saw it from the window?"

"I couldn't see the World Trade Center," she said, "because the shade was down on the window. But my teacher, Rebecca, lifted it up and I was looking at it and I saw the plane go right into it." Hannah mimed the motion with her fingers, which were holding a french fry. "There was a big ball of red smoke in the sky," she said. "The World Trade Center was in trouble. I could see it was in trouble. I told my teacher. Rebecca said: 'Don't look out the window. Everything's okay.' But everyone wanted to look, so we all went to the window. But I was the only one in my class who saw the plane going into it. Everyone else only got to see the red smoke. Then we all went out of the building, and that's when I got to go down the stairs the fastest I ever did."

David told me later that this surprised him, for it hadn't surfaced much in over a year.

"You know it's got to be in there," I said, "doing its work all the time."

Of course I was also talking about David. But David, true to form, had been keeping pretty positive and cool, publishing critiques on projections for the site; insisting on respect for the residential factor in the World Trade equation; and shepherding the building, 114, through one outrageous inconvenience, insult, insanity after another in an effort to move back. At a point where I lost track of how many homes he had inhabited since the 11th, I was helping David to move into Battery Park City. It was the thirty-second floor of a building adjacent the one in which Tex and Kevin had lived. If you

TOUCHING PEOPLE

looked down directly from the windows on the Hudson you couldn't see the riverwalk and it felt as if you were hanging over the water, which you practically were. Views of the New York Harbor were spectacular, but David told me how, late at night with the lights all off and the family asleep, he would sit at one of the south-facing windows watching passenger jets flying up the Hudson as if they were flying straight at him, so that he mentally rehearsed how to hustle his family out if they plowed into the building. What was atypical here was not that David would sit and watch and go through that mental process, but that he would tell me about it. In August of 2003, by which time 114 was still not habitable, David started, at last, to falter. It was bound to happen. If, as Einstein said, God does not shoot craps with the universe, it would have been impossible for the situation obtaining on Liberty Street not to have started to grind a dust out of David. Not that he was falling apart, but his lacerated life was too far from coming together—or perhaps it hadn't been lacerated enough.

Like others I had met who had lived through that morning, David had not returned to the work he used to do and he was determined, once the dust of September 11 was out of the air, to embark on a new and better life and to become a new and slightly better David. Why not? David had worked as a banker and a troubleshooter in business but he was open to my suggestion that he continue in front of my lens when I moved on to shooting dramatic features. We laughed about the irony of a man without a dime having to hurry up and make his next movie in order to generate gainful and satisfying employment for another. As there was more media interest in the artists next door (the *Times* Metro section was doing a series there), he offered his condolences that I had not chosen a more sympathetic subject.

"I chose you because you're taller than anyone else," I said.

In truth, my subjects were less an issue of choice than of what Emily Dickinson would have called *a happen*. That I had formed a few good friendships made it as much of a good happen as the fact that I was making a good film. I liked Michael Cook and the artists next door with whom I shared a profession—in fact Michael and I are still corresponding, meeting for coffee, and I am intrigued with how passionately political he has become—but it was 114 Liberty Street, *not* 120, to which Kevin first brought me, and that was where my camera had found a home.

A new life for David would have been a good thing—his wife, Sarah, was not thrilled with him, he said, when he worked his old jobs because he wasn't a happy person to be with then—but, alas, the dust of September 11 hadn't cleared yet for David, not literally, not in any respect. "I am extremely frustrated and tired," he told me. "I can't get traction on the building. Everything takes too long. Every time we stop we go back a few steps. From the amount of sleep I need I'm concerned that I am essentially fighting depression. The reverberations of those attacks continue to echo through my soul. I look for meaning, and I only see the world as a huge sinkhole. I despair of hope for humanity, which is echoed in my lack of hope for my own situation."

Next day I spoke to Donavin about it. He had taken a year of therapy that proved satisfying. He had moved out of Pearl Street and shut down his workshop in Brooklyn. He was unloading his woodworking equipment into a barn in Millersville near Lancaster, Pennsylvania, where he rented a small house. He kept in touch with Curtis and Tony, the supers at 114, but David had let him go and his work there was over. "I'm sorry to hear about David," he said. "I've been having bouts of depression myself that I never used to have. Erika wants me to go on medication, that's how bad it gets."

I said: "Remember how we talked about Ground Zero sucking people in, even those that have survived the attacks?"

"It's done its work on *me*, I know that," Donavin said. "It's amazing that you can live thirty-nine years of your life and in *one day* all of that's *completely* negated."

A few days previous I had spoken to Kevin McCrary after Tex had passed on at the age of ninety-three.

"What'd he die of?" I asked. "Or was it just old age?"

"No," Kevin said. "Once he had to move out of his place down there he was never the same again. He went progressively downhill after that. I think of him as the last casualty of 9/11."

Even Gautam, who never had the slightest intention of leaving New York and who was proud of his sturdy metropolitan spirit, was showing a darker side the last time I entered his shop. For one thing, Smoker's Choice was losing money. Gautam had told me that the store, before the 11th, had made family out of its patronage. Nian had told me much the same about his shop on Liberty Street. After the attacks a lot of Gautam's customers disappeared. And he had to pay for costly refurbishing of the store. "When people ask how is business, you say so-so. That means business is going down. The City gives me help, but not enough. You can't survive." And the general atmosphere was less than edifying. "*Lot* of people not working," Gautam said. "Or people come in they all worry, they're going to lose their business, lose their jobs." But it was also that the morning of the 11th was not receding. It was asserting itself with a stern, slow persistence. "Me and psychiatrist—big separation. I don't scare from anything, from *anything*. But I go now, psychiatrist, because the body is not the same. Everybody, something happens— a noise, a commotion—the people are afraid, the mind rushes back to the past. Whenever I see two, three police cars, ambulances for hospital down the street, I think: 'What's happening now?' And the mind goes back. The rescue workers. The firefighters. The wounded people."

In his poem "Two Tears," which he published soon after the attacks in *Manav*, an East Indian paper issuing out of Jersey City, Gautam had written: "Destruction blew at the speed of a tornado / Each one was confused / Terrible cries and shouts / No tears in any one's eyes / Deep echo of silence reflected in the world of pain."

"I used to be happy to come to work," Gautam told me. "Everybody talks. It's cheerful. Eleven years I've been here. All the time I love New York. Now, *first time,* I only come because I have to come. I don't want to see the city. In the mind, I'm afraid something happens. My daughter's twenty-three. My wife, we talk about leaving the city—first time. The way I walk? I walk like this."

Gautam mimed the weighty slouch I had noticed when I met him one morning, long before the rush, in the Chambers Street/World Trade Center station where he'd had his second store. I had been down there shooting the end of the line, the E trains that crawled in from Jamaica still telling you, with signs and announcements, that they were taking you to the World Trade Center. Throughout the station, **WTC** was still posted on the columns, but over your head, on a horizontal sign that hung from the ceiling and spanned the width of the platform, the words **WORLD TRADE CENTER** had been bluntly blotted out with black paint. I don't know the name of the functionary who gave the order—"Go paint it out"—but it was a crude, perfunctory adjustment to the catastrophe. If this was the quality of vision for the future of Downtown, there wasn't a future. One could argue that it was, after all, only an issue of three words, but if it doesn't matter what is said or unsaid on a subway platform where thousands of New Yorkers and citizens of the world will be walking every week, then it doesn't much matter what is said or unsaid on the campaign trail or in the classroom, City Hall, newspapers, the State of the Union, courtrooms, streetcorners, pulpits, the Pentagon. If you looked at the sign closely, catching the right angle of light, you could see the outlines of all the letters underneath the black redaction. This was a nice little piece of urban poetry, fine, I included it in my film, but is it not pathetic that the billions being thrown at recovery, removal, relief, redevelopment, research, counseling, committees, wars, advertising, education, propaganda and profiteering could not engender something just a little better than this, a block of black paint, in one of the largest subway systems in the world under the stage where the Twin Towers had fallen and embedded their great beams like spears into the street?

In that station the trains would screech to a halt, the doors would open and, if it was early enough, no one walked out, at most a few people. That morning Gautam was one of them, but it took so long for him to walk the platform that he and I were facing each other alone. We stood beneath the rudely corrected signage for a moment, faltering. Gautam seemed out of sorts, as if trying to comprehend what it meant that I was there and it put me out of sorts, too, to see him this way. There was a feeling between us that this was not the place to meet. In Smoker's Choice we were somehow protected. Here, it was as if we were embarrassed for having no explanation or reassurance about the event that had thrown us together. Here, it was as if we would have to tell the truth and we could not fit that into the camera. Perhaps I had interrupted an early daydream in which Gautam's Twins were still standing up above, two tall New Yorkers waiting to greet him when he walked out of the station at the graveyard of St. Paul's Chapel.

We walked to the gate together where Gautam pointed out the store, closed now for good, in which his nephew was standing when this whole thing started, but I didn't walk with him to Smoker's Choice, I waited on the platform, thoughtless, between the two bumpers terminating the E line. To walk to work with Gautam would have resulted in my own disintegration before we got to Beekman Street. I asked myself: *What the hell do you think you're doing?*

This was New York City. This was the subway. This was the world. Did I honestly think this camera would give me the means to deal with it? How did I arrive in such a disempowering dreamscape, this liar of a station that, however the EPA or the DEP abated it, would never have pure enough air for me to breathe? I, like the E train, had come from Jamaica: I was born there and lived there until I was seven. "How many more stops?" I said to my mother on the straw-woven seats whenever we rode the E to Manhattan. I would eye the exciting space between the cars enviously, nervous too, recalling the story I had heard about the guy who got his leg chopped off changing cars.

What should I have done, turned the camera on and shot the lamentation in Gautam's walk as he traversed the platform, wondering what the movie guy was doing here, aiming at the privacy of his morning?

Those were days, days of *Johnny Staccato, M Squad, Gangbusters, Zorro, Man with a Camera, Superman, Flash Gordon,* when it was Radio Row here, three hundred shops—Blan the Radio Man, Cantor the Cabinet King—overstocked with what were known as *brown goods:* World War surplus and souvenirs, shortwave, hi-fi showrooms, vacuum tubes, spare parts, *know-how*— and there was no reason at all to come this far down unless you were taken to the Statue of Liberty.

What's more, where's my crew? My producer? Where's a single other person at my side? Where's my switchblade judgment, my assassinative resolve? I couldn't catch the Towers, the jumpers—now I can't catch anybody even with a lens.

Twenty-three years ago I started to write a book, *Street Eater,* basing each chapter on a walk through the city. The book was going to end after I'd walked the length of Manhattan, I had written about half a dozen chapters and I was excited, but the Twin Towers humbled me. On the 107th floor of Tower Two, facing north, I sighted up the island. The sky was darkening. There was lightning and light rain was falling from nearby clouds. When I thought I was looking at the far tip of the island I was looking at the Empire State Building, a rude realization. *That?* I thought. *That's* your little book? What possessed me to imagine I could walk, and write, all that length of city?

Walking Lower Manhattan, shooting *Liberty Street* where my abandoned *Street Eater* had so energetically started, I was reminded of that old lost book and I saw that *Street Eater* was on hold, that's all, for a quarter of a century until I returned, under improbable circumstances, to finish it as a film. I was photographing many of the places I had walked because I wanted the viewer to see in what vital storied neighborhoods the Twins had collapsed. Wherever I went I tried to shoot what I called Kubricks: extremely still shots that, because of the way they were lit, the way they were framed and the way they would cut together, were more than just representative scenes of Downtown: they conveyed some of its power. Shooting these Kubricks—ambitious term, given that the camera was stabilized on a bag of lentil beans wrapped in a tube sock—assisted me as much into the art of filmmaking as shooting the site and my dramatis personae on Liberty Street. Often it was through these Kubricks that my *Street Eater* excursions, and what I had written about them, were brought back to life. I could remember getting a pass to Governor's Island, my father's place during World War II, which he lied and forged a paper to get into and then met my mom in a Village nightclub, Jimmy Kelley's on Sullivan Street where *The Fantasticks* later played and where Mom was doing what was then called *interpretive dancing* . . . or having lunch on the steps of City Hall, watching a demonstration called Dead City—Mayor Koch and the dancer Jeffrey Holder were there—for the preservation of rent-controlled studios for artists . . . or combing the Broadway curb for just the right piece of wire with which to pry open my car, into which I had locked my keys, and seeing **GROUND ZERO 2.9 MILES** and an arrow pointing north chalked onto the corner of Maiden Lane across the street from Barthman's clock, the great glowing ticker that's embedded in the sidewalk, the best clock in the city even when it's out of time . . . or running through the Austin Tobin Plaza in the rain after leaving the Twin Towers. Behind me, of course, was 114, where no one was living then: it was a commercial property. I couldn't recall ever seeing the street itself but I remembered quite precisely what I was thinking in Trinity Church, or on an East River pier, or on the Staten Island Ferry, or climbing up Liberty, or up in the South Tower where a Midwesterner cried out: "Man . . . I'd say we were *up* there—yes, Buddy—god*damn*," an oath that encapsulated the one thing Manhattan can do as well as any place: it can wow you. I remembered that I looked down to see Barthman's clock still glowing in the sidewalk, now and then blinking as someone walked across the corner, and that memory was why, after the Twins had fallen, I had wondered: "Did it break the clock?" and why, upon arriving at the site, I was eager to get to Maiden Lane again. "Still there," I said to Ray. "It's son of a bitching still there." On the 11th it was snowed over with dust and debris but the glass was unbroken and the clock continues to shine its eccentric testimony to American enterprise, a delightful artifact of advertising ingenuity and a little more than that, for it empowers the city sidewalk to speak, to tell you the time. Barthman's clock still blinks with the shadow of a foot when people hang a sharp turn across the corner, and you can still see it glowing from . . . from as high as you can go.

My friend Lance, who was the Ray in those excursions, explained to me, on Broadway, that "Ground Zero" denoted the Empire State Building, which was 2.9 miles away and was the target at which a nuclear attack would be aimed. I could remember thinking: "Just a little footnote on—literally, *on*— Maiden Lane in case someday someone needs the information." And I remembered awaiting a train in the Whitehall station, looking across the tracks at a painted tile with a country scene on it, a white house with a red roof and a flowered lawn with sailboat waters and mountains behind it, a scene that repeated every few yards, a row of country houses in a place where it seemed so incongruous then, in 1979, when the subways were filth-holes and it was unimaginable to put those pictures there. It was shattering to see it and like a scene in a novel I was nearly paralyzed. Now that I was back twenty-five years later, standing in a subway again, with Lower Manhattan my subject again, was I any abler at the task, this new and more sensibly confined *Street Eater* that was eating, more or less, one street? All that life— hadn't it given me, at least, just a little more power? It didn't feel that way. What had deceived me into thinking I could use this little instrument to register the aftershocks above me?

The painter Michael Cook had told me a story about the dog who had lived with him on Liberty Street for over five years. On the 11th this poodle made the getaway with Michael, who rushed out of the building when reports were suggesting that something was going to fall. As Michael's building was one door west of David and Mark's, his windows were that much closer to the Twins. "He was very well behaved," Michael told me about his dog, Indigo. "We were like refugees walking with this little cart of clothes and other things we had tossed into it at the last minute. We couldn't take any art: all of that became a part of the debris and was smothered in dust. The dog was so befuddled that he stayed right with us. We walked around in a daze amongst people covered with ash, our eyes, mouths, throats really burning, but we got water for him and he seemed okay. But when we brought him back down and I took him for a walk, he appeared to be overwhelmed. After five years he'd gotten to know every corner, every tree, every lamppost and everything else. We were on Broadway and Liberty Street. He couldn't piece together the situation in his mind. He knew there had been something there. Now it was all completely different. He just stood there and stared and sniffed. He couldn't comprehend what had happened."

Was this me then, too, standing there and sniffing on all fours, unable to comprehend what had happened? Why did I ever bother to read Plato, Aquinas, Descartes, Kant, Russell and Whitehead if they left me in the same situation as Michael's dog? At the least, I wanted my notion of the urban black hole to prove false. But in the Beekman Street store Gautam showed me, again, how it weighted him by letting the soul and the lift out of his posture. "How I walk, now, is not the same. No life. Now is only the body."

But his store is still there with the Indian Chief beside the door, although the Chief's American flag is missing in action. As Gautam was told (too often), it was unpatriotic to have an Indian with a flag, a story to remember if you think that anti-Arab vitriol replaced the old original kind. When Gautam was handing out supplies and the use of his cellphone and the Chief was covered in dust as much as they were, people weren't complaining about a thing, but memory is short when it's selective. Business has fallen even lower now—but Gautam is staying. As he searched for a poem in an office so small that two people can stand together only if the door is open, I said: "I won't stop in one day for a handshake and you've moved to Miami?"

"I'm not going to Florida," he said. "I'm not going *anywhere*. I'm going only here."

And yesterday, playing pirate with little Hannah, an older angel now, I saw her as cheerful as any other child. Earlier that day, David and I were looking out the great new windows at 114. The site was nearing the ceremony for 2003. We were talking about obstructions to the view in years to come. "We will definitely lose some of our sky," David said. "But then we'll have Greenwich Street back, so that'll give us a look-through in that direction." It was the old optimism. "Besides," he said, "it can be nifty to watch some really big buildings going up."

"And Hannah will know them," I said, "the way people remember the Trades. 'I watched them from the beginning,' she'll say. 'I remember when it was just a big pit. I saw them grow. It was right across the street.'"

12

NOTES ON DUST

I thought of Picasso at Ground Zero, not because September 11 enacted an urbicide of Cubism, forcing you to suddenly see the World Trade Center from an improbable number of angles simultaneously. I thought of Picasso because of dust.

Picasso said to Brassaï: "Dust has always protected me."

In Picasso's Paris apartment in rue des Grands Augustins the situation was opposite the one on Liberty Street. Even during the Nazi occupation, perhaps especially then, dust was his friend because it represented the status quo: no advance or attack on the security of life. Absence of dust was a sign of the intruder. Empty cigarette boxes, catalogues, journals, gifts from admirers, junk off the Paris streets—whatever Picasso kept (he liked to keep everything), he wanted their coordinates fixed, unchangeable. The negative space of dust-departed was an alert that the maid, a mistress, some snoop had been meddling. How can you look for things unless there is dust for you to know they will be there, exactly as you left them? And if you can't find something at once, how do you keep the day from falling apart? This man who touched everything of everyone in sight, who tampered incessantly with how the world sees itself, who inflicted catastrophes upon his canvases ("A picture is the sum of its destructions"), preferred, in the theater in which he operated, for nothing to move an inch unless under his own hand.

Picasso did well by dust (by cigarettes too). It was a long life, with more art per second than any other. Did his dust protect him? He said so, and in my book Picasso gets to say what's what. For lesser geniuses, for men who lack the charisma to turn the positive power of dust into reality, bullshit isn't much more than bullshit. Despite the example of Tex McCrary, who walked the streets of Hiroshima unconcerned and unprotected and yet lived to talk to me at ninety-two, I took it as a given that some of the people in my movie were going to die of dust.

There have never been clouds like those of the twin collapses. The riot of dust in that neighborhood, where there are roughly twenty thousand residents within half a mile, represented a synergy of some of the worst contaminants. When a technical report uses science-fictional phrases like *most hazardous substances known to man,* it's impressive. I wanted the guys I was meeting to take better care of themselves, but I could do no more for them than for anyone else in my life. One of my first exchanges with Donavin typified an attitude common to the area.

"How're your lungs?"

"Fine. No problem."

"No cough?"

"No, nothing. I've developed an immunity to dust. I'm a woodworker: I breathe it all the time. I'm half made of dust."

He was doing a Picasso but my guess was that the dust wasn't buying it.

"This is different," I said. "It goes in and stays in. Meanass stuff."

"Yeah, I know. I probably ought to get myself checked."

He never did.

"You might not see what it's done for thirty years."

"Right."

The conversation moved on. Even getting *the cough* didn't mean much to people. If it did, how would you continue to work? I queried a firefighter, an affable Hispanic guy with a master's degree. As a former fire inspector he remembered Liberty Street before the 11th: the Trade Deli, Pronto Pizza, the Food Exchange, Miami Sub. The building was built well, he said, an opinion corroborated by engineers who said that you could erect a highrise on top of it, and that was one reason why the beam that put a hole in it was not able to shock more of the structure into submission.

"Did you get the cough?"

"Not too bad," he said. "For the first few months I was coughing up blood every morning, then it stopped. I'm fine now. But I was worried about having more kids. I went to be tested. I think it's okay."

Many of the guys I was following in my zoom were not wearing respirators, and as for Liberty Street, Kevin never wore one, Donavin never wore one, no one in the teams of volunteers ever wore one, most of Donavin's men never wore one, at least not at first, and David never wore one (by *never* I mean I never saw it; in David's case I saw it for an hour one day). When I asked Kevin McCrary about it, he said: "It was cumbersome. It was hot. You'd only wear it when you were right there on the smokeline, on the pile."

I asked ATV Mike about it. "I didn't have the patience or the time to worry about a mask," he said. "My first concern was to see who I could find alive." Only once, at David's insistence, did Donavin wear a mask, and that was thin white paper. "That's useless," I said. "Are you getting a real one?"

"I think living is overrated," Donavin said from behind the paper. After going maskless for such a long time he looked strange, unconvincing, more like an offhanded reveler in Venice than a contractor keeping the dust out at Ground Zero. He said: "My therapist asked me: 'Are you suicidal or homicidal?' I said: 'Do I have to choose?'" He delivered these lines with perfect timing. At least he was taking his sense of humor seriously.

Organizations distributed respirators but the numbers were too few, and workers deprived of adequate protection were also deprived of accurate information on just how dangerous it was to take a breath. But to say that every worker deserved a respirator is not to say every worker would have worn one. Yet it was a pro-health suggestion but you can't send a man into a mudslogging war while reminding him to keep his skivvies clean. Trying to do that kind of work (if you can call it *a kind of work*) with a tight plastic appliance pressing hard into your face, limiting your intake of air and, in a sense, narrating it—for you are hearing every breath—can feel like a defeat in itself, not the best approach to keeping a million and a half tons of unstable debris from swallowing you. And respirators cover your mouth, preventing conversation. Working vigorously among men without conversing with them would constitute its own type of hazard, making a necessarily social act an isolated one that could soon self-destruct. Saying about men who were on or around the site: "They ought to have put their masks on," "They were *told*," "It's *their* fault," misses the fact that respirators rendered some tasks undoable. How do you sniff and taste dirt for human remains with a mask over your nose? How do you supervise, or shout out a warning, in speech that is muffled into gibberish? Respirators guaranteed daily disadvantages in exchange for a promise of intangibles—better lungs, longevity—that were irrelevant to the job to which these men were committed. I know that for me it was well near impossible to wear a respirator among men who did not. I would have felt as if I were watching them all die and, by extension, as if I were killing them myself.

A Brooklyn firefighter, Dennis, who was there the first day and for many days after, said: "It was chaotic at first. You'd be searching somewhere and then: 'Go down there and put out a fire,' or: 'Get a ladder up there,' or: 'Get out of there—the building might collapse.' We had our own masks [Scotts packs] for putting out fires in subbasements, but they only last eleven minutes. About twelve or one in the morning they started washing our eyes out and giving us these flimsy masks like doctors wear, but after three breaths of picking up stuff you were sucking it into your mouth, it's wet, you can't breathe, and so you throw it off. It's basically useless anyway. A lot of people say O *they didn't wear their masks.* Because you *couldn't,* not for long, not if you wanted to get people out. People say *that's the only reason he's breathing heavy* because they want to cover themselves. I used about four of them and then I gave up. I said: 'You've got to be kidding. I won't be able to do *any-thing*—I'm putting it on every two seconds.'"

When I discussed this issue with William Langewiesche, whose elegant, authoritative *American Ground* was based on living a daily life at Ground Zero, his attitude was less cavalier than Donavin's but it was no less stoic.

"It's hard to work in a mask," I said. "You can't converse."

"No."

"And you can't wear a mask in a group of guys who are not."

"Exactly."

"So how'd you do?"

"No problem. Like other people, I had a cough when I was there. As the dust settled or was put down by water, and the smoke, which was pretty nasty stuff, was finally suppressed, the cough went away. Everybody had the same problem. There was dust in the air. The dust makes you cough and it's not really healthy for your lungs. But there was this other aspect to it: we were hearing reports of massive health problems, all these people who were supposed to be having trouble with their lungs and dropping out of work at the site. We never knew any of those people. They were impossible to identify. Nobody that *I* knew at the site—*nobody* I knew—not one single person, dropped out for respiratory reasons. That doesn't mean that people didn't do it. I just didn't know them. It was a big place. But I think there was a level of skepticism about what was going on with that."

Langewiesche, who is the least affected, most pleasingly self-assured writer I have met, obviated the need for my follow-up question by taking his answer a step further.

"I talked with some of the public health people later on about that specific issue," he said. "I thought maybe I should not neglect it. It was one of the problems of unbuilding, certainly. I pointed out to this particular guy, who was very smart, Stephen Levin, up at Mount Sinai Hospital: 'Look—how much of this is really going on? For real? Don't tell *me* about it: I've been down there since the beginning, more or less, and I haven't been wearing a respirator and neither has anyone else, and it's okay, you know? It's not *that* bad.' '*But,*' Levin said. 'Don't be stupid.' He told me about specific cases of people who were probably prone to respiratory problems and can have very serious reactions to the dust. Some people had asthma to be begin with, and some developed asthma. He also pointed out, I think more significantly, that none of us know. In twenty or thirty years, are we all going to die of lung cancer?"

He would never think about it, but in writing about the men who converged on the site and simply did what was needed to put the city together again, Langewiesche added his own name to the list of Americans tributed in his book for their bold, individualistic adventure in democracy. With what degree of relish Death looked upon that list cannot be known.

There is a lot, too much, that I don't know about the 11th. The toppling of the Towers: was that a political act, was that a religious act, was it an act of Islamist nationalism or cultural imperialism or was it not an act at all but a series of interconnections of which the meanings differ drastically depending on where you intercept them, and must I now, for the sake of the sweet children to whom this book is dedicated, hunt for an answer and the beginnings of justice in the regions I would least like to go: the desert, the cave, the palace, the mosque, the internet café, the seminaries of homicide? I don't know. How Egyptian, Saudi, Afghani, Pakistani, or, for that matter, how American were the attacks and must I also hunt at home in the top-secret memo and the nondenial denial? I don't know. To understand what happened to the Towers must I also understand what happened to JFK? In mid-March of 2002, when he was asked about not having picked up, or picked off, bin Laden, President Bush said: "I truly am not that concerned about him."[26] Is this the example of resolve we should follow? With G-men eating through a budget of thirty billion a year, and with access to diplomats, couriers, mercenaries, entrepreneurs, moles, spooks, satellites, translators, bodyguards, armed forces, arms dealers, correspondents, state departments, sheiks, shooters, hackers, short-sell handicappers, rug merchants and terror-trackers all over the world in service of something they call, incredibly, *intelligence,* is it right for me to believe that the United States did not employ one single soul who went to bed on the 10th with a head full of what the morning would bring? Like the '98 fatwa from bin Laden, was this a countercrusade to liberate Mecca, the al Aqsa mosque and the rest of the Arab world from anything less than bin Ladenism? I don't know, but if a zealot wants to stroll out of the shade of the Koran into the cockpit of a 767 in order to kill me, shouldn't the fact that he *can* do it, impeccably, engender at least a few resignations and terminations in the powerful places where, with stunning displays of arrogance and freedom from oversight, people have been promising me, for over half a century, that I am well protected? In St. Gregory the Great, where my life was just beginning, the air-raid signaled us to single-file out of the room, line up on both sides of the corridor, roll ourselves up into little safety balls, and pray aloud for God to deliver us from the Russians, those loud fat bald men who hammered their shoes on tables and wanted to bury us with H-bombs. If, in the middle of life, sirens sound again for me, warning that *to live* is *to be hated by lunatics* and thus *to fear annihilation,* am I to roll myself up into another safety ball as the doomsday specialists, the Dr. Strangeloves, seek that nuclear payload in all the wrong places?

I want to sit with minds that have not been redacted, minds that can cool this insomnia of words that I arrange and rearrange in shifting tones, rhythms, implications, insinuations (e.g., *the jumpers—the cloud—piece of the plane—waiting for people but no one came—boxcutters—bucketlines—hijackers—pipeline—stairwell—sleeper cells—Sarasota—Bechtel—al-Quaeda—Rumsfeld—Brown & Root—Pakistan—found a thumb—Taliban—faces of the firefighters—fireball—slurry wall—FBI warning—blue sky that morning*), poking around for missing links in books, articles, timelines, congressional testimony, the photos of the hijackers, bin Laden's **WANTED** poster (Scars and Marks: None; Occupation: Unknown; Remarks: He is left-handed and walks with a cane), as if the winning combination will unlock, for me, the code of the 11th and will give me a little guidance I can carry into the world, carry as *sentences,* for I am beat by the wordless understanding I had sought in the streets of Lower Manhattan and I want philosophy, the very concept of reason itself, the fundament of civilization, to stand and deliver, for it is time for this experiment of Intellect to show me what three thousand years of it were worth. Then I want to put one beam back (you can put back the next), I want to catch one jumper (you can catch another), and I want to stop seeing the same writing on the wall: **EVACUATE — SEARCHED — TRIAGE — MORGUE.**

Meanwhile, I do know this much for certain: cleaning up after this "desert" dream, and the federal disregard that permitted it to happen, was very very expensive and it cost more than money. I would like it to be remembered that some of the cost was taken out of lungs in Lower Manhattan.

When, to take the edge off, I used to refer to "the death dust," pronouncing it in the wobble-leg tones of an old movie, there was a truth behind this capering: I thought of the dust as holding death, delivering death. Langewiesche, who would have agreed with Thoreau that *a man sits as many risks as he runs,* seems to have made his peace with it from the first. Responding to his own rhetorical question about dust-induced disease down the road, he said: "That's just the way it is. I'm going to die of something, I'll die of that."

In a previous book, *Sahara Unveiled* (New York: Vintage, 1997), Langewiesche admires how the people of El Qued reverse the conventionally anticipated relationship to sand and its invasive properties by welcoming it. They pile it under their carpets and take the grit of it into their food as a philosophical lesson. I think that, along with a strain of quiet defiance, an element of this approach permeated the site, following the wisdom that the best way to deal with an enemy is to befriend it. As I have suggested, it is hard to scale the power of conviction over the power of contamination. My friend Richard Selzer wrote a story called "Luis" in which a Brazilian ragpicker finds a star in a San Paolo dump, refusing to believe it is a radioactive element, even after his hands have fallen off. Hopefully Langewiesche, Donavin, David, Kevin, and everyone else who walked that world of dust will never need to suffer a similar test of faith, or of destiny either.

In my movie I wanted, at least, to show the outward, visible difference between ordinary dust and the dust of September 11 so that my viewers could see the World Trade Center as gray paste, white powder. I asked Donavin to guide them through the distinctions, which he did one day when he was working on the Liberty Street wall of David's apartment. It was October of 2002. In preparation for new windows, a long-awaited milestone in 114's recovery, Donavin was "demoing"—demolishing—two sets of sash frames— an old wooden one from ninety years ago and a newer, aluminum frame he had installed over that—in order to find the most efficient way of doing a hundred of them. He scraped and prodded the claylike substance that had caked on the aluminum and at one point he sniffed some of the paste on the edge of his putty knife. "Uh! There's the *final* test."

From his first day back in the building he was aware of what you could call the organic component that gave this dust a dark, storied cast, but it became more rather than less disturbing to him as the work wore on. I could sense it in the brief initialism with which he generally referred to it: DNA. If I were playing the part of Donavin in a film, I doubt that I could imbue those letters with such a degree of suppressed angst, latent anger, heartsickness.

"DNA."

At first it was three letters, then a sentence, a paragraph. The letters resonated differently each time he said them until, toward the end, they were a chapter in themselves, telling a story of nine months.

"DNA."

Listen to James Watson say it, then listen to Donavin: they are not the same letters. In a few rare moments he addressed it openly, but never expansively.

"Lately I've been thinking about . . ."

"About what?"

"I don't know. All the people that's in there. I don't even like to touch it anymore. I think I need to be out in the country. I think I need some trees."

Another of his tasks that day was to find out how much dust from the 11th had been sucked into the walls when those blasts hit the building. As part of the demolition he was prying out planks he had installed in the conversion from a commercial property. After crowbaring one of them he leaned against the wall and contemplated the store of dust. "That's *a lot*," he said reflectively. "I hadn't counted on that. Look at all that stuff—*caked* in here."

I always liked it when the battery-powered drills went to work and one of the big wood panels that substituted for windows was taken away. Instantly, there was only a little air between you and all the commotion across the street. I was happier to breathe that air than what was trapped in those apartments. As the tall modular panel was eased out, the room lit up and sounds of the site multiplied and were made more distinct and particular. Jackhammers, drills, hammerings on the inside played in counterpoint against the diversity of sounds down on Liberty Street and all around the site. I never tired of looking out those spaces, partly because the view encompassed so much of the city. You could check around the perimeter for progress: speedy repairs on the great Godzilla bite the North Tower had taken out of the World Financial Center . . . more glass going up in the atrium of the Winter Garden . . . windows returning to the Millennium Hotel . . . stones in the walk beneath One Liberty Plaza where a Brooks Brothers had served as a temporary morgue . . . small, almost invisibly slow steps on the Verizon, the red gauze and multicolored tarps on its faintly Mayan Art Deco façade giving its upper stories a mildly festive air . . . Fiterman Hall, its south façade ripped open by the falling of World Trade Seven, not seeming ever to get back together again. You could sight up Church Street, Greenwich or West Broadway, following the traffic that disappeared into TriBeCa, a faraway region that appeared even farther when identifying itself as a victim of the attacks. And there was always the sturdy, seemingly undamaged Federal Building, the unfailingly beautiful Woolworth Building, the churchyard of Paul's where the trunk of a sycamore uprooted on the 11th was not yet sawed and carted away. To shoot the city and the site through these glassless apertures was a way of reminding viewers they were looking at Manhattan and that September 11th happened, and Ground Zero was formed, directly outside of and *in* people's homes. To have Donavin in that frame, undrilling, yanking, complaining ("I fuckin *hate* drywall—that's why I'm a woodworker, not a *drywall* worker") or, much later, to have David lighting up a cigar I had bought for him and smoking it as he looked through his brand-new window—these simple images told as much story as I could manage. "That's really the whole movie," I once said to David. "A guy gets blown out of his home and one day he gets his windows back, he lights up a cigar, and he looks out at the city. He's still there, his home's still there, the city's still there."

Before that finale, I tried to show the dust wherever I found it. "If that camera doesn't have Ground Zero dust on it," Donavin said, "no camera in the world does." But I could not show the killing, not before, not during, not after the Twins fell. It was happening right there in front of my lens but I did not know how to capture it. Perhaps no camera could reveal the corrosive force of that dust on my protagonists. But I wished that, as the dust crawled its way into the works of my video camera, it would have shown, on the tape, what it was doing in the dark trusting hollow of a lung.

I liked going to the Waterfront Boxing Club over on New Street around the corner from the New York Stock Exchange. This was a gym with a specialty: white-collar boxing. Its funky brick walls were covered with posters from boxing films (Garfield, Brando, De Niro) and photographs of prizefighters. The stairways had an eclectic mix of handlettered maxims from fighters and philosophers. There was a billiard room. Driving rock music. The loud ring of the exercise bell. Jake La Motta on a postcard posing with a babe. But really it was a gym for men and women to get fit through the medium, and in a milieu, of boxing. Owing to the fact that my father, during the time he was a bookmaker, also managed a boxer, Jackie La Bua, I grew up with gloves and a punching bag around the house, but I went to the Waterfront only to shoot it and to talk. When a few pages ago I spoke to the Brooklyn firefighter, Dennis, I was, in fact, speaking to him in a ring at the Waterfront. The place was run by two brothers, Martin and John Snow. Martin told me a story about a pair of coworkers, Wall Street types who were not getting along. At a point where they wanted to kill each other, one of them said: "No, let's box." So they went to the Waterfront, they trained there awhile, then the Waterfront sponsored a Grudge Match. It was advertised, people came, the guys entered the ring and fought it out. "So," I asked Martin, "was it all very polite, like Gentleman Jim?"

"No, they beat the shit out of each other. Better there, though, than on the street."

Nine o'clock on the night of the 10th Martin trained a new girl. "Nice to have you as a member," he told her. "We'll see you tomorrow." She was twenty-four. "Twelve hours later she was dead," Martin told me. "Another kid, twenty-three years old, I trained him when he was at Gleason's. He's gone too. It was an ordinary day when they went to work. In anybody's wildest dreams did they think they'd be killed by *this?*"

When the South Tower was hit Martin was on Church Street a block north of Donavin, a few yards from David, directly in front of the Millennium Hotel. "We were getting hit with stuff," he said. "In the fourth grade we had a snowball fight. I thought I was running for my life then, but this was *really* it. I ran like a Girl Scout—forget about it."

When the cloud of Tower Two came to New Street, Martin took everyone into a small locker room and stuffed the doorway with shirts, concerned that if the Stock Exchange was also a target, New Street was close enough—too close for comfort. "Before we go we form a circle to say the Our Father," Martin told me. "We've got one Jewish guy, Bruce Feinstein, so we baptize Bruce with the Riptide Rush Gatorade. No sense to taking any chances—I was covering all bases. I thought we might be dying. So Feinstein says the Our Father with us and we all take off uptown. Everybody was out of their stores. Trucks and buses abandoned on the streets, which were white, pure white. There was no sound. It was an eerie type of quiet, like after the snow falls."

Before he opened the gym Martin had worked in asbestos abatement. Having the expertise, he later cleaned the Waterfront himself once he could pass the barricades. During my first conversation with him we talked about dust and the way it was being handled. Martin said: "The only way to *properly* clean these neighborhoods? Shut down *all* of Lower Manhattan, clear it out—*completely.*"

I am content to have alluded, in my film, to the failure of the agencies entrusted with policing the dust-protection of Lower Manhattan. I was open to the issue and I asked questions about it but I had to remind myself that this complicated story was simply not within the power of my movie to sort out. It already felt as if it were half a dozen films, and it couldn't accommodate the EPA, the DEP, the DDC, the DOH, the ATSDR, the NESHAP, OSHA, NIOSH, or any of that cavalcade of acronyms and initialisms representing agencies about whose interlocking and overlapping duties an outsider could only guess. Respecting health issues, they fell together, for me, under the serviceman's acronym: SNAFU, for SITUATION NORMAL ALL FUCKED UP. I did not know why maids were cleaning in buildings without masks. I did not know why people who did bother to wear masks insisted on wearing the wrong ones. I did not know why people who either knew or ought to have known better were scrubbing their places with soap and water, as if that sufficed. I did not know why sidewalks and streets were reopened when the buildings all around them were still contaminated. I did not know why exhausts of exit-air from HEPA filters were blowing toxic particles onto walkways in use. I did not know why that great exposed mess at 130, the Deutsche Bank—formerly Bankers Trust, a name that, taken as a sentence, summarized the one-way chat between business and the EPA—had been abandoned to insurance quarrels and left to tower menacingly and toxically over the neighborhood for over three years. I did not know why there were Agency Men sitting in beach chairs on the sidewalk of Cedar Street, or why, during a conversation to which I was privy, Donavin was thinking further ahead and much clearer about safety than the beachboys in charge. Now that vaccinating a kid for everything, dropping his eyes with vitamin K, sleeping him on his back, corner- and socket-proofing his house, and strapping him into a carseat are only a few of the safeties that are urged, if not forced, on parents, I do not know why strollers and baby carriages were permitted below Chambers Street. Representative Jerrold Nadler did as much as one sincere Democrat could do—issuing white papers, organizing press conferences, calling for funds, for cleaning, for clarity—to hold at least a few people somewhere accountable for what was being done to his district, but the Bush administration having recruited as watchdogs the worst opponents of the fields they were hired to protect, Nadler and New York have not found friends enough to decontaminate Lower Manhattan.[27]

The trouble with anecdotes about the cleanup is this: they're a little too perfect. David and I were having a cup of coffee one day when Donavin called. "Can you come here quickly, have the camera ready to shoot?" A team of specialists were hosing down the walls of 120 (125 Cedar) in the central lightshaft it shares with 114. What I shot was a Three Stooges routine in which three men were wearing street clothes, no masks, and the spray was blasting contaminants from one wall to another (one could see it building up on the windows of 114, which had recently been cleaned) and they were spraying each other, obliquely, in the face. The group of us standing there all said the same thing: *Do you believe it?* If *we* could doubt what's in front of us, why wouldn't you?

"Across the street they've cleaned over a million tons of debris," the painter Michael Cook told me in his apartment, "but we're standing here looking over the rim of that crater and we haven't had any help at all, we've been totally ignored by the city, the OEM, the DEP, the EPA. The least they could do would be to test the air, help us clean the building and get back in. But they haven't been responsive at any level—city, state, *or* federal. Pan around and see."

I could see and I could smell and I was glad he insisted that I wear my respirator. This was half a year along but the place was a bombsite.[28] What a tale. And with a past. Liberty Street, when it was still known as Crown and was part of the West Ward in a neighborhood of laborers in small wooden houses, burned down a week after the British occupation in September of 1776, its residents joining the flocks of homeless crowding into St. Paul's, which became a refuge the way it did on the 11th. Then it became a street of dwellings made of chimneys, broken masts, and canvas from old sails. During the days when thirty thousand hogs roamed the streets as an approach to sanitation it was decimated by so-called Asiatic cholera, typhoid, yellow fever. Government stores on Liberty Street were burned in the savage Draft Riots of 1863. Much much more down the years, now this. No wonder the walls of Liberty Street—the south side of the site's foundation, the subterranean Bathtub— had started to fracture, threatening to pour into the void whole blocks of Liberty life. Imagine a democracy that reconstructs the land from which they say the terror came while neglecting one of the oldest of its streets, a street called Liberty, a street that was closer than any other to the 11th. Two phrases alone, *before the Revolution . . . after the Towers fell . . .* made Liberty Street at least as much America as Pennsylvania Avenue. Michael Cook had spoken to television, spoken to the press, spoken to politicians—what was Michael to do now to get the attention he deserved, blow something up?

"The EPA started and backed down," Michael told me, "saying they'd give the DEP the indoors, *they'd* check the outdoors, but the DEP said: 'Let the landlords do it.' The landlords' test was bogus. Tenants' tests showed three times those levels. The landlords said: 'We'll clean it up but . . . but . . .' So we've had to do it ourselves. There's the Deutsche Bank sixty to seventy feet away filled with mold and asbestos—is it coming down or isn't it, and what happens to *us* either way? If I were in charge one of the first things I'd do, once I mobilized all the heavy equipment onto the site, would be to drive a big truck up to the front of this building and say: 'You people have a problem. Let's at least get your stuff out of there.' On the contrary: they've turned trucks away that've tried to get in here. They've been the greatest impediment of all. And there have been problems with *our* security, right here, from the 11th to this day, partly due to building management, partly due to agencies passing us off to one another. We've had things stolen, we've had things ruined—and this is *not* from the attacks, this is from people coming in. It's inhuman what we've gone through."

I did not know why Michael and that building full of artists were left to clean their own spaces, or why they had to fight for aid when there was aid for overseas and there was aid for airlines and there was aid for corporations to *please* remain in Lower Manhattan—even if they weren't planning to leave. They could not get government to buy them their safety suits, which were roughly one hundred dollars, while Attorney General Ashcroft—who had aligned himself with the white supremacist journal the *Southern Partisan,* which is no friend to the mix of inferior races in New York—was eagerly dispensing over eight thousand dollars on a set of blue drapes with which to cover up statues in the Great Hall of Justice because he didn't wish to be photographed with naked aluminum breasts. After the building at 120 was, finally, locked down and cleaned by Agency Men, Michael found dust there, and Donavin reported that the place was still a mess. "It's been trashed. Shoddy work. And the building is still filthy." They came too to 114, took its walls down and carried away whatever couldn't be cleaned. Then the residents of Liberty Street were finally informed that it was safe to rebuild, to move back in, but an independent study found asbestos in the dust, dust that David showed me just by lifting a floorboard.

Discussions about toxicity invariably confused me and gave me the impression that confusion was general. This intensely political story about betrayal of public trust had to be handled by other filmmakers, hopefully with the right-shape heads for dust science and bureaucracy. I am concerned here with issues of private trust. I have referred to the neighborhood as a dust-driven world and I am aware that, to a stylistic fault, I have freighted this narrative with a repetition of dust-related nouns and modifiers. With a talent for figures of speech I might have breathed poetic life into the dust, but I can only tell you that everything was dusty, and everybody was, in some way, cleaning up. If there was a more private picture than my camera could possess, there was also a larger, more civic picture of dust and a politics of dust as contaminated as anything in the air or under the boards of David's floors, where his kids were being encouraged to go play again in safety. They were not safe before, they aren't safe there now. What this means is that someone isn't upholding the Constitution, in which the safety of those children is effectively guaranteed.

Who that someone is can be gleaned from a report by the Office of the Inspector General (OIG) of the EPA. In *EPA's Response to the World Trade Center Collapse*, issued on August 21, 2003, the OIG confirms that the "EPA's overriding message was that there was no significant threat to human health" in Lower Manhattan but that the EPA lacked the data to make such a claim.[29] The report also states that the "EPA could have taken a more proactive approach regarding indoor air cleanup," an understatement, but a statement nonetheless by an organ of the EPA itself, so you needn't trust only my reports from Liberty Street.[30] Chapter 2 of the OIG report, which details White House influence in shaping EPA assurances and guidelines, supports my phrase for the chair of the CEQ: *the corrupt James Connaughton*, friend to defendants in asbestos suits everywhere, a man who deserves to be a defendant himself. Connaughton's attack team, the cynically named Council on Environmental Quality, deleted a crucial advisory for residents to hire professional cleaners. One cautionary statement about asbestos was substituted with advice not to worry about short-term exposure. Even the titles of press releases were rewritten to falsify. The report states clearly: "CEQ influenced the final message in EPA's air quality statements," and quotes the EPA Chief of Staff as saying that final approval came from the White House.[31] The National Security Council was part of the loop as well, for national security *means* welfare to Wall Street, even if it entails cheating the street from which it takes its name. Regarding a press release of September 16, the report states: "Every change that was suggested by the CEQ contact was made."[32] About that same release, one of the EPA's risk communicators said: "I did not feel like it was my press release."[33]

As you page through this extraordinary document, there is a crime story in chapter titles and subheads alone: "EPA Statements About Air Quality Not Adequately Qualified," "Data Available at the Time Did Not Fully Sup-

TOUCHING PEOPLE

port EPA Press Releases," "Council on Environmental Quality Influenced EPA Press Releases," "September 13 Press Release Also Revised to Eliminate Cautionary Statements," "Ground Zero Workers May Not Have Received Sufficient Information," "Unprotected Workers Cleaned Contaminated Offices and Residencies." And yet the report refers to this systematic corruption as *the collaboration process,*[34] and it invokes barely a single name in any agency, as if the problems were out there working on their own and in the question of who should answer for them, the *who* would be meaningless, a dodge that gives the report an almost fictional demeanor that would soon be imitated by the 9/11 Commission. Even Christine Todd Whitman, then head of the EPA, is stripped of her name. She is a *she*, but she is EPA Administrator. On September 13, 2001, EPA Administrator said: "From a real health problem . . . health concerns, we don't have to worry."[35] Parsing that sentence for its lack of good grammar might lead you into Freudian revelations about the speaker and the interests for whom she was speaking, but don't bother to mine it for the truth about dust. One statement in the report summarizes the situation. "Competing considerations, such as national security concerns and the desire to reopen Wall Street, also played a role in the EPA's air quality statements." It was quoted by Jennifer Lee in the August 9, 2003 *New York Times*, but the article was hiding in the Metro section alongside a piece about a cabdriver stiffed on a long fare.[36] The Bush administration had instructed this agency to lie about matters of life and death the way it had ordered every other federal agency to lie in order to safeguard corporate imperatives, but it was just another normal day at the *Times* Metro desk. At least they wrote about it—although Juan Gonzales had written it on the front page of the *Daily News* in October of 2001. *The desire to reopen Wall Street.* On September 15, EPA Administrator said: "There is no reason for concern."[37] On September 16, Assistant Secretary of Labor for OSHA said: "Our tests show that it's safe for New Yorkers to go back to work in New York's financial district."[38] On Monday the 17th, with little media outcry or congressional opposition, police and firefighters rang the bell at the New York Stock Exchange and money talked again.

In Jacob Bronowski's documentary series about science, *The Ascent of Man*, which he made for the BBC in 1972, there is an episode—it is also a chapter in the book of the same name—titled "Knowledge or Certainty." Typically,

Bronowski threads together an interesting array of notions, personalities, historical progressions. The organizing image is a train that ran between Berlin and the University of Göttingen, where some of the best minds in Germany were active until the advent of Hitler in 1933 when, as Bronowski puts it, "the tradition of scholarship in Germany was destroyed, almost overnight." About the railroad commute on which exciting new approaches to science had been heatedly discussed, Bronowski says: "Now the train to Berlin was a symbol of flight."[39]

In his charming, unhurried way Bronowski elucidates an irony: at the same historical moment in which Max Born was seeing that theoretical physics was starting to look like philosophy, and Werner Heisenberg formulated his Uncertainty Principle (which Bronowski calls the Principle of Tolerance), Hitler "and tyrants elsewhere" were promulgating "a principle of monstrous certainty."[40] Bronowski ends this sequence with a discussion of his friend Leo Szilard, who in 1934 filed the first patent for a nuclear chain reaction, followed by a decade of trying to keep the bomb from being used. Szilard wanted the bomb to be exploded in such a way that demonstrated its power and motivated surrender without killing more people. Tex McCrary told me that MacArthur wanted the second bomb to be used in a similar way: as a demonstration of might. When I asked him why it was dropped on Nagasaki, he said: "President Truman said: 'The only way to win a war is to kill people.'"

But a disillusioned scientist and the ruins of Hiroshima aren't quite the end of this sequence. In its final few frames, which are as moving and pertinent as anything on film, Bronowski, dressed impeccably in a fine woven suit and with a handkerchief in his breast pocket, wades into a grassy pond at Auschwitz, squats down, plunges his right arm into the muck, and draws out a fistful, saying:

> I owe it as a scientist to my friend Leo Szilard, I owe it as a human being to the many members of my family who died at Auschwitz, to stand here by the pond as a survivor and a witness. We have to cure ourselves of the itch for absolute knowledge and power. We have to close the distance between the push-button order and the human act. We have to touch people.[41]

I was thinking about Bronowski one morning on Liberty Street when I was climbing up the ladder to the roof of the chiller. I had set out that morning to change my strategy, at least for a day. I had hitherto avoided seeking out, taking home, or even touching, for very long, the pieces of life that had fallen out of the Towers. Seeing a part of the first 767 saying

AMERICAN AIRLINES

AA

FLIGHT SERVICE

TRADITION OF SAFETY AND SERVICE

had done me in sufficiently for savoring artifacts. But this morning I wanted to finger every inch of every article that passed under my gaze. It had rained and the chiller roof was a brown puddle. I put the camera down and waded around in it, pulling things out and removing them to dry ground: a small chain, plastic from a computer, pottery from a planter, twists of metal, a book cover, furniture fragments, including what appeared to be the parts of a wooden desk. Spotting a piece of cardboard protruding from the mud, I reached in and drew out a paper picture frame. I wiped off the mud and found a Polaroid of a man who is standing beside his daughter. The girl is sitting on a horse. The man is chubby, dressed in a turquoise undershirt. A crucifix hangs from a chain on his chest. He has dark hair and a mustache. He looks Hispanic. He looks proud. He looks pleased. In his left hand he is holding something. His right hand is keeping his daughter secure in the saddle. She is a pretty, curlyhaired brunette around the age of four or five and she is thrilled. The horse appears to be less so, casting a weary eye at the lens. The climate is tropical. Nothing is written on the picture or the frame. A lump of something fused to the Polaroid paper that at first appears to be flesh is, on closer inspection, probably a small bit of cloth or other material.

I carried the picture home in a handkerchief. When I stopped to have a glass of wine in a bistro by the Brooklyn Bridge, I unfolded the handkerchief, turned the picture away from me, and showed it to the girl behind the bar without having much to say. She had seen the Towers burning from the roof of her building but she had never gone to the site. I let her look for a minute, then I folded it back up. When Donavin joined me at the bar I showed it to him. He looked at it quietly. I have shown it to very few people since.

I was not able to penetrate the mystery of those faces by finding them in the listings of the dead, but that told me nothing. For all I knew, father and daughter were in the mud I had wiped off the picture. Had the South Tower fallen a little farther to the south, or to the east, I might have been contemplating an unknown pair of faces that looked like Mark and his daughter Lucy, or David and Hannah, or Donavin and Little Man. It is the kind of photograph you believe is telling you something but to understand the picture you need to understand the world. I have kept it because it needs to be kept by someone, and for me it is a reminder that Jacob Bronowski was right: even in the sludge of devastation that signifies the worst of human behavior—homicidal certainty—perhaps there, most of all—you have to reach for people, and you can rest assured you will find people there.

ASKING QUESTIONS

David Stanke contemplating Ground Zero.

13

DAVID FRANK

At Work in the North Tower

Here it is, right here, here's the test—what're you going to do?

My conversation with David Frank, whom I met through Kevin McCrary, began on Liberty Street in front of 114, continued over the South Bridge and through the World Financial Center to South End Avenue. We resumed it the following day, September 18, 2002, in a Midtown hotel.

David was a national accounts manager for a company called Quantum/ATL, which occupied a suite of four rooms on the south side of the seventy-eighth floor of Tower One—the North Tower—where he was preparing for sales meetings on the morning of the 11th. He spent much of the day with a blind coworker, Mike Hingson, and Mike's guide dog Roselle. David was living in Los Angeles at the time and he had flown to New York for the meeting.

JOSYPH: *(On Liberty Street)* This has got to be strange for you, walking around with nothing here.

FRANK: I read the signs and I start gulping emotions again, but it's indescribable, it's . . . as if you don't feel it anymore because it's what you *are* now: it's burned into your bones.

JOSYPH: I just came from the music director of Trinity Church, Owen Burdick. He said that the sound won't go away for him, but when I asked him whether he could imitate it he said no.

FRANK: Those are my thoughts exactly. I was on the seventy-eighth floor when the plane hit. I have a good musical sense, but when I try to duplicate the sound it's impossible. Except in a dream that I had three weeks after September 11. I was in a movie theater in Los Angeles. We were disturbed in the screening by debris falling from the ceiling, so we all got up and began to leave. Then I heard the plane again in my dream. That's the only time I've been able to hear that sound again. The other great indescribable was the South Tower falling. And yet, up on the roof with Curtis [the super at 114] just now, he said: "I heard this sound and I started to run." I said: "You had never heard that sound before, had you?" He said: "No." I said: "But you knew *exactly* what it was." He said: "Yeah, I knew exactly what it was." We *all* knew what it was. It was a calamitous, hellish sound. It couldn't have been anything else, and the fear it touched off was overwhelming. Couldn't stop it. My feet left the ground and I ran for my life.

KEVIN MCCRARY: *(Taking articles out of a bag)* These are slides that fell out of Windows on the World. Here's some business cards from the Towers. Two of them didn't make it. And here's a piece of the plane.

FRANK: A piece of the plane? I look to you as a historical repository. Make sure you catalogue all this stuff.

(Next day)

JOSYPH: Why did you have a camera with you?

FRANK: The whole intent of being on the seventy-eighth floor was to show our equipment to computer resellers who were representing our products to the likes of Morgan Stanley and American Express. I was going to take some video just to garner a little enthusiasm.

JOSYPH: After the building was hit, was there an impulse to take out the camera?

FRANK: Not right then. Later on I shot a few seconds from the street, when

I was on Broadway. But after the impact I went to the window strictly to see what was going on. Seeing the South Tower with a burn mark alerted me to the scope and scale of the problem.

JOSYPH: Could you see flame?

FRANK: A little bit, but no penetrating wound into the Tower. It was collateral damage, a large jet fuel splash, like an inkblot with a flame in the center.

JOSYPH: Did you hear the plane?

FRANK: No. We were on the south side of the building, the plane came in on the north. Even on the north side I don't think the sound would push forward—unless it was right on top of you.

JOSYPH: I know a tobacconist, Gautam, who said it rumbled like a 3.0 earthquake.

FRANK: The impact was *phenomenal.* Everything happened at once. The lights went out. There was the sound, which was unique. I was shaken off my feet, then the building began to travel, it just kept going toward the south, toward the harbor and the Statue of Liberty.

JOSYPH: Was it one second and back, or was it long enough for you to think the building was going to fall?

FRANK: I say *travel* because I wouldn't call it a sway. It literally began to move. I'd say it lasted four, five, six seconds in one direction, giving us plenty of time to think—*I* certainly did—that the building was pushed way past its architectural limits. We've all experienced swaying in tall buildings. This was much more dramatic than that. I thought the building would snap in two. There was no sense that it was going to stop. These things were happening in microseconds, but I thought: *Okay, it's going to stop now—no, keeps going—no, it's going to stop—no, still going—it's going to stop—O no it's still going!*—and then you think *we're done, we're going to fall seventy-eight floors with the rest of the building on top of us down to the bottom.*

JOSYPH: Were you standing still at the moment it was traveling?

FRANK: No, I recall very vividly how I put my left leg out one step to brace myself from falling toward the windows, we were leaning that far. When the building finally did snap back I had to brace myself again as it went the other way. I put my hand against the wall as it returned toward the north.

JOSYPH: So there really was a sense of sliding down?

FRANK: To a degree that I decided the building would snap. In the midsection of the structure it would peel away and fall. Other people recorded the same sensation. It sounds ridiculous because you think of a unified skin all the way up and down the building, but it was so stressed out that if it had gone any farther it could have broken. We leaned so far down that we could see the Statue of Liberty coming up in the window. Normally when you walked toward the window you could see the Statue of Liberty, but I was farther back in the office at that point. So as we were going down, with a bit of the Statue of Liberty coming up in one of the windows, that was a strong indication that we weren't in the right position!

JOSYPH: You were *not* supposed to see that.

FRANK: Not from that angle, no.

JOSYPH: Did you run?

FRANK: There was nowhere to go. In my view, we were in place, riding this thing out. The building was struck, it began to lean south, it snapped back to the north—I'm not sure if we went back and forth again—but I recall the incredible sound of it lurching down. That building *groaned*. It's like being in an old elevator that resets itself to the bottom floor. You know how you lurch down sometimes? The entire structure did that and the building shuddered to a stop. It left a very peculiar sensation in my mind that the bottom of the building was unhooked from its foundation and that the building was minutely swaying, as if the bottom were not quite anchored. The view outside was all this debris and fire and papers flying around and something dangling from up above, like a venetian blind cord hitting the window: bang bang bang bang on the outside of the building. Tremendous sense of instability.

JOSYPH: So even though your floor had not been hit directly, you knew this was a bad place to be. You didn't think: "It's a bomb and we'll wait for instructions."

FRANK: No, there was no ambiguity. We didn't know a plane had hit. My first thought was a gas line explosion, but I dismissed that instantly. We smelled gas, and when I looked out this fluid was streaming down on both sides of the window. I didn't know it was jet fuel. I didn't get that till later. When I saw collateral damage on the side of the South Tower, and the aura of orange light signifying a huge fire above us, I knew it was something *very large*, involving both Towers, and there was no doubt about it: we had to get out. But of course we didn't do that. We stayed behind for a while trying to turn off our equipment. *(Laughs)* Interesting decision!

JOSYPH: But it's consistent with other stories. Kevin's father, Tex, fussed around looking for camera equipment. So did Kevin. David Stanke, from 114, retrieved his iced Americano from the table at Starbucks and took it with him on his journey through the streets, under the Towers. Donavin had a cup of it in his teeth as he climbed above the crowd on Broadway just before the first collapse.

FRANK: I'm sure Starbucks will be happy to hear of this.

JOSYPH: Did you start to leave and then say: "Wait a minute—maybe we won't be back"?

FRANK: Yes, we had grabbed our things and were standing at the door when I said to Mike: "If it's a terrorist attack or not, you're not getting up here for at least a few weeks. Shouldn't we turn off the equipment?" But I couldn't find the plugs—they were in the floor beneath the units—and Mike couldn't locate the switches, so we wasted maybe a full minute with this. It seemed like an eternity. It could have been the wrong thing to do. It was kind of a cloudy moment. Maybe I was resonating from the initial impact. Everything, obviously, turned out right for us, but we made some foolish decisions and we lived. Some people probably did all the seemingly right things and they didn't.

JOSYPH: Despite the seismic shock to the building—

FRANK: Yeah, well it was much bigger than 3.0. That would be a little trembling. Where *we* were this was not a little trembling, this was major stuff.

JOSYPH: Still, what you said to Mike bears out that there was no sense, then, that the building would ever come down.

FRANK: No, there was no thought of that till the instant the South Tower started to fall.

JOSYPH: What did the jet fuel smell like?

FRANK: It's a bitter odor. If you inhale a lot of it dehydration sets in quickly. It really saps you.

JOSYPH: Did it smell as if it were burning?

FRANK: No, we were below the impact area and the smoke was all going up. I take that back. There *was* smoke in the hallway of the suite, enough to raise an alarm in my mind. I'd never been in smoke like that. It wasn't heavy and we had plenty of room, still, to breathe, so I didn't realize it at first, but then I saw that we might succumb to it. My impulse was to get on my hands and knees and crawl, but we didn't have to do that.

JOSYPH: In the stairwell you didn't have windows. Was there a sense of claustrophobia?

FRANK: Things were pretty clear until around the mid-sixties, where we hit a traffic jam and we came to a grinding halt. There were thousands of people with nowhere to go. But they were well behaved, very civil. Several of the women were crying hysterically but they were all in line and people weren't climbing over each other. When people saw Mike's condition they began to yell *there's a blind guy and his dog,* so we started coming down, hugging the inside railing as people pushed aside to let us by.

JOSYPH: Did that help you to get down a little faster?

FRANK: I would have to say yes, even though, as the burn victims came down, we had to crunch ourselves to the side, and as the firemen were coming up—we must have passed about thirty-five to forty firemen hugging the inside of the stairwell—we had to push to the right too. So we made many stops. And Mike could only move so fast. But overall we were ahead of the people who let us down, so it was a benefit to us that Mike's condition was recognized. To this day I don't know if all the people who let us by them survived.

JOSYPH: Do you remember the smell from the collapse?

FRANK: As unbelievable as the sound was, the smell was too, and as impossible to describe. The bottom line is that it was ugly, hellish. The rubber, the insulation—the concrete itself was burning, steel was burning, people were burning. Our lungs were *on fire* for a good two weeks. We had inhaled the cloud and it had everything in it, including human remains. And that smell contributed to the anguish afterwards. *You couldn't get rid of that damn smell!* It was in my *shoes,* it was in my *hair,* it was in my *clothing.* I mean, I *really* wanted to get rid of that smell. It *touched* you, it *caked* you, and that was the smell of *death,* of *rot,* of *decay.*

JOSYPH: Did you recognize it when you returned in October?

FRANK: O yes. I saw four or five crews working simultaneously. The amount of fire going on! They were stripping away layers of dirt and every time they picked up stuff, more smoke would come up along with rebar and wire and God knows what else, and the smell would waft its way over the site—it made my skin crawl. Maybe that was the worst, because you could turn away from the site, look at something else, and you could hear other things, but that smell would get in your clothes and there was no escaping it. You could talk for hours about the smells of that day. Or about the sounds. But as Curtis and I were saying yesterday about the sound of the South Tower, everyone in the street knew exactly what it was and it's a sound you can't duplicate. Metal poles breaking, pulverization of concrete—that's just a concept, that isn't the sound itself.

JOSYPH: If it was ten or twelve seconds for 110 stories, that staccato sound must have been pretty fast.

FRANK: I was processing things so quickly that it's hard to measure time, but I heard two very large explosions and in the fraction of that second it wasn't clear that they were related to the Towers, but then the ground began to tremble and everybody knew what it was and we disappeared.

JOSYPH: You didn't know they'd be coming straight down, like a textbook demolition.

FRANK: No, I knew the Towers were a quarter mile tall and I did the math really quick. We weren't a quarter mile away, we were on Broadway with a row of buildings between us. That was way too close. If it were falling northeastward it could fall over those buildings or push them toward us. As it happened, none of the larger debris made it to us, but the cloud sure did. There's a great shot in the book *A Nation Challenged* of people running, I think it's Fulton and Broadway, next to St. Paul's.[42] I might have been in the corner of that shot. You can see the cloud coming around the corner. Whoever took that shot was covered within a second or two. That cloud was racing at thirty or forty miles per hour. It was *bookin,* as they say—it was *moving.*

JOSYPH: If you were forced to compare that sound to something, what would it be? Jackhammer? Express train?

FRANK: Express train is good. Later that day I escaped to friends of mine by Columbia University. Their apartment looks out over the elevated section of the 1 and the 9 lines as it approaches the 125th Street station. It makes a lot of noise, a sound of air rushing and metal on metal. That rushing metallic noise: it sounded similar to that. For quite a while that sound threw me into a mini-panic. When I returned to the site in October I was standing on Broadway and some vendors were showing pictures of the World Trade Center when I heard this sound. I'm in a panic, looking around, thinking another building's coming down—because the place is still unstable. But I'm thinking I'm in a movie because no one's rushing around—there's no reaction at all. Know what it was? The Broadway subway. The noise was coming up through the street. It was freaking me out. I thought it was another tower collapsing. So it was similar to that, but it was also unique and with a dimension of the macabre. That sound was mixed with the shrieking of people. Myself, I didn't say a word, not a peep.

JOSYPH: But Mike can't see. How much did you narrate?

FRANK: All the way down in the North Tower I was describing the situation. We had to stop many times, Mike would ask what's going on and I would tell him everything: the burn victims coming down, the firemen coming up, the minutiae of debris on the ground. The dog could step over stuff, but I'd be saying: "Mike, there's something here—lift your foot up a little more." It wasn't like stepping up on a curb for him. This was unusual stuff. The dog was very very good but I didn't want to take any chances. I felt very much tied to Mike. He didn't particularly *want* me to be that way—he resisted it—but I decided that in spite of my being an irritation, perhaps, we had to get out of there. And there's no way I'm leaving him behind.

When the South Tower began to fall I *did* leave him behind.

Yeah. I completely abandoned him. I just left the ground and flew around the corner. And then came back.

JOSYPH: You came back.

FRANK: I came back, yeah, I came to my senses a little bit. I left him for maybe a full second or two. It was enough to go around the corner. Then I thought: *If I survive this and Mike doesn't, how can I live with that?* The other question was: *How can I possibly turn around? If I turn around I'll be killed, that's it—I'm dead.* So I turned around. *(Laughs)* And just as I turned around Mike's dog, Roselle, had brought him around the corner. I think she may have just followed me. A moment before, there was Mike, the dog, me, and this black lady looking at the North Tower burning when the South Tower began to fall. She shrieked and disappeared. I ran. Then I turned around and there he was, Mike, so I didn't have to go too far back to get him. And as soon as I got to him—just a couple of bounds back— the cloud hit us.

JOSYPH: So for one instant, thought left you—

FRANK: Totally.

JOSYPH: —and biology took over. But as soon as thought returned, it was: Mike.

FRANK: It was both, it was me *and* him. How could I live if he died—*how could I live with that?* And how embarrassed I was! Ashamed of myself that I'd left him behind.

It's what your life's all about. My wife and I are students of meditation, we've been at it a long time and over the years you develop a greater sense of compassion. Well, here it is, right here, here's the test—what're you going to do? Are you going to keep running or are you going to turn around? When I turned around and I saw him, there was a microsecond of thought that I had done the right thing *for myself,* and if I died, okay, you know? Fine. Just that one bright sense. Then the cloud hit us and it was on to the next decision. There was no time to dwell that day. Things

ASKING QUESTIONS

were moving so fast that you were processing four, six, eight thought-streams at a time. So with all these moments I've gone back and opened them up to get a better view.

Another moment was when we made it down the stair into the Fulton Street subway and the cloud followed us in. It was completely black, you couldn't see in front of you, you couldn't breathe, and I was sure I'd made the wrong decision: *this was a big mistake*, we would never get out of there. I didn't think we'd be crushed or suffocated, I just thought we would pass out and that would be it. There wasn't a question about it—it wasn't a doubt, it wasn't a fear, it wasn't some anxious anticipation—it was knowledge pure and simple: it was the signature of death. I even said something to Mike. We'd gotten safely out of the building but I had made the wrong choice and now this would be the end. And I felt it was my fault. But we kept on moving and a guy named Lou, a janitor—I call him an angel—helped us out by pointing the way to a little room at the end of a hall.

Wholly apart from the emotional impact, you could talk solely about the mental observations, from the mundane to the cosmic. Your mind cracks open and you're illumined by the adrenaline, the fear, the exhilaration and the sense that you are in an historical moment. When the building started to fall there was no doubt about it.

JOSYPH: When I first started shooting and I saw how this city was reduced, actually, to trash, I viewed it as an important piece of history. You could either walk away or you could dive further into it and live it while it happens, rather than hearing about it later. So I'm interested in the fact that as the South Tower fell you had a sense of historic moment: it was unique and you were right in the heart of it all.

FRANK: When the plane first hit I was partly tied into my own stuff, but that negativity was shaken right away and several thoughts came in. One of them was: *This is historic, this is big.* It wasn't a large developed thing, just a little impression—*this is historic*—then I dropped it because there was so much to do. But when we got down to the bottom and I pulled Mike out of the line—we had escaped the whole complex—and I looked back at both Twin Towers over my shoulders—we were right underneath them and I saw them both ringed with fire and these jet plumes coming out and joining together—I knew immediately that it was an Arab man and it was related to the Palestinian-Israeli conflict. Because the crescendo of violence in the Middle East was huge, in my mind, before the attack, and I was alarmed about it. When I saw that vision behind me, I knew that it was a terrorist attack without hearing any news about it at all. I knew more or less who did it and something of why. And that it was a major historical event.

JOSYPH: No thought that it was an accident?

FRANK: None at all.

JOSYPH: In any field in which enlightenment is important, satori can come from years of study and meditation, the right word from a master, or it can come from a frog just croaking in the moonlight or someone who simply bops you on the head.

FRANK: Yes, who bops you on the head. *(Chuckles)*

JOSYPH: So would you agree that enlightenment can also come from a 110-story tower that's collapsing on your head?

FRANK: O sure. I think satori's a good word. My understanding of satori is that it's a mental event that illumines you over time. It could be a couple of minutes, it could go on for days, but there is a vast opening and a level of observation that you didn't have previously. It subsides into so-called routine, but you've incorporated it into your daily life. This was a huge event. My mind was in that space for several weeks afterwards. Tremendous openness to life.

JOSYPH: But when you try to translate or extenuate satori, it disappears or becomes something else, doesn't it? It's the openness itself that's the point.

FRANK: It's the openness I tried to hang on to. But that's a meditative state, and like all such states you have to *not* try to prolong it. *Don't hang on to that either!* But it's very tempting because it's so extraordinary and highly enjoyable. Your cranium is broken open. The mind that I had going into that day was completely different than the mind I was left with at the end. The petty complaints, the arguments I was having with a difficult person at work who I didn't respect and blah blah blah, all the considerations that would tie me up in the business—at seven o'clock Tuesday night *that was all gone*—all gone. And I was wide open. I mean *wide* open. And that's the perspective that I have carried forward, by and large. There's no way to return to that stimulus, that intensity, but the openness can be there.

JOSYPH: A lot of people talk about getting over it, finding closure, returning to normal, but there is another side to that day: people came into their own, people rose to the challenge, people learned things. I don't think it's pressing for metaphor to say that the same attack that blew open those buildings could also blow *us* open as human beings, and it doesn't have to be a negative thing—if you live through it.

FRANK: Yes, if you live through it. In terms of a country being attacked, all the conventions of reacting to that came into play, of course. But on another level I saw an attack of human beings on themselves, a perpetuation of the violence and confusion of humankind, irregardless of the borders, the buildings, the technology and all of that. Yet despite being such an ignorant act it yielded tremendous insight. So how do you judge these things ultimately?

In meditation, whenever you have confusion, the best way to step onto the path is by not *expressing* that confusion, verbally or physically. You don't hit someone over the head with your complaint. You restrain your impulses and you take that energy to the meditative path and begin to transform it into awareness. Which yields compassion and a different view of action. From that point of view these guys did the wrong thing. If they had a complaint, that's not the way to carry it out. But given the fact that it happened, what do you do now? The energy's out there—it's raging all over the place. Well, you can fight it back, or you can begin to work with it and see a very different perspective arising from the energy— *phenomenal* energy—that was released that day.

JOSYPH: In a song that I wrote for my film, there's a chorus: "World Trade burning the sky / Desert man wants to blow me up I don't know why." *(Frank chuckles)* That was a common feeling: why are *they* doing this to *us*. Are you saying that, on reflection, it's more a question of what we're doing to each other?

FRANK: That's the big picture to me, the big big picture. I find it interesting to hear people saying: "These guys are filled with rage and anger, they're irrational and they attacked us." I categorically reject that. I don't think events like this happen in isolation. These people planned this, they were highly motivated, deliberate, intentional. That doesn't come out of severely irrational behavior. I see a complaint back there. You can judge the complaint and say yes or no, it's valid, it's not, but there was a complaint. Of course I don't condone the fact that they carried out the complaint the way they did. That's not the way you get your message across effectively, because now, for better or worse—worse for them if they had a complaint—no one wants to hear anything about it. The Arab population, in our lifetime, is terribly repressed. There's a big human problem there. That's been buried. Frankly, that's to our overall detriment. If they had a complaint the world needed to hear it.

JOSYPH: Can I say that you don't regret the whole experience of the 11th?

FRANK: I don't regret it at all. If you say that you regret it you're denying the experience and shutting yourself off. It is scary to let all that energy into your mind, but it's impossible to deny. You either yield to it and conquer it as a result, or else you fight it until it dissipates, but then you're losing an opportunity to grow. In a classic moral sense what these people did was wrong. Historically I can't recall an attack like this, here, on civilians. I don't want to diminish what happened at the Pentagon, but that was a military target. If only the Pentagon were hit it would have been a national tragedy, but people have a different perspective on a military target. This was a uniquely civilian target and uniquely architectural, in a unique city, for the first time on the home turf of arguably the world's freest country. On the other hand, I can't regret being a part of that vast, multidimensional experience and having the opportunity to see into humanity. How often are you offered that in an age? So, no, I'm not shrinking from the experience.

JOSYPH: How is Mike doing?

FRANK: He's doing well. He's involved with Guide Dogs for the Blind. He's left the computer industry, like I have. He likes what he's doing. Less stress, more enjoyment of life.

JOSYPH: Was it that day that made you quit?

FRANK: It pushed me over the edge. When severance came down I took it with glee to find a new means of livelihood and do some volunteer work. Or maybe something like what you're doing.

JOSYPH: How did you meet Kevin McCrary?

FRANK: A New York City police detective, Carlos Aviles, took me on a personal tour of Ground Zero, then he introduced me to Kevin at St. Joseph's Chapel. Kevin was interesting right from the beginning. I felt in him a really sympathetic colleague, a recorder of the day and the events ongoing. Very generous of heart. And, he was infuriating! You'd try to get something done and, like you said, there's no direct path from A to B with Kevin. And while you're on the phone with him he's having *three* conversations at once. But he's a very generous soul. As a survivor I felt a need to come back here in October that people didn't understand on the West

Coast. "What do you want to go back there for?" Kevin helped me to get through that by taking my hand, so to speak, bringing me up to the top of his building and showing me that perspective. He took me into his apartment and showed me these remarkable pictures. He and his father, Tex, have dozens of World Trade Center murals and photographs. About the construction before Battery Park City and how these buildings just arose out of the Hudson.

JOSYPH: When you were looking at the site with Kevin from Gateway Plaza, was there a part of you that thought: *Good God, I escaped from that?*

FRANK: To see the support beams for the elevator shafts . . . to see the general markings of the North and South Towers . . . to see this great ring of buildings around them, wrapped in safety nets because the Towers, when they fell, were *throwing* things—tremendous volume of material—into the air, all the way over to Battery Park City, ripping open the sides of buildings several blocks away because they were thrown from so high up in the air . . . I keep trying to find words to describe the devastation. From Kevin's point of view I could see across to where the shops were. It's heart-wrenching to think that's where Mike and I came out. It boggles your mind. *That's where we were.*

JOSYPH: Does it help to talk to people who were there?

FRANK: O yes. Talking with Curtis and Donavin, instantly there were sympathetic colleagues. Our interest in each other was immediate. "O, you were on the seventy-eighth floor?" Curtis being blown down the stairs of that building, opening the door just in time so when the force of energy hit him, it didn't crush him against a closed door, it threw him down the staircase, which probably saved his life. These details—instantly I can identify with a close call. These guys had several of them and so did I. For the people on the West Coast it's more of an abstraction. My employer at the time didn't get it. They didn't offer me time off. I had to shake the tree for that. When I came back to work after ten days off I had to ask for more time. Until Christmas, even though I was able to write about it, speak about it, I had a *profound* sense of disbelief in body and mind about it. *I* couldn't accept it. But my employer—they just didn't get it. It was a businesslike response. They didn't understand the inside story, the trauma. My position has been: I'll tell my story to anybody who wants to know, but I don't need for people to view me through that filter. Now, whenever I speak about it, my primary message is about the firefighters.

JOSYPH: You were conscious of the physical weight they bore.

FRANK: The clothing alone is, I believe, at least twenty-five pounds, maybe more. Then they carried axes, picks, oxygen bottles, lengths of hose. When you think of seventy-eight floors, or ninety floors, you don't realize it was a staircase, a landing, another stair and another landing and that zigzag makes one floor. For every floor you had two staircases. So we went down 156 staircases. To get to the impact zone in our Tower, firemen had to go up 180 staircases with maybe fifteen to twenty steps per stair. It's a phenomenal exercise. By the time we saw the first fireman, in the forties, he was hanging on to the inside railing in the middle of the staircase. I looked him right in the eye, he looked at me, and he just said: "Are you okay?" That's one of the great visions of that day. Because *he* was completely spent, but he was only thinking about *us*. So I was privileged to see tremendous acts of evil and tremendous acts of compassion within an hour and a half. Both brought to us by men, not by gods and devils.

JOSYPH: The firefighters knew where they were going.

FRANK: And that wasn't lost on us. It was almost as if a conductor were there, because at one point the entire stair erupted in applause and we were cheering like a ballgame. The walls were very smooth so the sound sent chills up and down your spine. We were saying: "God bless you," patting them on the back. We knew they were going into hell because before they had arrived we'd seen the burn victims coming down. They were going to an unfightable fire. They were there for us, trying to pull people out. People say they're *supposed* to do that, but this was something your training can't prepare you for, the scale of events was *so* big and extraordinary. I believe that's more a divinely inspired moment when you're acting at that level and you and all your comrades are there at high risk. They knew the odds. They knew the chances of getting out were not good. I don't think heroism fits it very well. The word is overused. That day just blew away language, too. Did you notice that? When the Towers fell, the silence was absolute. It was external silence, it was internal silence. Speech left people's brains. They were dumbfounded. People in the street were just looking toward the World Trade Center, wounded, bleeding, heartwrenched. There were no words. They're still hard to find. So when you say *hero,* it doesn't make it for me with those guys. That's too trite. You can just say what they did.

ASKING QUESTIONS

JOSYPH: When you went to work in the building that morning, did you take the Twin Towers for granted, or did you examine the architecture?

FRANK: I don't know what made me do it that morning, because I had never been a fan of the World Trade Center—I'd had a romantic attachment to the Empire State Building—but I guess I was developing a better appreciation for the sheer engineering triumph of the structures. I parked my car in the Edison Garage. Then across Liberty Street, right there, is the south side of the South Tower. I stood in the lot for a couple of seconds looking straight up to the top of the building. I didn't think it was beautiful, I just looked at it, like taking a snapshot. There isn't much to see: a flat plane of vision against a beautiful blue sky. I took that picture in my mind and I walked on up the street, past the Marriott Vista and into the North Tower.

JOSYPH: Some of the people in my film—Kevin, Donavin—often wondered what would happen if the Towers were to fall. Have you thought of them as vulnerable, attractive to terrorism?

FRANK: I got to the Twin Towers around 8:05. When I reached the office I decided to go back down to Security and see if I could make things easier for the reseller partners who were coming up to the suite. I wanted them to be on time. I was standing on the seventy-eighth floor sky lobby, waiting for the elevator, when the thought came into my head: "What a target these buildings are." Just like that. The thought then left me. Of course it was a sensitivity to the '93 attempt. I can't claim any prescience. It was a moment that turned out to be more interesting only in retrospect.

JOSYPH: There was no fear attached to it?

FRANK: No, no. They were so big! They stood out so much! And it was tied to '93.

JOSYPH: Now that they're gone, how has that absence affected your sense of the city? You're not a lifetime New Yorker but you had an awful lot of New York in one day.

FRANK: New York is profoundly changed. It's a very different place from an emotional standpoint, and the way the city sees itself has to be different now whether you liked the buildings or not. You always saw them, they were part of the skyline and part of the statement, the boldness, the commerce of the city and how people congregate. Now they're gone. But the impression doesn't just go away. I get emotional about it. Like right now . . . It's a really soft sorrow about it.

I love this city. It's a difficult place, it's an exhilarating place. The sorrow is part of the exhilaration of the city now. It's *a condition* of it. Maybe that'll shift into a hope for the future, if and when there's a replacement. But I can't see that sorrow going away in my lifetime. I carry it with me all the time. Not to indulge in it, but it's persistent whether I'm here or in Los Angeles. It's a huge part of my life.

JOSYPH: Do you feel more camaraderie with New Yorkers?

FRANK: You wonder what a New Yorker is. You live on Long Island but you see yourself as a New Yorker. Someone once said that if you live in Boston, you have to do certain things to become a Bostonian. If you live in Washington or Chicago there are things you have to do there to become a part of those cities. But anybody can become a New Yorker, there are so many facets of the city and so much here to identify with. I've lived here and I've paid taxes here, too, so even though I now live in Los Angeles, my heart's here, it's not in Los Angeles. Los Angeles is a great, under-rated city—but I'm a New Yorker.

JOSYPH: You're not scared off?

FRANK: No, no. They've done what they wanted to do. Why bother with it again? The other view is: let'm try. I take a very conventional view on that: you can't live out of that kind of fear.

JOSYPH: After those buildings collapsed, *and then they came after you,* there must be a sense of *well, what else can you show me?*

FRANK: Yes, and short of a nuclear event, I can't imagine anything bigger. On an ethical, on an almost biblical level, this was an event for the centuries.

14

WILLIAM LANGEWIESCHE

National Correspondent for the *Atlantic Monthly*

I thought, this is an amazing *experiment in what it is to be America.*

William Langewiesche is one of the few people in this book whom I did not meet while shooting my film in Lower Manhattan, but I had wanted to speak with him from the time that I read American Ground: Unbuilding the World Trade Center, *which appeared in three issues of the* Atlantic *between July and October 2002 and was published as a book by North Point Press later that year. It is such a distinctive document as to constitute a genre in itself, and it is one of the few accounts of Ground Zero that attain the level of art. By descending into the heat of the removal operation, absorbing it firsthand on a daily basis, Langewiesche built something beautiful out of the ruins. The task of writing was, to me, as important as any other on the site and I wanted to know how he functioned in that environment.*

Our conversation took place on May 19, 2003 in Washington, D.C. in a hotel a few blocks north of the White House. Langewiesche was deeply into another project, for which he was in transit, stopping briefly in D.C. But having consented to revisit this subject with me, he gave it the intellectual rigor and the emotional honesty that is evident in everything he writes.

LANGEWIESCHE: My wife came into the room and said: "They're bombing New York." I said: "Is it nuclear?" I thought it could be much more massive than it turned out to be.

I quickly discovered what the story was. It was obvious right away that this was an intentional act. Speaking as a pilot, it was practically inconceivable that an airplane would hit those towers by mistake. It was also obvious that these were not pilots who had flown into the Towers. I cannot imagine *any* pilot with a gun to his head who would do this. There would be no reason to. Might as well just let them pull the trigger. So a few things were clear to me: that it was a terrorist attack, and that the terrorists were at the controls of the airplanes. Of course I felt the shock that everyone felt.

The calls from my editors at the *Atlantic* began within minutes. The question was, how do we, as a magazine, respond to this? For me, the first order of business was to complete a piece that I had been working on, and that's the downing of EgyptAir flight 990 out of New York for Cairo. I had been in Egypt for it, it was nearly finished, and I brought it to completion across several days. While the airlines were shut down in the U.S., I was grounded in California finishing the EgyptAir piece ["The Crash of Egypt-Air 990," the *Atlantic Monthly*, November 2001], which became our tangential response to the attacks. The question then for the magazine was whether to use me to go to northern Afghanistan to set up with the Northern Alliance—this was, of course, before there were any troops there—or, perchance, to take a look at what was going to be an interesting problem, which is what do you do with the aftermath in New York, in the middle of this dense city, which is also a rich city, and somewhat of a neurotic city (we all know the pressures lead to that). How are you going to clean up in New York City, of all places? I thought I was headed for the Northern Alliance, but it was worth a few days to take a look at New York.

There were thousands of journalists there, and there were lines at One Police Plaza for credentials, which the City of New York was requiring for any journalist who wanted to be led through the site. I don't normally have credentials. I can't really use them for the kind of work that I do. I never go to press conferences. I never lay out questions in advance for a formal sitdown interview. My writing is very different from all that. It's more impressionistic, it's a much longer form—I'm not a standard reporter, never have been. This credentialing process—the badging system—worked quite well for the daily press, but writing with six-month to one-year leads the way I do, it was clear that the type of controlled access being offered—probably by necessity—was not going to work. So I was going to northern Afghanistan. I never did get press credentials.

Eventually I walked into the site. It took me a couple of days. I found my way in and looked around. It was obvious to me, as it was to everyone—it was no great stroke of genius—that the really big problem was the weight of the debris. Whether to find the living or the dead or simply to clean up the site, the problem was that the stuff was very, very heavy and it was tangled. Human muscles and normal machinery weren't going to cut it. The bucket brigade, the volunteer process, was much to be admired from an emotional point of view—very valiant, admirable human thing going on there—but it had no effect. As far as actual twisted steel and concrete, it was a question of bringing in the heaviest equipment, like mining equipment. So I asked around: who's bringing it in? Everybody who knew said, well, there's this outfit called the DDC: Department of Design and Construction. I don't know New York City government, don't care about it, and certainly didn't know about the DDC. I've lived in New York and I've known it all my life, but I'm not a New Yorker, I don't write for New Yorkers, and I'm not interested in New York politics. But I asked my assistant in Boston, which is where the *Atlantic* is based, and word came back that the commissioner's a guy named Kenneth Holden.

What's a commissioner? Somebody who's in charge of a New York City department. Bureaucracy. They call themselves commissioners. Fine. Commissioner Holden. I introduced myself. I work for the *Atlantic Monthly*. I would like to explore the possibility of writing about the debris removal, the unbuilding. I said that writing this story would be like writing history in the present tense, that I would make a commitment to staying a long time, and that it would be a significant article for the *Atlantic*. And, by the way, I would need full, unrestricted access to the site, to the files, to the meetings. I couldn't work with restrictions on such a project. Within hours came a call on my cellphone: I'm Kenneth Holden, I know exactly who *you* are, and I know the *Atlantic Monthly*—I've been reading it for years—so when do you want to meet?

We met at the site. He walked me through the perimeter. That was at PS 89, the makeshift headquarters for the debris removal—which, again, was always my subject—and we had a private talk in one of the little kindergarten rooms, in which I said: "The ground rule here is that anything you want to be off the record *will* be, but by taking me in here—and this applies to anyone—you are exposing yourself to risk. Because *I* don't know, *you* don't know, *none* of us at this stage knows what's going to happen." This is early, so it wasn't even obvious that they'd be in charge. Certainly the results, which turned out to be successful, famously so, were not obvious at all. It was flat-out emergency. It was chaos and confusion. It was sleepless nights, very tired days, and a sense of great disaster having hit the city—and of death. There was no guarantee of a happy ending. I said to Holden: "If this project fails, if something goes wrong here, I will write about it either way. I'm going to write what I see." He said that he knew the kind of writing I would do, he'd been reading it for years, and he was aware of the consequences of bringing in a guy like me, but he felt that this was important and that it was worth doing.

JOSYPH: How did you go from seeing the site, hanging around for a few days and taking off for Afghanistan, to deciding *this* was the story? Did you look at the site and say—

LANGEWIESCHE: No, it wasn't obvious there. Once I talked to Kenneth Holden and saw the scene in PS 89, that was it for me. Not the site itself, but that incredible, creative scene at PS 89, where it was improvisation to the extreme. All groups were there. It was happening in meetings, it was happening in the hallways. There was this creative turmoil, and I thought, this is an *amazing* experiment in what it is to be America. For better or worse. Maybe for worse. But there's no spin around here. It's not possible. It is the raw form of naked America, for whatever that's worth, at this stage in our history, in a very specific way, and I have the opportunity here to look at America.

Of course it was also a New York scene, but what interested me was *not* that, it was that it was an American scene. And I really think, all the more so after the experience of the World Trade Center, that New York is *not* a separate place from America, as it's so often said to be, but in fact is the ultimate America. It is the distillation of America—the nth degree of America—America to the extreme. When I say American, it was the willingness to allow improvisation to happen. That's what was showing up at the World Trade Center. Admittedly it was mostly New Yorkers who were doing it, but it was really not a New York thing, it was an American thing. The bureaucratic structures were around, and there were people who bought into them to various degrees, largely depending on their level of intelligence. At the beginning they were formalities. Later they became real. But the reality was just underneath those formalities. It was very visible at PS 89, and it was visible on the pile. There was really no choice for me. This was much more interesting than anything I could have seen or done in northern Afghanistan, which is the sort of territory I'm quite used to traveling.

JOSYPH: I was going to ask how and when you found this theme with which to organize your story. What you're saying is that you found it immediately, and it's the reason that you stayed.

LANGEWIESCHE: Yes. It was most visible early. It became less visible as time went on and the place became regularized and, finally, in an incredibly boring way. But there was that vitality and improvisation in the beginning. Yes there was terrible tragedy. Yes there was death, and sorrow, and anger—all of those emotions. That wasn't what interested me. I've covered terrible things over the years. Wars. Airplane accidents. I've seen a lot of victims of violence, and I have never wanted to say to the victims or to their families: "How do you feel?" It's obvious how they feel: they feel bad. "I feel *bad* that my son or my daughter or husband or wife has just been killed. How do you *think* I feel?" That question of how do you feel, which was really the focus of so much of the press—*I feel bad, I feel bad*— I wasn't interested in that, partly as a matter of respect for the people, partly as a matter of content. In a situation like that, people have a reason to feel bad and there's not much to say about it, other than to wallow in it. I didn't want to do that and I didn't think it was interesting. This other thing was very very interesting and it was quite positive—even if it was going to fail. I'm not a natural patriot. The title *American Ground* that we finally came to was not, as it seems to be, a patriotic title, but a description of reality, a piece of American reality. American ground for better or worse.

JOSYPH: The high energy that you saw on the site—it was pervasive around that part of the city.

LANGEWIESCHE: I think it was. I'm not sure because I wasn't out in the city. My world was inside those perimeter lines. The city seemed far away to me. I stayed at a little hole-in-the-wall hotel in the Village because I wanted to get away from the site. I'd walk home late at night on the surface, to not be underground, just to be out in the city somehow. I was by myself, it was very solitary and I wanted it that way. I shunned company after those days. I would eat my dinner alone in some late-night restaurant and go to sleep. I did this for six months. That pattern did not allow me to get much of a feel for the city. I do think that there is, of course, great resiliency in New York. You could see people getting on with their normal life. The return of aggression, even, on the city streets was a welcome thing, as in the return of hornblowing soon after the attack. But basically I don't think I can judge New York City, because I wasn't in it. I was in this other place.

JOSYPH: When you did go out into company, how did it affect conversation, in terms of people's interest in where you'd been?

LANGEWIESCHE: When they found I was working down at the site they wanted to talk about it—*I* didn't. I had my fill of it, day in, day out. I needed a break from it, mentally, and I was not very communicative. So if they *didn't* want to talk, I wouldn't have noticed. Of those who did engage me, I found two types. Some were completely open and curious. Others thought they knew and had very much the wrong impression, but they persisted in the belief that they knew, and this was the view that was pushed by the media: a simple view of heroics. Remarkably, intelligent people indulged in that view insistently. I tried not to give in to these conversations at all. I'd rather talk about . . . sailing.

JOSYPH: On the site you could come and go and see whatever you wanted. How did that work, given the level of security?

LANGEWIESCHE: I always had the right credentials, but I wasn't wearing the Star of David: the press pass. I was given the standard working credentials like every other workman on that site. As you know, there was a constant process of trying to tighten things up, and as the perimeter changed the credentials changed, but it was never a problem for me.

JOSYPH: Some of your excursions, such as the hunt under the pile for the chiller plant with all that Freon in it—a destination of rather dubious safety—demanded work gear, flashlight and so forth. How are you functioning down there as a writer?

LANGEWIESCHE: I always have a notepad and a pen, because I would feel naked without them. But there were many times when the conditions were too rough to write. It's too dark, you're climbing, you're on your hands and knees. In those cases, upon emerging, I would sit down—on a piece of broken concrete, typically—and write what I had seen. I didn't need to write essays about it. Compact, detailed notes. As I began to realize who my characters were, from a literary point of view—and I knew them all quite well—we would sit down in a café or somewhere off the site and over a beer, a glass of wine, a coffee or a dinner, we would have long, long conversations—hours—and I would tape-record them.

JOSYPH: Were you converting your notes into a working prose?

LANGEWIESCHE: No, no, I never do that. It would have been impossible. I was working too hard accumulating the notes. I was observing, listening, moving: involved.

JOSYPH: By the time you get up to your hotel in the Village—

LANGEWIESCHE: Midnight, one in the morning—

JOSYPH: —you're not sitting down to write.

LANGEWIESCHE: No. But I'm used to that. I do this all over the world. I'm often in areas where I'm physically very active and there's no way you're going to sit and write great prose. I don't need to. I create an accumulation of information—notes, tapes that turn into transcripts or indices of tapes—plus external information, file work. Once I'm finished at the site, whether it's some desert overseas or the World Trade Center, I then mine that huge mass of information in the little time I get to spend with my family. I take notes on the notes, so to speak.

JOSYPH: You're not daunted by all that material accumulating?

LANGEWIESCHE: No. After all, what is it that you and I are both doing? We're looking at something that is much more complex than any material we can accumulate, and we have to reduce it. The process of reduction is enormous. That's the nature of the job.

JOSYPH: Why did you include those biographical sketches of the book's key players?

LANGEWIESCHE: Well, because these were real people and I wanted to bring them to life, and people are what their histories make of them. The amazing thing is that these people, who came from all these different walks of life and were *so* different from each other, found themselves working together in this very unusual place. It was the story of the entire site: everybody there was coming from a different place. Even if you say people were mostly out of borough, blue collar—what does that really mean? What that means, in New York, is that a lot of them were born overseas. The backgrounds, the perspectives, were widely varied and yet people were working together quite well. That's the story of America. So I was interested in these backgrounds. And they were lively. You would never expect it. Who was Mike Burton [executive deputy commissioner of the DDC], the "czar" of the World Trade Center? Where did he come from? What was driving him? You couldn't know that without knowing a bit about his background. Ken Holden—probably the most unlikely guy to be a New York City commissioner. One would expect a commissioner, in New York, to be some kind of cigar-smoking backroom dealer. Not at all with Holden. Here's a guy who, some years ago, was verging on a punk rocker type. Brilliant intellectually—mentally *superb,* and very literate. How does *he* get to be in charge? Or the guy from the South, David Griffin, with barely a high school education, who takes over the entire demolition as a consultant. Uninvited: talks his way in. How does *that* happen? I went down to the Carolinas to talk to his old man and check that out. You've got to understand the background, know who you're working with. I'm not a newspaper writer.

JOSYPH: The sketches seem to me a way of verifying your theme. And your response suggests an answer to another of my questions: what would have happened with a Ground Zero elsewhere—in Paris, for instance?

LANGEWIESCHE: Yes, I've thought that often. It would have been very different. We know in the case of the French especially there would have been an overlay of rationality, of logic. This whole hierarchical, Napoleonic system would've been put in place, and the site might've been locked up until that happened. It would have been effective. The French build fantastic cities. They're great engineers.

JOSYPH: The Germans too.

LANGEWIESCHE: The Germans too, so it's not that they wouldn't have done a good job of cleaning up, but it would have been very different. In New York we were looking at this creative messiness, this celebration of chaos that lasted for a surprisingly long time. You would not have seen that in France or in Germany. In other parts of the world—some place with a big earthquake—say Turkey, or Mexico—you would have seen an intervention by the army. They would have imposed a different kind of order, and probably less effective than the civil order the French or the Germans would have imposed, and certainly less effective than what we saw here. Here the military was kept on the outskirts. Their job was to guard the perimeter. The Army Corps of Engineers had some role on the inside, but you didn't see a lot of guys in army uniforms. In many parts of the world you would have seen that. I don't know enough about the British, but I suspect that what we were looking at, in the response here in New York, is not just an American thing but originally some sort of British thing.

JOSYPH: They didn't say: "Wait a minute, stop: let's look to the very top."

LANGEWIESCHE: Right.

JOSYPH: "Who are the smartest guys? The most important, the most credentialed?" It didn't happen that way.

LANGEWIESCHE: No, it didn't. It was: "LET's put a wall around this place, and let those who rise, rise." I'm not sure that it was so much an intentional choice, but it was allowed to happen. Those who are actually getting the job done will rise. There were people on the inside who never understood that, and they were isolated by their lack of understanding. They *thought* they were in charge, but they were commanders without troops. It was very obvious at the Trade Center site, typically with some of the higher-up bureaucrats, guys with stars on their shoulders—I don't just mean in uniform, I mean also civilians—who didn't have the adaptive capabilities to understand that this is a different place, not the rules as they'd played them before. They would command the troops, and the troops might even say "Yes, Sir," but the troops didn't do what they were asked to do, they did what they felt like doing.

JOSYPH: Talk about this system when it's threatened from above, when this huge multinational corporation, Bechtel, is offered a multimillion-dollar contract to serve as intermediary between the DDC and construction. Beyond the fact—if you can get beyond it—that there's a connection between Bechtel and the bin Laden family, creating a situation in which the same family that knocked these buildings down is being promoted to profiteer by cleaning them up, no one at the site *needs* this intervention. But it's being pushed. What's the dynamic, in that extraordinary moment, when that is resisted? How did the DDC get away with saying no? Why didn't Bechtel come in over their heads?

LANGEWIESCHE: Bechtel came very very close to taking over. It was down to hours, and various times. I couldn't write about the Bechtel thing because it was *so* complicated and so quickly became a story of New York politics. Bechtel was an example of another form of American ground. The Bechtel episode was a frightening illustration of what I think of as a legalized corruption of the American system. It was perfectly legal, sure; however, fundamentally corrupt in a way that we know exists throughout the American political process today. Maybe it always has, I don't know. It's certainly there now, and I think we all understand the dynamics. This was a classic example. It was absolutely a parasitical thing. There was *no need* for Bechtel to be there. It was not just the DDC who thought that, it was everyone, including the other construction companies and the construction workers themselves. It was just *absolutely* clear. When Bechtel tried to come in, things were getting under control. The other construction companies were large multinational corporations, and I'm not sure that in their deepest souls they were all that different—I don't know. The point was not so much one construction company, Bechtel, versus the others. This was a place where innovation and practicality had triumphed at that point, it was working, and here comes a clearly war-profiteering move. What the politics were behind that—to whose advantage it would have been to bring Bechtel in—I don't know. They were backed down by the rising volume of objection. It would have turned into a big political embarrassment to the City of New York.

It was a shameful period in the World Trade Center story.

JOSYPH: How early did you know that the *Atlantic* was going to do something unprecedented: devote three issues to this story?

LANGEWIESCHE: Early, early. I have very close relationships with the editors there, personal and professional. It's a very happy marriage. Cullen Murphy in particular, and Mike Kelly—who was the editor in chief and who, a few months ago, was killed in Iraq—were very close to this from the beginning. All three of us decided early on that we had a very interesting thing happening in New York, that we had the possibility to write in a meaningful way about the United States, without spin, and that this would be the *Atlantic*'s response to the aftermath of September 11. This is something tangible, rather than generalizing about anger in the Arab street. We were going to describe something real here. Not that that anger isn't real, but we wouldn't have to generalize on this. So we decided the three parts early on. In conversations with Cullen, late at night, in Bryant Park, we decided how the three parts would differ, and the basics of that structure. It was that decision, within the first few weeks of my arrival, that allowed me to filter what I was seeing, to keep my eye on the ball and not be distracted by the many directions it would have been possible to take at that site.

I always knew, for example, that I was to write about the World Trade Center only from a physical point of view: the deconstruction. It's like getting an assignment to write about a concrete wall: it's a difficult one for a writer, but that was the assignment. Not to write about heroism, tragedy, sorrow. Not to write about the deeper political significance on a geopolitical scale—Arab anger, why they attacked us and so forth. It was to write about the cleanup. We also decided the organizational devices within that basic approach. What would we put in each of the three parts? We worked that out, and it helped me a lot.

JOSYPH: And yet the three parts don't seem divided programmatically. Nothing's hard and fast.

LANGEWIESCHE: No, there's flow-through between the three parts. It was a very carefully worked out organization, mostly by me, in terms of detail. But that's part of the job of writing. I always assume I'll lose my reader at the drop of a hat if I make a mistake. It has to be aesthetically pleasing, it has to be interesting, it cannot insult the reader's intelligence. You establish vocabularies, then you return to use them again as a private confidence with the reader. Although it was a very long magazine series, it amounts to a short book, but a complex one, organizationally, so that the reader cannot reconstruct how it was put together.

The *Atlantic* is a rare magazine, an unbelievable place. Right now, under these editors, it's having its golden time. It is enormously thoughtful and has great integrity. In the fact-checking, for instance: it was huge, huge. Five months of full-time fact-checking, for two people, on just this one piece.

JOSYPH: Even a historian addressing a popular subject—the Civil War, for instance, where there are guys who can tell you the number of notches on Grant's revolver—still has a sense of working in privacy, more or less alone. Here you undertook something with all eyes upon it, knowing that, however superficially people looked at the issue, it was of international interest and the work would be scrutinized. Did that affect your frame of mind?

LANGEWIESCHE: I didn't even think about it. My job is to go to some place or some event, to explore it as fully as I can, as one person alone, to form opinions about it and to express them with complete honesty to the reader, and then to get out of the way. I don't see my job in a grander, public sense. I am not an encyclopedist. I am not an academic. My job is also to write melodically, to be aware of narrative structure, that sort of thing—the intangibles of writing. I have also learned that I don't need to worry about writing on a subject which has been heavily covered by others. It never is a problem, because I'm writing on a different level.

JOSYPH: Is there a sense of pride when you're out there on the debris pile with someone like Holden, or Burton, having a talk with them, pride that you have, at least, earned their respect?

LANGEWIESCHE: No. I'm not being falsely modest. No, there's no sense of pride. There are other emotions. There's a sense of deep-healing connection, which is not artificial. There's a compassion that goes both ways and a satisfaction of trust, real trust being established both ways, trust that I never violate. There's the genuine friendship that grows up, always, in these stories. In my life as a writer I have made many close friends, about whom, eventually, I have written. It's very hard to write about people without becoming, in a sense, their friends. Because you think about them. To know almost anyone is to love that person. As a writer you have the opportunity to know them. You can ask questions about which they would otherwise be saying: "Why do *you* want to know?" But pride of being there? Not *at all*. I wanted other writers to be there. I wanted the newspapers to be there. One of the really silly mistakes that Giuliani made, early on, was when the perimeter was built. It was necessary to do that. For the place to function there had to be an exclusion of people. They couldn't have had everyone running through—the chaos would have been too intense. But it did not have to be an exclusion *of their eyes*.

There are two ways to exclude people's eyes. One way is to build an opaque perimeter, and they did that. The other way is to keep the press out, and they did *that*. They were both mistakes. Giuliani did well—he deserves credit—but he made these silly statements, sort of insulting the gawkers, he called them, or something like that, as if they were not decent people because they were trying to see in from the outside. I remember thinking, how ridiculous. There is no more sane and healthy reaction for Americans than to want to look at what happened when the country was hit on September 11. It was perfectly normal to want to see inside. I think that anybody who was in New York needed to make that pilgrimage, that trip downtown. Not to do that is a mystery to me. Giuliani was wrong. Eventually they built their famous viewing platform, but it took them forever. Meanwhile, the press was excluded throughout, except for these little rapid tours, wearing their bright-colored press badges and carrying their cameras. They would fly in, fly out, getting the externalities, missing the point of anything of real interest there. There was never a real question that this debris would be removed, so if it was this week or next, who cared? They were missing the really important stuff, the cultural stuff that was happening there. It was not their fault. They were being dragged so quickly through it.

JOSYPH: You couldn't even photograph from Broadway. Was that an attempt to control something bigger than they were?

LANGEWIESCHE: I think that was tied in to the fact that there were so many dead there. But it was a misunderstanding, because the dead were, for the most part, *not* visible: they were buried. They would come out in dribs and drabs. Nothing shocking, really, unless you were right on top of the situation. From the point of view of people on the outside, once the initial horror of the jumpers was over, once the buildings came down, it was not a gruesome place. Only if you were right where the remains were being removed. Otherwise, the dead were not visible. So that was a misunderstanding, that it was somehow macabre to be photographing. There would have been no opportunity to be macabre, and I don't think people wanted to be macabre.

JOSYPH: On the spine of the book there's a six-shot sequence, taken by you, of the South Tower skeleton coming down. Did you generally have a camera?

LANGEWIESCHE: No. I had a photo pass. I could have used a camera, openly. I brought a camera a few times and took some snapshots, put it away and never brought it back. That was a job for others and there were some good photographers there.

JOSYPH: How did it work with Joel Mayerowitz?

LANGEWIESCHE: He took those very beautiful pictures, but his attitude toward it was completely different from mine. After it was over and we had decided to use his pictures for the first of the three installments, I met him in his studio. He was very emotional about it and wanted to do this brother thing with me. I did not want that at all. I didn't share his emotions, nor his sense of brotherhood. I had a very different reaction to my experience at the site. I didn't have this sweeping sense of brothers-are-we.

JOSYPH: Some of your descriptions—the abandoned breakfast tables at the Deutsche Bank, for instance—have a photographic degree of detail.

LANGEWIESCHE: Well, you see, that's a place where notes could be taken. I was utterly alone there. It was the ultimate of solitude. Which is why I went back there so often. Even though it was ghostly, even though it was so badly damaged, it was always a refuge. I had plenty of time to take notes there, and I took very careful notes, because it was clear that I was going to use those scenes. I wanted to know *exactly* what they were like.

I remember once in the Sahara desert—a place in which I've spent a lot of time—coming to an oasis and sitting down in very hot conditions and having the time to write down, in a notebook, the sounds that I heard. I wrote down, in detail, *all* the sounds. There are times in the writing process when you can do that. If you can select the time to do that efficiently, knowing these details will be useful, it can be great.

JOSYPH: The Deutsche Bank loomed over all of the buildings on Liberty Street. Were you looking through that gash?

LANGEWIESCHE: Above it, too. But the gash was big, it was multiple floors, and I went through all those floors many times. I would sit there at the edge and look out at the site and relax, basically. Have a little solitude. Other people did it too. It was a known hangout.

JOSYPH: Some of the guys in your book explore the site with a kind of fear-lessness, almost a delight. To know that, you had to have followed them. Did you ever say: "Forget this—it's not worth it for one more paragraph"?

LANGEWIESCHE: No. The truth is, though the site was technically very dangerous, especially the underground, nobody was shooting at us. I've seen worse. I never felt threatened at all. There were times, underground—and I was much, much underground—I liked the underground, as many people did—there were times when I felt claustrophobic. But you realized, okay, here's the situation: I'm underground, and what's over my head is unstable, unexplored, there are vibrations going on, there's an ongoing fire, and if it takes *this* minute to let loose, I'm going to die. *But.* What are the chances it'll happen at this minute? Very small. After the initial collapse, there was a sort of instantaneous stability. The place was rearranged. It continued to collapse for months afterwards, inside, underground, but those collapses were not constant. And it was a big site, so it would have to be your unlucky day for you to be at that one place where it collapsed. Don't forget: nobody was killed. So it just goes to show that the attitude I'm describing was not some brave, macho attitude. It was, in fact, a realistic appraisal of the dangers. Which were significant, but not awesomely dangerous.

JOSYPH: The job was done faster than expected, it was done beautifully and, strange as it is to say, it was done enjoyably. They *wanted* to move more trucks. Guys were bragging to me. That was all they could do. They *loved* doing that.

LANGEWIESCHE: It was a peak experience, a very positive thing for many people. Rightly so. Not so much for me. For me it was a day in the life. It's the work that I do. But for many people at the site it was the liberation of their lifetimes, and they were liberated in many ways from many things. It was also the energizing of their lifetimes, and the giving-of-meaning of their lifetimes.

ASKING QUESTIONS

JOSYPH: Did you meet guys who didn't know how to handle it when the work tapered off?

LANGEWIESCHE: Of *course*. There was a sense of depression that set in over the entire site. As things were normalized and people were being asked to leave the site, and then, finally, everyone had to leave, there was enormous sadness that it was over. Also, it was never forgotten that people had died. People were very sensitive to that. There was no callousness there about the larger significance of the attack and the results of the attack. But there was also this other sadness. End of the good times, in a way. The fondness between people. The shared something that Mayerowitz was talking about.

JOSYPH: And a freedom from certain kinds of restrictions and connections.

LANGEWIESCHE: *Many* kinds. Freedom from office work. Freedom from normal construction site supervision. Freedom for firemen from the firehouse. Freedom, also, for people from their families. Freedom from domestic responsibility. Even if you went home at night to your wife and children, they understood that you were doing something larger than you, and that you had a reason to come home late and to leave really early in the morning. And there was sexual freedom. On the outside there was a whole lot of that going on. There was freedom of every kind.

JOSYPH: One of the guys in my movie threw up in his shower when they opened up Liberty Street. Getting people back was part of his job, but what the hell was *he* to do now?

LANGEWIESCHE: It's just like people coming back from war. It's a well-known phenomenon. Wars are a very positive experience for many people. It's not all hell. It has always been that way. Not just for bad people, but for good people, too, there are positive aspects to the experience of going to war. Well, these people at the site were going to war—without the shooting.

JOSYPH: I knew some guys who were working in the parking garage, over on the north side underneath Six, and they nearly got me down there. Did you see it?

LANGEWIESCHE: O I was in there many, many times. I was underground I don't know how many times—a hundred times? I was all over the place. So, sure, many times I saw the garage.

JOSYPH: Was there anything normal about it?

LANGEWIESCHE: O yes, cars went the full range from almost normal—dusty but pretty much undamaged—to terribly damaged or burned out, to cars hanging over the lifts. Some were vertical. There were collapses there, so cars went down in the collapses. Every range that you can imagine. The only common thing was that everything was covered with Trade Center dust.

JOSYPH: Why did you like the underground?

LANGEWIESCHE: Everybody liked the underground. The great majority of the people at the site were there because they wanted to be there. Everybody was an active, enthusiastic volunteer, one way or the other. Maybe through a terrible sense of tragedy, but they wanted to be there. If you wanted to be there, really, then you wanted to be on the pile. Not on the periphery. Not in the Red Cross tent, the Taj Mahal. You wanted to be on the pile, for obvious reasons. If you wanted to be on the pile, you wanted to be underground. I met a few people who would have felt too enclosed, but, basically, everybody who could get underground went underground.

You know why the underground was fantastic? The underground was the ultimate of that site. The whole place was interesting and appealing in some ways because it was physically so exotic, not just culturally. The exoticism, the strangeness which is so well known to people because of the photographs aboveground—the gothic walls, all of that—was much more intense underground. The underground was pretty much invisible to cameras and remained that way throughout. Too dark, too tight, too dusty, too smoky, too dangerous, too hard to get to sometimes. But it was the nth degree. It was all the chaos, exoticism, and surreality of the pile in three dimensions, underground, and in darkness. It also had the beauty and the attraction, for a long time, of being unexplored. The unexplored is attractive throughout the world. Find a piece of unexplored continent and everybody's going to want to go there. We unfortunately don't live at a time when you can do that. But we could go underground at the World Trade Center. There was real exploration to be done there. So I think it was a natural thing that people, including me, gravitated underground. That was the place to be if you had the choice, and I had the choice and the freedom to do it.

JOSYPH: Was there a part of you, as a writer, that wished you had been there on the 11th and had seen the day itself?

LANGEWIESCHE: O yes, sure, yes, I would have preferred that. It would have been a most interesting starting point. But it's not a personal thing: it's for the readers. I think I achieved that service for the readers by writing

Diesel excavators grapple with tangled steel as the site still burns.

about Ken Holden and Mike Burton. After all, they were the characters. The only *I* that comes into this book is when occasionally *I* express an opinion, or *I* talk to someone. I'm a very externally directed writer. I do not talk about myself if I can avoid it.

JOSYPH: Addressing, now, the pilot in you and the man whose father wrote a classic on aviation, *Stick and Rudder,* let me ask you about those jets. How good did those guys have to be?

LANGEWIESCHE: Not very good. Any baby could've done it. That was one of the things that amused me from the beginning. The wise press was mouthing off about the incredible skill and training this took. And of course they can easily find aviation experts to go on television and confirm that, because it's to their advantage to pump up what it means to fly an airplane. I, who have flown airplanes from birth and who breathed and lived flying for so many years, understand the soul of the machine. The soul of the machine is a docile soul. It's designed to be that way and it *is* that way. Airplanes are flyable. An airplane like that, at high speed, is all the more flyable. Speed makes planes easier to fly, not harder. It was a clear day. They weren't landing or taking off. It took *very* little skill. Anybody can read a GPS [Global Positioning System]. In fact, I think those guys were suckers, because they overtrained, from an aviation point of view, for what they did. They seemed to buy into the myth a bit too much. I had that impression from the beginning. It was simply *not hard to do that*. Yes, if you had *no idea* of how to fly an airplane, maybe you couldn't have done that. But to take an airplane at high altitude, high speed, on a nice day, and to fly it into New York City and hit the side of a giant building—*it ain't hard*.

JOSYPH: Why is it easier when it's faster?

LANGEWIESCHE: It's a little complicated. The response of the airplane at high speed is going to be better. These guys were way over the speed limits, so they could have gotten into trouble, but up to that point—getting in trouble because of the speed—they would have had no indication of that. They weren't test pilots, they were out there in airplanes that were over speed for the very low altitude, and they were dealing with dynamic forces on their control surfaces that were unusual, but it didn't take any skill to deal with them. Until the airplane comes apart it flies better and better at high speed. That's a simple way of putting it, but you can say that. And the airplanes didn't come apart.

The guy in the South Tower, apparently, almost missed. That was a function of speed. Because of that hard left turn, where he smacked into the building in the end, he clearly had misjudged the closing rate with that building. He had come out of another turn. One of the things you see from people who aren't used to speed in an airplane is that they underestimate the amount of space, over the ground, that it takes to turn one of these things around, because of the speed. So it seems that he made some slight miscalculations that way. But because he gave himself enough of a straight run at it, it didn't take a huge amount of skill to hit that building. The guy coming in from the north, he just went straight at it from a long way back. No problem, no problem.

JOSYPH: What would it have looked like in the cockpit?

LANGEWIESCHE: I have thought of that often. I think it would have looked in the cockpit much as it looked on the outside: intensely real. There's a clarity inside a cockpit to all views. It's the ultrareality of the cockpit. I think there would have been nothing dreamlike about it. And for those on the outside, watching those airplanes hit, there was nothing dreamlike about it. They were very real. There is no question that this was happening in more like a hyperreality than any kind of a dream state.

JOSYPH: What about the complaints that very little was done after those planes were hijacked?

LANGEWIESCHE: The conspiratorial view that this was half-intentional, that we allowed this to happen, is *utter* nonsense. It confuses many things. It exhibits a fundamental lack of understanding of the nature of the sky, the size of the sky, what is air traffic control, what are air traffic controllers as men or women, what are military people, what's the nature of the military organization, and how effective is the military. These people are investing enormous competence in the American military. It's perfectly competent, but it's a very large organization, and like all large organizations it's quite stupid. There's no way around that. It's true for the air force, it's true for the army, it's true for large companies. It's almost beneath comment, the idea that this was in some way planned. The planners aren't that good. The choreography is way too tight for that notion to be at all realistic. Nonsense.

JOSYPH: Why did you say it was paperwork that brought down the South Tower?

LANGEWIESCHE: When the official investigation that was run by the ASCE, the American Society of Civil Engineers, looked into the thermal realities of what had happened, the best evidence in both towers seemed to indicate that the big blossoming of fire outside the towers was harmless. It was good for the towers. It was just the burning of fuel harmlessly in the air. Those fireballs looked dramatic on camera, but they were sort of meaningless. The blasts consumed a large amount of the fuel in those airplanes. The rest of the fuel was atomized in a really intense way. There was some pooling—some of it went down elevator shafts, that sort of thing—but basically it was atomized across these multiple floors by the violence of the impact, and then ignited. The effect was a very rapid burn-through. The temperature achieved was high, but of short duration. Jet fuel is kerosene. It burned through quickly. I believe I was told it burned through in two or three minutes. I think in the official report they gave a slightly larger number to be conservative, which was probably appropriate. These are always estimates in any case.

That alone would not have caused a significant weakening of the steel, which is what is required for the buildings to fall. But it ignited, across large areas—multiple floors—all the things that could be ignited, which included furniture, carpets, computer casings, separations between these awful cubicles that people have to work in, and that included, of course, unbelievable amounts of paper. Paper was the focus of the studies that were done on the fire, and it was found that massive fires like these—

these were fires out of the Apocalypse—huge, huge fires—fires made of paper, would be sufficient to weaken the steel. Of course the buildings were already badly wounded. A certain amount of the support structure had been eliminated by the impact. The remaining support was holding up the weight of the upper floors, above the impact zone. When that intact support was weakened by the fire, across time, it let loose in both cases.

JOSYPH: Your writing never pushes for any kind of emotionalism. The reader never even hears whether or not you're upset. Did you ever get wiped out?

LANGEWIESCHE: Never. Never had the slightest inclination to. After the book came out I was asked that question many times in interviews. Charlie Rose spent a lot of time trying to get me to be emotional about it.

I'll tell you the times that were most difficult for me, emotionally. Occasionally I accompanied the families of those who had died so they could contemplate the scene. This happened quite a few times, because people knew that I knew the site. I never wrote about this because it was off limits, irrelevant to my subject. Personally, for me, of course it was sad. But basically, no, I had no problem sleeping at night. I had no nightmares. I saw, of course, much death, much mutilation and all of that. I was heavily exposed to it for many months. I felt no consequences of that, none that I can identify. People could say, well, one day I'll wake up a raving lunatic because I was so badly wounded and I'm suppressing all that. It may be, but I doubt it. People get used to death, you know? People get used to horror of all kinds. People also get used to chaos. Life does not only consist of a tranquil, middleclass, orderly American existence. It may be because I've traveled so much for my work that I'm very aware of that. And I'm not sure that I seek a tranquil, middleclass American existence.

JOSYPH: But that's why an interviewer would *love* to see you welling up with tears: so we don't have to fear what's different about you. Crying's a great leveler. You too can crack up over a sad experience.

LANGEWIESCHE: I'm sure that I can. In this case I had no inclination to. I'm not invulnerable to these emotions. I just didn't feel them. Period.

JOSYPH: Did writing this book teach you something that you can apply to the next book?

LANGEWIESCHE: I don't know the answer to that. Progression as a writer is such a subjective, intangible thing, very difficult to talk about. I do feel that the quality of my writing and my ability to communicate with my readers is improving. Where *American Ground* fits into that progression I don't know and I don't think about it. I hope the books will keep getting better. I don't want to be known only for *American Ground*. That's just one small book.

The day I sent in the last of that manuscript—the *day* I sent it in—I simply stopped thinking about it. I did my work, I said what I wanted to say—I had the luxury to be able to say it—and then I moved on. Literally. I remember exactly where I was when I sent in the last bit, by computer, over the internet. That was it. I had a glass of wine. I went outside. It was late summer. And I didn't give it another thought.

First Resident of Battery Park City

The first time Ground Zero was ever filed in a news report,
I filed it: from Hiroshima.

My initial conversation with John Reagan Tex McCrary took place on December 1, 2001, in Tex's new apartment in the Gateway Plaza complex in Battery Park City a block from Ground Zero. Tex was ninety-one. Our last talk was at his wife Jinx Falkenburg's house in Mill Neck, Long Island. I have augmented these talks with material from a third conversation in the Edison Hotel in Midtown Manhattan. Tex talked anecdotally and, as his son Kevin told me: "He's a walking history lesson," but the reader will have to decide to what degree Tex's version of events—the conception of the Twin Towers, for instance—has been colored by the talents of a former publicist, TV performer and tabloid editor.

When Tex died in July of 2003, the owner of VIP Yacht Cruises, Mark Philipps,
who had loaned Kevin the cart that he drove at Ground Zero, volunteered a boat
to take Tex's ashes into New York Harbor, where they were sprinkled into the water
by the Statue of Liberty. We began our talk after Kevin posed his father in front of
a picture Kevin had taken on the pile. Whether or not, as Kevin believes, Tex was
ultimately destroyed by the 11th, here, in the new space he was eager to move into
for its exceptional view of the site, Tex's voice was full of future.

TEX: The whole idea of Battery Park City was born in Hong Kong after the
    war when I took Sam LeFrak and showed him how to build on landfill. I
    had landed the first four-engine bomber, my B-17, in Kai Tak airport in
    Hong Kong two days after the surrender was signed. I don't know whether
    you've ever been there, but it's like trying to thread a needle to land at this
    short little airport. The runway was pockmarked with craters. I had three
    planes in my flight section. Two of them went down on the nose. We had
    a big party that night in the Peninsula Hotel. It's right on the water. We
    put notes in beer bottles and threw them out the window into the harbor
    for fun. I came back two years later and you couldn't see the water be-
    cause already the Chinese were building highrise on the waterfront. So I
    took Sam LeFrak, who built LeFrak City, to Hong Kong and to Manila to
    show him what you could do with landfill. Got all the engineering, archi-
    tecture and economics of building highrise on landfill. Came back and
    sold the idea to Governor Rockefeller. And that was the birth of Battery
    Park City, where I was the first tenant.

KEVIN MCCRARY: And the second to last one out!

JOSYPH: When you showed LeFrak the potential of landfill, were you pre-
    senting it as an entrepreneur, or as a man who was interested in the de-
    velopment of Manhattan and in a good idea?

TEX: You just hit on the key phrase. My uncle, as general counsel of Texaco,
    moved Texaco from Houston to the Whitehall Building at the tip of the
    Battery. He brought me with him. The first thing that I felt about New
    York was something you just said: "A good idea." At the top of the White-
    hall Building was the Whitehall Club, where every great shipping line had
    their flags on the walls. There were big brass telescopes at every window,
    and the harbor was full of foreign ships with foreign flags and foreign
    names. I said then and have said it in various ways afterwards: New York
    City is the last frontier town in America for a good idea. It still is. And
    what I'm watching out that window, and what you saw in Kevin's picture,

is Easter morning. It's the rebirth of a great idea. And I want to be a part of whatever happens. Simple as that. At ninety-one.

JOSYPH: Before they made the grid, all the city was a lot like it is down here: curved streets, alleys, trees. It's the oldest of New York and the newest. Maiden Lane—that old winding street led right to the Twin Towers. It's like a village of its own, but it's more like six of them: South Street, the ferries, Fulton Fish, Battery Park, the old Newspaper Row, Wall Street, City Hall, that walk up Broadway, from down at the Custom House, past those great old buildings coming up toward Chambers . . .

TEX: Right. Absolutely. *(Forms his arms into a crossroads)* To me, New York City has always been what the French call *croix de vie,* the cross-section of America. Not New England, not Texas, but New York City. And in New York City the microcosm of the whole city is Lower Manhattan. It grew up behind a wall, literally. And it was torn down, and made another wall, which my son Kevin photographed: Ground Zero.

Ironically, the first time Ground Zero was ever filed in a news report, I filed it: from Hiroshima. I was the first one into Hiroshima, the first one into Nagasaki: the first American into both those places after the bombs were dropped. I took in a team of top war correspondents, but I knew why we were going. In the briefing, which was top secret, the target was Ground Zero. So I filed the first report from the first Ground Zero *and* the second: Hiroshima and Nagasaki.

JOSYPH: You're moving closer to the catastrophe. You're not abandoning ship.

TEX: I repeat: it's Easter morning, it's the rebirth of the city. And in a sense it's the rebirth of America. When Nelson Rockefeller had the idea for the Twin Towers—incidentally, there is another man you should talk to, because this story has not been written. He is the founder of the World Trade Center concept: Guy Tozzoli, who is now chairman of the Association of World Trade Centers around the world. He named the Twin Towers the World Trade Center. It was his concept to have Twin Towers.

JOSYPH: People forget that the Twin Towers used to be called David and Nelson.

TEX: *(Smiling)* That's right, that's right.

JOSYPH: That was journalism, but there *was* a strong connection with the Rockefellers.

TEX: The Rockefellers *created* Downtown Manhattan. They *owned* most of it. There's a dirty joke that really made the decision. Because Nelson once made a wisecrack, which he was good at. He said: "I want to build down here on the Hudson, in the beating heart of Manhattan, where Main Street and Pennsylvania Avenue cross, at Wall Street, five days a week. I want to build the tallest building in the world, and I want it to remain the tallest building for as long as I live, and I expect to live for fifty years." He was a young man, you know? And he had already been tagged as a governor by the fact that he had an Edifice Complex—to build build build. Nelson's father—which most people have forgotten—completely changed the pattern of New York City when he built Rockefeller Center. He moved the focal weight of the city to the West Side. He *crossed* Fifth Avenue. Time goes on, there is talk of building the tallest building in Chicago and in Asia. That's when Nelson said: "In Downtown Manhattan, where so much of my family is involved, I want to build the tallest building in the world." Guy Tozzoli, who I want you to meet, said to this group that Nelson had assembled: "Governor, there is no way that you can guarantee that *any* building will remain the tallest building for fifty years. Somebody's going to top you by one floor."

Guy was an early whiz kid with computers. He was a young hotshot who had studied urban growth. He was the one who figured out there was not enough real estate left in Brooklyn, Queens or Manhattan to build a container port for the future, so he pulled all the figures together and he literally moved the Port of New York from Lower Manhattan to Bayonne, New Jersey. So people paid attention to him when he talked, and he never minded speaking out. And he said, in this meeting: "Governor, you can't guarantee that *any* building will remain the tallest for fifty years. But, Governor, only you have the personal wealth, the political connections, and, frankly, the pizzazz and the chutzpah to build twin towers. Nobody will build the tallest twin towers in the world."

And Governor Nelson and everybody did just what you're doing: "Mmmm . . . yeah . . . boy . . . that's a hell of an idea . . . " Now, I don't know who made this joke up, but Nelson enjoyed it enormously. The joke was: "And Governor, twin towers will give you what every man dreams of: a double erection." Laughter. I said: "Repeat that." General laughter in the place.

JOSYPH: So you were there when the remark was made to Rockefeller?

TEX: I was there. I met him because I had studied architecture at Yale. I was a part of the group of ten or fifteen people trying to figure out, what do you do? One was Austin Tobin.

JOSYPH: The plaza was named for Tobin. He ran that whole project. Tobin and Guy Tozzoli.

TEX: That's right. And that's the way it happened. I honestly believe that joke made the decision, along with my further knowledge of landfill construction. That's the beginning of the rest of this story. *(Points out the window)*

JOSYPH: There are people who want a memorial and they don't want to build here.

TEX: No, no, rebuild, rebuild. On one wall I'm going to have Kevin's picture of Ground Zero. On another wall I've got a twelve-foot picture of Battery Park City before the World Trade Center was built. It was shot by Joseph Karsh with a camera that had fourteen-inch negatives built to photograph Mount Everest from a helicopter. So that'll be the beginning and the rebirth. Then you look out the window. The great thing about that picture that you saw blown up is that it's laminated. When people look out the window and then they look at the picture, they are reflected in the surface of the picture and they become a part it. *(Tex moves to the window where the site is in full force)*

KEVIN MCCRARY: What about when you landed on the helicopter?

TEX: I landed the first helicopter in the Downtown area on the top of the Telephone Building over on Barclay Street. You see that building right down there? *(Points to World Financial One)* That's Dow Jones. The *Wall Street Journal* is the most important newspaper in the world. It is the voice, the conscience, the memory, and the future of Wall Street. And that's the importance of what you're looking at out this window here. You watch open-heart surgery and a heart transplant on the economy of America, right there.

JOSYPH: You have no doubt it'll survive the operation?

TEX: No doubt. What to build? I don't know. But I want to be in a front-row seat to watch it happen. *(Gestures out the window with vigor)*

JOSYPH: Why did this happen?

TEX: History is full of . . .

I was the first American into Hiroshima and Nagasaki. I took twelve top war correspondents into those two target cities. But I had taken them to Dresden first to show what conventional firebombing around the clock had done to a European city. I don't think this is . . . fate. But I think that when the World Trade Center was built, Twin Towers, you set a target. *(Gestures out the window)* It got hit.

JOSYPH: How did you know there was anything wrong that morning?

TEX: I didn't really, except that I went to bed every night foreboding, you know? Worried. I found it difficult to get to sleep. As people do, I invented a way to put myself to sleep, to wash my mind in the old roundelay: "Row row row your boat / Gently down the stream." I did that over and over.

That morning, in Battery Park City, twenty-five yards from Ground Zero, right along the river, I was literally rolled out of bed from the shock of the first Tower. I jumped up. For some reason I had gone to sleep with my camera, a Polaroid with a fifty-millimeter lens, on the floor by the bed. I grabbed the Polaroid and jumped out in the middle of the first wave of debris from Tower Two. I yelled for Kevin. I had run out with Kevin but I lost him. Kevin had started playing the Minuteman. I was literally knocked over. I went on my hands and knees, and the debris from Tower Two was over me. I found it hard to breathe, hard to swallow, impossible to see. I was moving along on my hands and knees, crawling to the water, because I had seen the Japanese people in Hiroshima crawling to the water. The police found me, dropped me over the wall into a Coast Guard boat along with dozens of other people trying to get away. I was dumped on the Jersey shore into a police ambulance. I woke up twenty minutes later in the Jersey City Hospital. People were checking names off. The head of the hospital recognized my name because I had founded the North Shore Hospital in Manhasset, so he knew who I was. He was a very jovial Irishman who picked me up and took me to his home. His wife was a nurse. She looked after me. He gave me his business card. It said:

McLaughlin Funeral Home
James A. McLaughlin, Jr.

And he made a wonderful joke. He said: "Mr. McCrary, keep that card. We're not quite ready for you *yet,* but I have a funny feeling you'll be back. I'll be waiting for you."

JOSYPH: And yet you're full of new projects.

TEX: My motto, for my whole life, was the only line I wrote in Jinx's book. It was the last line: "To be continued." That's been my whole motivation for everything. And that's the excuse for *this* continued story.

JOSYPH: Did you hear the second plane?

TEX: I heard the second plane and I photographed the South Tower coming down.

JOSYPH: Rather than turn and run, you turned and photographed: that's the instinct of a photographer.

TEX: Yes. That was my job during the whole war.

JOSYPH: You did surveillance of bombing raids over Germany.

TEX: I had been in charge of all photography doing reconnaissance for the air force.

JOSYPH: You took one shot, you turned to run, and it knocked you down?

TEX: I took the shot literally on my hands and knees, and I was engulfed by the cloud of smoke and cinders. Not hot. I never felt heat. There *was* heat. I didn't feel it. I was smothered in soot, which was warm but not hot.

JOSYPH: When you took that photograph, you knew it was the Tower and not just a piece of it as some people thought?

TEX: I knew, because I had seen the Towers building. I knew the architect, Yamasaki. I knew the whole story.

You know, I've been lucky. I've been through World War II, Korea, Viet Nam. I have a picture of me with the senior surviving Japanese admiral in Shanghai surrendering to me before MacArthur got to Hiroshima. I'll show you the picture.

JOSYPH: Was there anything visually about Hiroshima or Nagasaki that was comparable to Ground Zero here, or was it completely different?

TEX: Completely different. This Ground Zero is compressed. At Hiroshima and Nagasaki it was total devastation. Total. Trees were stripped of all foliage. What had been trees looked like gallows. I remember one of the guys that I took in with me, Bernie Hoffman, from *Life* magazine, who has a photograph in a book I wrote called *The First of the Many*. We were walking down what had been a street and I turned to him and he had three Leicas strung around his neck, wrapped in tinfoil. Not entirely as a joke we wrapped our crotches in tinfoil too. Which didn't last long because this was August. I said: "Hey, Bernie. I brought you around the world to photograph this story, you haven't shot a picture." Bernie said: "Truth is, there's nothing left to photograph except the people, and that's not something that *Life* magazine or any *other* magazine *or* newspaper will print. Because it shows so graphically the horror of what we have done. *Life* will never print pictures of what we have done to these people." Then he said: "I wish my camera could catch the odors. People have been burned here. This place that was a city of 250,000 people smells like a barbeque pit. People—human flesh—*burning*."

JOSYPH: The photographs he did take weren't ever published in those days, were they?

TEX: No. You may remember that John Hersey came in a week later and got pictures from Japanese photographers and wrote the story. Sure enough he couldn't sell it. *Look, Life,* the *Daily Mirror,* the *Daily News*—nobody would print it.

JOSYPH: Eventually he got it into the *New Yorker.*

TEX: He went into the *New Yorker.* He sat with the editor, Ross. But the business mind in back of the magazine was Raoul Fleischmann of the Fleischmann's Yeast family. I happened to be there. He said: "Mr. Hersey, I don't think your manuscript needs pictures. You write in photophrases. If you will let us print your story I will drop all advertising from one issue in order to accentuate the power, and the graphic impact, of the words you have so brilliantly used."

There are two ways of writing. You can write with words or you can write with the camera. Sometimes words are better than the camera. You know the old rule: "One picture is worth a thousand words." Not true. The right word will *create* a picture in millions of minds and memories.

JOSYPH: Did it surprise you to see the piles of pictures Kevin took?

TEX: He's done beautiful work. He's got a picture that captures it: "The Last Beam Standing," which is a marriage of words and pictures that I like to think I invented.[43]

JOSYPH: You promoted that notion when you were editor at the *Mirror,* having a caption that helps a picture to speak even clearer.

TEX: That's right. I had a formula that wound up in Eisenhower's cabinet when he was in the White House: PHCQ. Picture. Headline. Caption. Quote. The picture captures your eye. The headline captures your ear. The caption tells you who. But the quote tells you the reason for the story. I used that in everything I did. When Nixon went to Moscow he made a television address to the people of Russia. I wanted that to be big news, so we met Nixon at Andrews Field, put him in a helicopter, and landed him on the steps of the capitol. That dominated the news. PHCQ. This is the formula that Kevin fell into. He fell into another force that showed, after 9/11, like it showed in England during the Battle of Britain, which I covered for the Hearst newspapers: a volunteer spirit. Kevin didn't have an assignment from me or from you or from any newspaper. He was, with a camera, a volunteer. And a damn good one. And that's the reason he didn't necessarily have to sneak through the police and the firemen. He was *given* access because they knew that Kevin would tell their story.

JOSYPH: Tex. Say it: you've got to be proud of Kevin.

TEX: I am. I like to think he is developing into a photojournalist. My beginnings in the newspaper business were on the *Daily Mirror,* where I started the habit of giving a credit line for photographers under the picture. I figured that's the way to increase morale without it showing up on the budget. And it sure worked.

JOSYPH: Ground Zero was some developing ground for Kevin. Fumes, hot beams, emotional turmoil, and then there was the law. It was tricky using a camera.

KEVIN MCCRARY: I had an open shirt and the camera was on a strap against my chest with my mask over it. Every now and then I'd pull it out and take a picture from down here *(by the heart).* I never put it up to my eye because I knew I'd be seen. I was at Carnegie Hall last night. Security there was worse than Ground Zero. I was three rows from the front, taking pictures of a commemorative for 9/11. So I shot the same way, from all these odd, inconspicuous angles. Most of them came out. Most of them came out from Ground Zero, too. But I was very discreet and selective about photography, even though I had handed out twenty or more cameras to firemen. I didn't have a gun on my side or a badge on my chest or a fireman's hat, I just had a hardhat and the accoutrements of a volunteer, which put me in a lower status and made me vulnerable, so I tried not to be too obvious about it.

TEX: There was a mad scramble to photograph Ruth Snyder in the electric chair. The *Daily News* got a shot, grainy, out of focus, but a full page of what we call *a gasper.* During the Bruno Hauptmann trial [for kidnapping the Lindbergh baby], again there was a scramble to get Hauptmann in the chair. I had one of the best spot news cameramen in the history of tabloids, Nick Sardos, who came to me and said: "I've got to find a fellow with a glass eye."

I said: "What're you talking about, Nick?"

He said: "I have found a way to put a lens in a glass eye and a little piece of film, and I've *done* it. But now I've got to find a fellow who wears a glass eye."

I said: *(Laughing)* "Nick! Come on!"

JOSYPH: He was serious?

TEX: He was *perfectly* serious. This was the year that a lot of people started wearing a homburg hat because Anthony Eden had worn one. Nick Sardos taught me how to put a Leica inside a homburg hat with a hole in the top.

JOSYPH: How would you work the shutter?

TEX: You'd hold the camera in your lap, you know, like this *(hand behind cap),* and have it set to infinity. I got the first picture printed of the Supreme Court sitting. *(Kevin laughs)*

Steve McGuinty was one of the old hands in the Far East. After the war, he found out where Hideki Tojo [the Japanese prime minister and minister of war] was hiding. This was outside Tokyo, in the hills around Fuji. So we got into Jeeps and we drove through the fence around his house. As we broke down the door to this little house we heard pistol shots. We ran in, and Tojo was slumped on the floor. He couldn't get at his sword, and so he had shot himself. We were slightly horrified, but only slightly, and then McGuinty went over and grabbed him and turned him over and he started bleeding all over the floor. McGuinty, a veteran of *Daily News* coverage in New York, said: "A bullet never bleeds going in, it bleeds going out, and I wanted to make a better picture, so I turned him over." *(Chuckles)* And we got a wonderful picture of the blood! The irony was that by rolling him over we drained the blood out of his lungs. Otherwise he would have died. This brought him back to life, and he lived long enough to be hanged.

(Holding a photograph) This is the picture I told you about. That's me, then. That's the senior surviving admiral in Shanghai. This is the interpreter. This was really the turning point. We didn't *need* to drop the second bomb. Jimmy [MacArthur] knew it and didn't want to do it. Jimmy wanted to save the second bomb for Mount Fuji. Put the second bomb down just over Mount Fuji, take it off the horizon, and the Japanese people would know the power of the bomb and would have the feeling that there was more where that came from.

JOSYPH: Who pushed to drop that second bomb?

TEX: President Truman said: "The only way to win a war is to kill people. The Japanese will keep fighting until we kill more Japanese." End of story.

JOSYPH: At first, you were hopeful about the neighborhood. So was everyone else. The acrid smell, the disruption, the sight of that destruction—none of that could drive those people out. But the economic situation is doing it.

TEX: Right. For Alan Greenspan, the whole of Downtown Manhattan is Ground Zero: the economy.

JOSYPH: Apart from representing enterprise and daring, the Twins were people's home base, their town. They were *your* front yard. What did it mean to have them across the street?

TEX: It was a unique community, I would say unique in history, but it was *my* community. I knew the shoeshine boys. I knew the waiters and waitresses in Windows on the World. I'll never forget going to the ramp outside of Windows on the World with a then famous Italian architect. I remember he waved his hands and said: "You know, some day this is going to make an historic ruin. More than Vesuvius, more than any volcano, what a ruin this will be." Well, that's what happened. A community was destroyed, and I think there will never be another in New York City. From the carpets on the floor to the Windows on the World, it was unique. And bin Laden was absolutely brilliant to do it the way he did. He knew that those Twin Towers were a symbol, not just of Wall Street but of the meaning of a great city.

16

JAMES CREEDON

New York City Paramedic

Who was this person whose hand I saw?

My conversation with James Creedon ranged over the streets of Lower Manhattan in the places that are critical to his story, including West Street below the South Bridge and the Hudson River waterfront in Battery Park City. Our initial conversation in December of 2001 is augmented with material from subsequent conversations during the course of the following year, including a walkaround with Kevin McCrary and an exuberant talk with Donavin on the rooftop of 114.

James grew up in Washington Heights. He was twenty-four and living in Brooklyn at the time of the attacks, which he initially heard about on a radio beneath his open window. He is now becoming an M.D.

CREEDON: Trying to get to my battalion, traffic was so backed up that I got behind a police car and wound up coming up through the Battery Tunnel.

JOSYPH: After you parked, were you running?

CREEDON: We're always told don't run into a scene, take your time, look around, make sure it's safe to go in. You don't want rescuer number 1 to become victim number 2. So I came in slowly. I saw the Towers burning. I saw body parts and wondered how they got there. I walked in closer and under the South Bridge I found a lieutenant from my command. He gave me a bag of equipment, a radio, a helmet—which saved my life, I think— he said: "Do the best you can," and off I went. I saw confetti coming off the building, shards of metal and glass glittering and shining. The flutter- ing of the metal was like birds turning into the wind when you see sun- light off their wings. It was beautiful in a terrible way. Smoke and paper were fluttering out toward the water. There were identifiable body parts all over the area. People were jumping out of the building. You wanted to stay covered wherever you went because at any moment someone could fall on you and kill you. One of the first firefighters who died on the scene was killed by a body that fell from a building. We were also concerned be- cause there was cyanide in the '93 bomb. The way it exploded vaporized the cyanide, but terrorism can try to use a secondary device to kill rescue workers, so we were afraid of it this time.

I was looking straight up at the buildings, which are over a thousand feet tall, and being that close to them was astounding—the enormity. I could see the debris falling. Fire engines all over. People running this way, that way, but at the same time a sense of order: people knew what had to be done. Firemen over there, paramedics over here, just trying to do their jobs. We had staged ourselves under the South Bridge for protection. Standard highrise fire, you stage from the ground floor with a triage sta- tion and an outside station. The only reason I was at the outside station was that my lieutenant said: "You go here." He could have said: "Go in- side and back them up," and I wouldn't be alive.

For ten or fifteen minutes I'd been moving people away from the area when we felt a rumble and heard a roar that was louder than anything I've ever heard. The ground began to shake and it looked like a giant dark black hand was reaching out over me. It was surreal: the metallic glimmer of the building, the black smoke, the debris directly over us. We didn't know the whole building was coming down. I thought there had been an explosion. All we knew was that we had to leave the area.

JOSYPH: What was the sound—like a series of explosions?

CREEDON: It was . . . inexplicable. I remember exactly the way everything was. I remember it in slow motion. We were standing there. We all had our helmets on. A busy scene, but orderly. Then, all of a sudden, we all looked up. Now, why did we look up? At some point you sensed it, then you saw it, then you heard it. Or you heard it and then you saw it. It all happened at once. There was this moment when we started to feel the ground move. Then we heard the rumble. It built and built and built, like when you hear a roll of thunder coming from far off getting stronger and stronger and stronger, except it didn't fade away, it just kept roaring, closer and closer, louder and louder, and as it built the ground was shaking more and more and things were getting blurry because everything was shaking, you couldn't see, the sound was coming, so we started to run from the South Bridge to World Financial One until it physically *hit* us. It wasn't just *over* us, it was *enveloping* us. I started to feel small rocks coming down on top of me, as if someone were throwing stones at us. They got bigger and bigger until a large one hit me on the head, which is why I think the helmet saved my life. As we were running everyone was knocked over at once by the shock waves. I was thrown off my feet by the stairs at World Financial One.

JOSYPH: Was that from the building reaching the ground?

CREEDON: I think it was, but in the moment it was hard to know. We hadn't a clue that the building had come down. I just felt this push, and I saw it happen to other people as well. It was the force of this huge amount of concrete, metal and debris collapsing on itself, pushing all the air out and knocking people over.

JOSYPH: Did it lift you up first?

CREEDON: No, I was thrown forward.

JOSYPH: Was it like being shoved, or was it like being shot?

CREEDON: It was like you were a little kid and this giant was running behind you that took your back and just pushed you. It wasn't like being *hit (slaps the back of a hand into the palm of another)*. It was like running and being *thrown—pushhh!*—off your balance. As I was running my lieutenant dove under a fire truck, others under the walkway—everyone was seeking the best cover they could find. In the end we lost seven ambulances and two command trucks, as well as four guys from my station and, as you know, hundreds of other rescue workers.

JOSYPH: Were you under anything?

CREEDON: No, I was out in the open. My helmet got knocked off. I lost my radio. I lost my stethoscope. I lost my telephone. My bag of medical gear was gone. As I was thrown, a cloud of pitch black descended on us so you couldn't see anything. Couldn't breathe. Eyes burning. Mouth burning. Skin burning. I was on the ground covering my head. I put my shirt over my face. Debris was raining down on us. People were screaming. You could hear ambulances and trucks exploding. You could hear girders falling. It was a noise you couldn't imagine. I remember thinking *this is it, this is the end, I'll be dead*, just waiting for it to happen.

JOSYPH: You *could* have been one of the casualties.

CREEDON: It occurs to me all the time. One lieutenant dove under a fire truck: he was okay. Another person dove under that same truck and his legs were crushed by a beam: he didn't survive. People right next to me were killed by falling debris, and it didn't require a girder to fall on top of you: a stone the size of your fist falling from eight hundred feet could kill you easily. That's why I credit the helmet with saving my life. That was a huge thud on my helmet before it was blown off. When things calmed down a bit the rumble started to fade but it was still pitch black and there were still people screaming.

JOSYPH: But you still couldn't see what had happened to the building?

CREEDON: You couldn't see an inch in front of your face, there was so much soot, ash, dust. That cloud of debris was moving at sixty miles per hour and we were directly in its path—we were right next to it, a few hundred feet away. It was a different level of force than being a few blocks away. When I went to the hospital later, pieces of stone and debris were removed from my back that were embedded in my skin through my uniform. When I see photographs of the area, it's inconceivable that people survived. It was a matter of the building tilting half a degree this way, not the other—a matter of luck as to whether you lived or not.

JOSYPH: When you were on the ground, was it like you were in a windstorm, or was it a onetime blast?

CREEDON: It was like when you're a kid in the ocean and a big wave is coming and that front of the wave hits you and pushes you and there's all that water behind it surging and thrusting you forward. But that was just the beginning. There were rocks and stones and dust and shards of glass and papers flying past you. It was like sticking your head out the window when you're driving down the highway, only instead of just the air it's all this stuff forcing its way down your throat, into your eyes, into your ears—it just kept going, maybe it went for thirty seconds. And while the lighter things are flying past, the heavier things are crashing and you can hear the roar of fires from gas engines blowing up in ambulances and fire trucks—total cacophony of sound. The roaring of the wind. The falling of debris. The exploding of ambulances. The yelling of people. The alarms of the firefighters. The pitter-patter of stones all around you. Your helmet. Your hands. Your own breathing. Your thoughts racing through your head. When the smoke started to settle and turn a hazy brown, by the light of the burning ambulances we could start to negotiate a way out. And we had flashlights. Of course at this moment, in many of our minds, the thought was: *is there anthrax in the air, is there nerve gas we're not going to live through five minutes from now?* All the medical things were going. *When will I not be able to breathe? When will I start having seizures?*

I started moving toward the waterfront but at the time I didn't know *where* I was going, all I knew was that we needed to group people together, link arms, and move through the debris. There was a physician from Columbia Presbyterian. There was a firefighter. There was a police officer. There was one civilian. Anyone we saw we said: "Come on," we'd grab their arm and move along. Looking at it now it's hard to imagine what it was like. There was debris everywhere but it wasn't a few inches, there were mounds of girders and paper and burning trash—everything you could imagine. You could hear the fire alarms, the people screaming for help, the sirens. We walked down Albany Street. Toward the water we came upon an Au Bon Pan and then another place [the Garden Café on South End Avenue], where the glass in front was broken. None of the faucets were working so we took bottles of water and sprayed people's eyes, telling them to flush out their mouths but not to swallow in case there were toxins in the dust. Rescue workers had fallen back around here to treat people and put them in ambulances, but a lot of them couldn't see, so we'd flush out their eyes and they could go back to work. You would just say: "*You*—put this water into a bucket and drag it outside." "*You*—find people who need a drink and give them this water but tell them not to swallow." The pulverized concrete dust and burning ash had forced its way into every part of your body. You were coughing, you couldn't breathe, your lungs hurt, you were vomiting, your nose and ears were plugged, you couldn't hear, you couldn't see. Once you realized that you were okay, the first thing you wanted was water. As soon as you got it you felt as if you could do your job again.

At the Hudson River waterfront, by the promenade, we started loading people into boats—tugboats, security boats, emergency service units, Fire Department—every kind of boat you can imagine. At this point only the South Tower had fallen, but I was at the water now, so my job was to get all these people out of the area.

JOSYPH: Aren't there stones in your back?

CREEDON: I was bleeding from the side of my head, I had burns on my hands and on my neck and all along the side of my head, I was bleeding from my back, I twisted my left leg, and it turns out I damaged my left knee and ankle.

JOSYPH: Then why didn't you leave on a boat?

CREEDON: In an emergency situation you want to get the walking wounded out of the area, but when it comes to yourself it's a different story. Maybe I was in a little bit of shock, but mainly my job as a rescue worker is to help people out of there. I knew people had lost their lives, including our guys. We heard all the alarms off the firefighters' uniforms, a whining sound that comes when a firefighter hasn't moved for thirty seconds or so. They were everywhere, all around you, like birdcalls. For those who knew, that was a heartbreaking thing. Just from that sound we knew immediately after the Towers had come down that hundreds of firefighters had lost their lives—or, worse, were trapped alive. No one was in the mindset to get on a boat. Our job was to get the twenty-five thousand people in the area to safety. Concern for myself came later.

JOSYPH: What about pain?

CREEDON: When someone said: "You're bleeding out of the side of your head," I said: "Don't tell me—don't tell me," not because I have a problem with blood, but because I didn't want to know how badly I was injured. Right now I'm walking, I'm thinking, I'm helping people—I'll find out later what's happening with me. Actually, as I was walking along I thought my ear had been torn off and I didn't want to think about it.

At one point I had a two- or three-year-old girl in my arms with the mother right near me. The mother had been screaming, so I said: "Give me your child, I'll put her into the boat and you'll be next." As I was stepping up to put her into the boat, just about to reach her over the rail, we got a warning that the second Tower was starting to come down. "Run! Run!" Everybody started running—the mother, me too, with a wet rag over the girl's mouth—trying to outrun that cloud. At the time we had no idea the buildings would come directly down. If the second building col-

lapsed you could be thousands of feet away and still be killed, so we were
running as far and as fast as we could. The mother disappeared so I just
kept running. Then I walked for ten minutes around the ferry terminals,
down by the docks, trying to find the mother. People were saying: "Where
do we go—where do we go?" In the end I passed the child off to a stranger,
a woman in the crowd, saying: "Please take care of this girl. I don't know
where the mother is. Right now *I* can't take care of her. We'll find the
mother later." I had other work to do. I couldn't go on this mother search.
And I was struck by the fact that there was a mother somewhere in that
crowd who had lost her daughter, and I was holding a daughter who'd lost
her mother, and some random stranger in this intense situation who was
worried about her *own* life, and knowing this could be a responsibility for
days, was willing to step up and take a child she didn't know.

CREEDON: After a few hours of treating people at a triage in New Jersey we
were redeployed back to Manhattan, to a firehouse near the Fulton Fish
Market. We got off initially at the south end of the island and we walked
the rest of the way.

JOSYPH: What was it like crossing back over?

CREEDON: It was a surreal scene. There we were in the middle of New York
Harbor on a state trooper boat, it was about four o'clock, and it was like a
war scene, like pictures of Pearl Harbor. You could see the island of Manhattan without the Twin Towers. In place of them was a giant plume of
smoke that wafted over the island and out over the water. You didn't know
if other attacks were coming. Since the collapse, this was the first time
that I felt really scared. *I can't believe I'm going back to the island!* But I was
glad to be sent back. This is where I work, this is my responsibility, these
are my people. They had said that we were all contaminated with anthrax,
so our attitude was, well, if we're already contaminated, let's get back to
the island—why should we stay in New Jersey?

JOSYPH: How was the air walking up?

CREEDON: The air was terrible. It smelled like a huge fire, stronger than I'd
ever smelled it, and it was coming off our clothes and all of the gear we
had. We had breathed in so much. Our eyes were all red. Some people had
scratched corneas. All of us were coughing. One paramedic who I met on
Staten Island had been injured in both collapses but there he was, stand-

ing up, still trying to help people. That's one thing that will always stay with me: the bravery of people who had been injured not once but twice and who had lost their partners or close friends or family, but here they were, still risking their own health to take care of people. That was how it was. Everyone wanted to know: *how can we help?* We were all upset when we were told we had to go back to the hospital to be seen. None of us wanted to leave. I was treated and I stayed overnight but I returned the next day. I helped out with medical care for a while but then I joined the bucket brigades, passing buckets along, digging out debris, trying to find people. I stayed there overnight and I did that for two days. Thursday afternoon I was standing in the middle of a debris pile, digging where the North Tower was, when we thought One Liberty was going to come down. A warning system was set up. They thought they saw the building shift and all of us went running. I reinjured my left ankle, so I ended up in St. Vincent's Hospital.

After that I worked at Ground Zero for weeks and weeks, putting in sometimes sixteen-hour days, staying here, not going home. You'd sit down somewhere, take a nap, fifteen minutes later you'd be back up again with something else to do. It's a bit of a blur now. As one worker said, from September 11 to Thanksgiving it was one long day. Lots of coffee, lots of macaroni and cheese—for months—terrible diet—comfort foods—it's what I liked as a kid. Mochas and macaroni and cheese—wow!—all's right with the world! Or Red Bull. They would bring in ten cases of Red Bull, swarms of people would take four or five in their pockets, then they'd get back to work. "Is there any more Red Bull?" Caffeine, sugar—no one would drink it normally, but down here *that* was the drink everybody wanted.

There was a mutual respect with everybody. The people passing out drinks were profoundly respectful of the people who were digging and vice versa. It didn't matter whether you'd been there when the Towers fell, all that mattered was that you wanted to help. Agencies that may have had conflicts in the past had found this commonality. There was a democratic spirit: an FBI agent, an EMS worker, a Red Cross worker, a volunteer, a state trooper, a firefighter, a deputy inspector, an officer on the street— different levels of different fields would be on a line together taking supplies off a boat. No one cared what anybody's rank was. If I'm not working there, I'll work over here. At one point someone laid out butcher paper for everybody to write on. It was like that on the windows of the

ASKING QUESTIONS

World Financial Center. People wrote messages and opinions in the dust but they never crossed anything out. If there was room, you used it. It was very democratic. **BOMB OSAMA**—**REST IN PEACE**—**KILL THE ARABS**—**WE DON'T NEED ANOTHER WAR**—you would see them side by side. You'd be surprised at the range of opinion.

Then I worked for the Office of Emergency Management at the Family Center on Pier 94, where people who were injured or who lost loved ones came for help. During this time I was struck by how grateful people were. They'd come up to you on the streets and hug you, or they'd hold up signs on the Westside Highway—hundreds of people, day or night—as we drove away from Ground Zero: **THANK YOU RESCUE WORKERS**. I'm always honored to be called a hero, but the credit goes to the people who lost their lives in the line of duty and I prefer to reserve the word for them. The people we lost from our squad are irreplaceable. They came in every day and helped people in New York City. They weren't just paramedics, EMTs, rescue workers. Many of them worked in volunteer fire departments outside the city, or volunteer agencies here in the city, so the loss echoes beyond just our own ambulances. Two of them were up in the mezzanine of the South Tower moving people out, and that's where they found them months later, lying not too far from each other, compacted into the pit of Ground Zero forty or fifty feet down. How they know it was the mezzanine I can't imagine.

JOSYPH: What did your car look like when you came back down the next day?

CREEDON: It was covered in a foot of debris, a foot of ash and a foot of dust. The inside was all toxic. Many cars were not returned to their owners: they were said to be too toxic. I had to wear a dustmask inside the car but none of the windows were broken and I was lucky, I was able to drive it out of the area.

JOSYPH: If you had gone away to medical school prior to the 11th, would you have regretted not being here?

CREEDON: The guys who were uptown when it happened and had to hold down the fort there wish they could have been down here. Everyone wanted to be here. If I were away when it happened I'd have wanted to get back here any way I could. I would have swam back if necessary. Being a paramedic is part of your identity. It's not just a job that you go to and come home. Most paramedics have studied for years, they have first aid bags at home, they help people in their neighborhood, they do volunteer work—they end up working sixty, seventy hours a week. When something like this happens *your whole person* is compelled to help out. *Having helped out at one of these incidents, I'm lucky to have lived through it, and if* something like it happens again and I'm away, I'll probably stay put because it's important to take a longer view. I can do a lot as a paramedic. I can do more as a physician. The world will keep moving when I'm in school. I need to stay committed to what I'm doing.

JOSYPH: At what point did you see the hand?

CREEDON: Walking toward the area I see this red rag on the ground. As I get closer and I see that it's bloody, I'm thinking *I guess they treated somebody and they dropped it.* When I get closer I see the head of a femur sticking out of the rag. It's someone's leg on the ground. First it's a red cloth, then it's a bloody rag, then it's a leg. I'm still hundreds of feet from the buildings. As I get closer I see the hand. When I see the hand I think of the Sistine Chapel of Michelangelo: the hand of Adam reaching up to touch the finger of God. God is breathing the gift of life into Adam. How ironic that here is this hand, cut off toward the elbow, lying on the street with nothing around it, three blocks away from the World Trade Center, positioned exactly the same as the hand of Adam. It's not a clay model: *it's someone's hand.* Someone who's probably not alive anymore. The other parts of the body are pretty far away. I saw the irony, immediately, of the reference to the Sistine Chapel, but it didn't settle into me till later, in talking about it, when I realized the contrast between this famous image for the giving of life representing now, in reality, the loss of someone's life.

I'm not a religious person—it didn't instill a religious feeling in me—but it's made me think, over the months, about questions of religion, identity, fate, possibility, circumstance, luck, uncertainty—all of these things are in this image. Every time I talk about it, it becomes a deeper subject. Who was this person whose hand I saw? What was that hand doing an hour ago when it was on a plane, or twelve hours ago when it was hugging someone goodbye, or days ago when it was holding its child? Some person, just like you, is going along living their life when suddenly they're in pieces over a five-block area of New York City. When I have nightmares, that's the image that comes back to me again and again.

JOSYPH: If I were writing a novel with this scene, my character would probably think: *Well, do I pick it up and carry it with me?*

CREEDON: If you get to a car accident and you see a hand on the ground, you pick it up and you pack it up in a certain way because you're hoping you can take this person to the hospital and get it reattached. Here you have a hand, but where are you going to put it—why are you going to save it? There's nothing to reattach it to. Then, no one was thinking DNA evidence. You think: *Well, that's someone I can't help—maybe I can help someone else.*

You try to put it together. Was this someone who jumped and part of them was blown here? Was it someone in the first plane that came from the northern side, heading south, and this is part of that person flying out in the other direction? For me, I looked at it, I knew what it was, these thoughts raced through my head, and I let it go. I'm in the world of the living. My job is to help people who need to get away from the building. This will come later.

JOSYPH: The shoes had a power too.

CREEDON: They were reminiscent of the pile of shoes in the Holocaust Museum. The shoe is a very basic, very domestic object. But when you put shoes together they represent people: hundreds of thousands of feet. They become icons. As the Towers came down women kicked off their shoes to run away more quickly. They left these shoes behind. When we came back down and were cleaning up the area, searching for people, there were shoes all over the place. They eventually got collected and put together, so they took on a larger meaning, like this hand. If the hand represented thousands of people who died, the shoes represented forty thousand people who didn't die, who were taken out of the area by rescue workers. And they represented the fear whereby notions of propriety and correctness and the need to wear certain kinds of shoes fell away. They weren't concerned anymore whether they wore the right shoes for their outfit, they were concerned with saving their lives. When the Twin Towers were burning all these different daily opinions and categories of weight, gender, age, ability started to fall away. Now it was a question of who's going to help a person on the sixtieth floor in a wheelchair, who's going to carry the person who falls down from smoke inhalation. Are you going to help *them*, or help yourself? I think the World Trade Center brought out qualities in people that they didn't know they had. The shoes speak to that for me.

JOSYPH: Are the nightmares bad enough to wake you?

CREEDON: O yes, they wake me up, they wake my girlfriend up. Nightmares of having the building collapse on me and being trapped inside, knowing you're going to die but it might take days, running away from a falling building—anything you can imagine. And for the first few weeks if I heard a rumble from the subway I could feel my heart racing. You'd be sitting on a bridge, a truck would be idling behind you and the motion of the truck would make you feel that the bridge would collapse at any moment.

JOSYPH: Or those steel plates that thunder under trucks in the street.

CREEDON: Those plates. The smallest thing. To this day there are moments when a rumble sends a shudder through. And when I see maps of the area, I remember what it felt like.

JOSYPH: Maps, not pictures?

CREEDON: Photographs don't really speak to my experience. I didn't see the planes coming in. I didn't see the Towers fall from far away. So that doesn't bring back being underneath. What brings it back is being under any tall building, remembering that angle. That big black cloud, like an umbrella opening up—it wasn't *over there,* it was directly *over me.* Or when I saw that overhead map we were looking at [by St. Joseph's Chapel]—there's where the Towers were, there's the South Walkway, there's the path I took—it's like a flashback. The whole world slows to a pause. I can feel myself running.

The night of September 10th I was a twenty-four-year-old kid working 911 and loving it. All of a sudden I look up and this building is about to collapse on top of me. There's more to becoming an adult! I went from being a kid to someone who might be ending his life—*and,* within the next thirty seconds. Some people die slowly over years—they know it's going to come. Some people die instantly and never know what hit them. But there's this in-between where you know you're going to die within the next few seconds. Millions of people have been close to death, but to have this moment when you see a building coming down on top of you and you think that's your last moment on earth—everything you want to do you won't do, everyone you want to see you won't see—to have this moment of pitch black where you're just waiting to die and you have this time to think, feeling angry and cheated—I couldn't even call someone to say goodbye—I wasn't panicked, but . . . if there was ever a moment that crystallized the notion that you ought to live life to the fullest, this was it. Rescue workers have something called Critical Incident Stress Debriefing. After something like this you talk to counselors, each other—it continues for weeks and months, checking back in, to help ease the burden.

But it doesn't erase the burden. This is something I'll never forget. I'll be seventy years old and still remembering that moment.

There is also a component of guilt. Maybe I should have returned to the collapse and dug people out rather then helping at the boats. Maybe I shouldn't've gone to the hospital that night. Dreams reflect that. And guilt that I didn't lose my life. Young guys with young kids lost their lives and *I've* gotten away with an injured knee, a sprained ankle, burns—barely touched. But I don't think the world would be a better place if I had died in the World Trade Center collapse.

JOSYPH: And you did your job.

CREEDON: Yeah, well . . . it's one of those jobs where you always feel you could've done more.

JOSYPH: The little girl that you helped must be a positive memory.

CREEDON: It's the most concrete image of doing my job that I have. It wasn't until I got to the waterfront, loading people onto a boat, that I started to feel *yes, this is why I'm here*. When the North Tower came down and I had to cover the girl's mouth and run with her, that was my job: this child was my responsibility. *If I do anything today I'm going to keep this child from dying in the World Trade Center*. And I did. She and the woman I gave her to were both very upset, they were crying and they were both covered with dust, but neither of them was injured. And the image has stayed in my head. If I ever doubt that I did my job that day, I can point to that and say there's one three-year-old girl who got away safely and reunited with her mother, and that was because of me.

JOSYPH: How did this experience support or subvert your politics?

CREEDON: Tell me what about the deaths of three thousand people in the United States makes the deaths of three thousand people in Afghanistan more palatable?

It's very easy for people who were not here, or who didn't directly lose people, to talk about the desire for vengeance. But after the attacks it wasn't just a matter of getting Osama bin Laden. People were saying kill the Arabs, kill the Muslims, bomb all those Middle Eastern countries. It revealed a racism or xenophobia in this country that was just beneath the surface prior to September 11. People who felt this way before the attacks were now accorded a forum. But how many countries are willing to ignore the United Nations, ignore the international community, ignore international law, ignore the laws of war and the laws of human rights and singlehandedly, with one or two allies, launch a military campaign against a country that's been devastated by decades of war? The United States, under George W. Bush, decided to do that. He pushed it through with a rhetoric that fired people up. The way to find vengeance and justice was to kill more people. Get Osama bin Laden, kick the Taliban out of power and if people get caught in the middle, too bad. To make up for it we'll drop them boxes full of peanut butter. So here we are months later and thousands of people have died in Afghanistan. People around the world who were afraid of the United States are now more afraid of the U.S. war machine coming to *their* door. North Korea, the Philippines, maybe the Sudan, maybe Iraq and Iran, maybe even Colombia. September 11 has become an excuse, a means by which to argue for a new world order, and it isn't being shaped in the United Nations or in democratic forums: it's being shaped in the Oval Office. So when I hear people saying that we need to get vengeance for the death of these people, I say, let's do it by changing foreign policy. Let's recognize what we should have recognized in Viet Nam, or further back, in the late '40s and '50s: that if U.S. policy is to seize more power, it's at the expense of creating more enemies. One expert told me that the chief thing that leads to terrorism is hopelessness. I think we're creating more ways for people to hate us.

JOSYPH: Was there any time of the day on the 11th when you were angry?

CREEDON: On the 11th the anger didn't come till that night. I was angry that we'd lost our men, angry that civilians had been attacked, angry that so many had been killed. Also, my father was a civil engineer who inculcated in me an appreciation for what he did. Thousands of working people spent years of their lives on one of the most amazing buildings in the world. When the Towers came down I thought about my father, I thought about the steelworkers at Ground Zero, I thought about the engineers and maintenance workers for whom it represented everything they've worked their whole life for. For steelworkers to see the major legacy of their lives just crumble, I could see where that could make them angry.

To lose people to an event like this and to almost lose your own life is sure to make you angry. But it was important for me to move past my anger. People were saying we have to nuke Afghanistan, nuke the Middle East—I just didn't feel like that. I'm not a pacifist, and I have no sympathies for Osama bin Laden and for terrorism in general. That's not the

The site filters through the surviving section of the South Bridge, which leads over the Westside Highway from Liberty Street to the World Financial Center. It was here that James Creedon was assaulted by the collapse of the South Tower.

point. The point is that we are trying to live in a world of hope, where the answer to violence is not more violence in return. I would say to people: "Have you seen what a war looks like?" *I* had never known what a war was, not until I saw the World Trade Center collapse. It was really a defining point for me, to see innocent people lose their lives because of forces beyond their control. It made me realize that when you see bombs on television it's not just a movie.

There's a famous quote: *An eye for an eye makes the whole world blind.* That's not just a utopian vision of living in peace, it's a realistic assessment of the fact that when you engage in a violent campaign against the violence of September 11, you feed the conditions for more September 11s, sending us into this spiral of international violence, war, terrorism. Have we really followed a path to justice? I was angry about September 11, but I was more angry to hear George W. Bush say that we're going to take out the Taliban and Osama bin Laden at any cost. I was more angry to see the Muslim people in my neighborhood spit on because of their religion. I was more angry to see Sikhs in California attacked and killed because they wear a turban. That has nothing to do with Osama bin Laden. In Afghanistan all these people were being killed in the name of justice and democracy, but these were the same people who had fought against the Taliban for years. So it's about feeling angry and yet thinking about how best to change the world. The United Nations felt angry about these attacks, as it has about others around the world, and many of its members criticized what happened but they weren't ready to ride behind the United States, launching a war at all costs. To believe that one equals the other is to fall into the trap of rhetoric. It's not clear thinking.

JOSYPH: Would it have been a good time for the United States to respect the UN?

CREEDON: It's been a good time for decades. This would have been a particularly good time. The United States worked to build the United Nations. After seeing the destruction of World War II, the leaders of the world decided we needed an international forum. During the Cold War, the United Nations became a pawn caught between two superpowers. Because the United States has so much power and provided so much money to it, the UN couldn't function the way it was intended to. The end of the Cold War became this historic opportunity to make the UN an international body, to enlarge the principles of democracy into a world forum. Instead, George W. Bush has taken a cynical approach to the UN, saying that when you support what we're doing, we'll use your name and your image of neutrality to support our goals, but if you don't support us we'll push you out, we won't pay our dues, we won't publish your views in our newspapers.

For example: the U.S. was found guilty of terrorism and human rights abuses in Nicaragua by the World Court, a body the U.S. helped to form. Did we say we're sorry, the World Court has found us guilty, we're going to pay the reparations? No, we say it's invalid, we refuse to participate, we refuse to fund it, we refuse to abide by its decisions. But if this isn't the time to use the UN, I don't know what is. I hate to sound like a leftist pouring information out of my ears, but these are facts. The U.S. has refused to abide by the World Court's decisions, even though we helped make it happen. Another thing is the definition of terrorism. The United States has been a part of trying to write the definitions. When we find that, under those definitions, *we'll* be found guilty of terrorist acts in Central America, we refuse to accept those definitions. Decades of allegedly humanitarian policy saw the destruction of hundreds of thousands of lives, all in the name of American democracy. It didn't bring democracy and it didn't bring a better life. Now we're turning to the Middle East. It's important to ask what role we have played in *creating* these problems.

JOSYPH: We tend to demonize people that we've armed, funded, and trained.

CREEDON: Well that goes for the entire history of the United States, people we supported who we now view as enemies. We can look recently at Saddam Hussein, purportedly now the great Satan, and yet he was supported by the United States. We put in power the people we want, and when they turn on us it's time to put a new person in. The U.S. consciously destroyed the water supply in Iraq in contravention of international law. I spent a summer in Guatemala working with indigenous health care workers. I was shocked to find out about U.S. support of death squads against human rights workers. This isn't rhetoric, this isn't paranoia: you can find it in the historical record. I'm no expert in political affairs, but when I see the cowboy politics of George W. Bush—"Wanted Dead or Alive"—"You're with us or against us"—to me, that's not the way you build an international movement against terrorism. We in the United States who suffered this attack need to take it as a historic opportunity to rethink the U.S.'s role in the world, and the first thing we need is to stop this march toward international war.

JOSYPH: If the same event that gave people the war fever gave you caution, it must bother them.

CREEDON: In some ways it's lucky I was there. It's a way of legitimizing my opinion about it. When they say *if you were there you would want a war too*—well, I *was* there. When they say *if you had been injured*—well, I *was* injured. When they say *if you knew someone who died*—well, I did. When they say *if you had been angry*—well, I *was* angry. It's hard to trump the genuineness of my experience. But I think there are many people who feel as I do. I've talked with rescue workers, police, firefighters, paramedics, EMCs. They may not voice it the same way but a lot more people have doubts about the war than you hear publicly. For many of us who were injured or lost people in the collapses it was a humanizing event where we had a moment of clarity and it cast doubt on the idea of war. It wasn't *we've been attacked, we need to attack back*. The gathering at Union Square started as a memorial to those who lost their lives but it changed into an antiwar memorial. It happened organically, not from people traditionally on the left but from people who, when they saw the loss of life, said: "Why do you want the destruction of more life?" I don't think that's idealism. Idealism is to say that we can do nothing and the problem will go away. Realism is to say let's not use a war that will create more hate and more anger against the U.S. Let's take a path that will resolve this problem in the long run.

JOSYPH: You sent out an email that got passed around.

CREEDON: It was just a simple statement. Next thing I knew it was everywhere. I said that if we want this war to bring our loved ones back, or because we want the world the way it was before September 11, it's not going to happen. I guess the message resonated. I've had a chance to speak to a lot of people.

JOSYPH: Have you been rebuked in any way? Scolded? Harassed?

CREEDON: Of course, of course. I was rebuked by people at work. Many rescue workers are ex-military or have family in the military or are fans of George W. Bush. I've been criticized by them. I've gotten hate mail. But I think people generally respect me for what I believe. I always try to speak respectfully about people who don't agree with me because I think respectful dialogue's the most important thing for us to have right now. I was lucky. One person in the command took me aside. He said: "I saw you on C-SPAN." I thought: *I guess it's time for a new career.* He said: "I want you to know that I don't agree with everything you're saying, but if anyone gives you a problem, come to me." As long as I spoke for myself and not for the people I work with, I didn't have to worry. That's why I'm careful. Who am I? I'm a member of New York City 911.

JOSYPH: How do you respond to the clamor for certain culpable individuals, like bin Laden? Do you let him go? Do you hire a shooter to track him down?

CREEDON: Here we are months later in the campaign against Afghanistan, thousands of lives destroyed, and yes I'm glad the Taliban is no longer in power, but bin Laden is still alive and I don't think we'll get him any time in the near future. So if it's a war against bin Laden the war has failed. If it's a war against terrorism it failed from the get-go. It's the idea that through force and anger and fear and killing people we'll stop the use of force and anger and fear and killing people. Even the language itself is wrong. Instead of a war against terrorism, I'd like to see an international movement or coalition against terrorism. Instead of just destroying terrorists, how do we destroy the conditions that create them?

ACKNOWLEDGMENTS

As the writing of this book partly arose out of the making of the documentary *Liberty Street: Alive at Ground Zero,* many of my thanks are in the credits of that film. Special thanks to the late Joe and Philomena Viola, and to the late Tex McCrary and Jinx Falkenburg. I also want to especially thank John Landrigan at the University Press of New England, and Michele Brangwen; Jane Carpinelli; Ralph Carpinelli and Sandee Jungblut; Richard Selzer; Rick Wallach; Richard Soden at Eye Vision Associates; Kevin McCrary; Donavin Gratz; Hannah, Sarah, and David Stanke; David and Mark Wainger; James Creedon; Gautam Patel at Smoker's Choice; David Frank; William Langewiesche; Michael Cook; David Munn and Fred Crist at Metalsmiths; Scott Murray, Rudy Wohl, and Mickey Quinn at Weeks Marine; Bolivar Arellano; Brigitte Stelzer; Owen Burdick at Trinity Church; Stefania Masoni; Martin Snow and Dennis at the Waterfront Boxing Club (now Trinity Boxing); the Ten House; Curtis and Tony at 114; Nian on Liberty Street; Ike on Broadway; Big Frank Silecchia for his generous donation; Jim O'Connor at St. Joseph's; Chris York; Jason Mazzone; ATV Mike; the dockbuilders Hector, Adam, Brendan, Anthony, and Tom; Rudy Weindler; Chris Chivers; Stephan Mueller; Michael Mulhern; Ray Sage; Kevin Koplin; Steve Zalaznick; the guys at *The Personal Computer Show;* Emmanuel Goldstein at *Off the Hook;* Mark Wagner at Voorsanger & Associates; Abel Ferrara for those good words in passing; Steve in Bowling Green; Terry Kennedy; Chuck Verrill; Mary Dierickx; Winfried Heid at Galerie Signum Winfried Heid; Dr. Arthur Miller; Faye Anderson; Erica Knerr; Richard Selzer; Eric Eason; Maryann Arrien; Ray Privett at the Pioneer Theater; the great people at the Melville Starbucks; Raymond Todd for coming along at the start; and Barbara Mann for staying with me for much longer.

NOTES

All illustrations are courtesy of the author from the film (or from footage shot for the film) *Liberty Street: Alive at Ground Zero*, directed, photographed and edited by Peter Josyph (Lost Medallion Productions, 2005).

1. When Jason Mazzone, assistant professor of law at Brooklyn Law School, talked with me about the Constitution and the Founders in relation to 9/11, terrorism, and the security of the city, he spoke about Lower Manhattan, where he had clerked for a judge. "The historic heart of the nation is there, even more than, say, Washington, D.C. It was in those streets that the nation was nurtured and given birth and grew up. The court-houses, the homes of people who were at the New York Convention and other important New York statesmen, the various people buried there—this is such an important part of our heritage. And to see it covered in ash, with fires going on and people running for their lives, it's almost as if it strikes at the heart of the Constitution itself."

2. In *Philosophy in a Time of Terror: Dialogues with Jürgen Habermas and Jacques Derrida*, by Giovanna Borradori (Chicago: Univ. of Chicago Press, 2003), Professor Borradori has a stimulating conversation with Derrida about September 11, but Ground Zero is not discussed. Professor Borradori confirmed to me that the subject of Ground Zero did not arise when she spoke with Derrida in his New York City apartment in October 2001.

3. See the revised edition of Danny Lyon's *Destruction of Lower Manhattan* (New York: powerHouse, 2004). Lyon's photographs were taken in the summer of 1967 when he was living at the corner of William and Beekman streets. At the time, Lyon wrote: "The Trade Center site is practically impossible to work in. PATH has the ruins guarded, and the wrecking is going on so fast that buildings disappear overnight" (p. 12), a situation I encountered at the end of the WTC. The Sonic Memorial Project, in a section of their website (sonicmemorial.org) devoted to the WTC, has an audio archive called "Radio Row," with a map, photographs, and other documents. Mike Wallace's discussion is at www.pbs.org in the 9/11/03 online forum for *American Experience*, which broadcast "The Center of the World," the WTC segment of *New York: A Documentary Film*, by Ric Burns.

Steve Zalaznick, an optometrist at 114 Liberty, was twelve when his father, who owned a cafeteria, was forced out of business to make way for the Twins. Steve was in his office, bracing himself against a support column, when Tower Two collapsed. His practice lost patients from that building, especially from Aon, which suffered some two hundred casualties. Steve naturally wondered whether he, like his father, would be ruined by the WTC. In talking about his father's plight he made an interesting slip. "All of a sudden his practice is taken away from him," he said of his father's lost cafeteria. Total Optometric Eyecare is now on Park Avenue.

4. See Jacobs's postscript to *Cass Gilbert: Life and Work*, edited by Barbara S. Christen and Steven Flanders (New York: W. W. Norton & Co., 2001).

5. Quoted in "Carving Up the New Iraq," by Neil Mackay, *Glasgow Sunday Herald*, 4/13/03.

6. Quoted by CBS News national correspondent David Martin on the *CBS Evening News*, 9/04/02, and printed online as "Plans for Iraq Began on 9/11." Defense Secretary Rumsfeld's remarks were found in notes made by his aides at the National Military Command Center at 2:40 p.m. on the afternoon of September 11 (www.cbsnews.com).

7. On 12/04/01 at the Orlando Convention Center in Orlando, Florida, President Bush was asked about his thoughts on the 11th. He said: "I was sitting outside the classroom waiting to go in, and I saw an airplane hit the tower—the TV was obviously on. And I used to fly, myself, and I said, well, there's one terrible pilot. I said, it must have been a horrible accident" (www.whitehouse.gov/news/releases/2001/12/20011204-17.html). On 1/05/02 at the Ontario Convention Center in Ontario, California, Bush was asked again about his reaction on the 11th. After making two jokes, and after a pitch for his "reading initiative," Bush said: "There was a TV set on. And you know, I thought it was pilot error and I was amazed that anybody could make such a terrible mistake" (www .whitehouse.gov/news/releases/2002/01/20020105-3.html). Two weeks earlier, in an interview he gave on 12/20/01 for an article by Bob Woodward and Dan Balz in the 1/27/02 *Washington Post*, Bush had said that Karl Rove brought him the news of what appeared to be a small plane accident, to which the president allegedly responded: "This is pilot error. It's unbelievable that somebody would do this." Bush also said that he told Andrew Card: "The guy must have had a heart attack" ("America's Chaotic Road to War," *Washington Post*, 1/27/02: A1, A11). And in an interview with CBS's Scott Pelley in September of 2002, Bush said: "I thought it was an accident. I thought it was a pilot error. I thought that some foolish soul had gotten lost—and made a terrible mistake" (www .cbsnews.com).

President Bush's waver between contradictory anecdotes about that morning isn't addressed in the 9/11 *Commission Report* (New York: W. W. Norton & Co., 2004), although the report does state that the president was told, before entering the classroom, that a commercial flight had struck the WTC. Bush has contradicted this conclusion. For many conflicting accounts of federal behavior on the 11th, including seven different stories of how Bush was notified, see Paul Thompson's *Terror Timeline* (New York: HarperCollins, 2004), or "An Interesting Day: President Bush's Movements and Actions on 9/11," by Allan Wood and Paul Thompson, 5/09/03, at the Center for Cooperative Research (www.cooperativeresearch.org). For a critical view of the 9/11 Commission's approach to presidential mendacity, see Benjamin DeMott's exceptional "Whitewash as Public Service," *Harper's* 309, no. 1853 (10/04): 35–45.

White House chief of staff Andrew Card has worked up a speech, which he delivers in near hagiographic tones, as if he were speaking to children, about the president's behavior on the 11th and on September 14. "And the President cancelled his event that day in Florida," he says, incorrectly, about the 11th. "Got on Air Force One. He flew high in the sky out of harm's way while we could assess what was happening on the ground and how our government had to respond" (www.whitehouse.gov/results/leadership/sept14cardtranscript.html).

8. See n. 7, Bush's Ontario talk.

9. After he left the site on September 14, Bush drove uptown to the Jacob Javits Center to meet more workers and some of the families of the lost. When the Uniformed Fire Fighters Association of Greater New York endorsed President Bush for reelection, they gave him a firefighter's hat saying UFA COMMANDER IN CHIEF BUSH. The Fraternal Order of Police, with a membership of over 300,000, also endorsed him.

In conversation with Amy Goodman on an 8/26/03 *Democracy Now!* broadcast, John Ginty, of the Uniformed Fire Officers Association, grappled with Bush's role, through his Council on Environmental Quality (CEQ), in the campaign of misinformation discussed briefly in this chapter (see n. 10 below) and more extensively in chapter 12. "I would hope it never got to his level, the White House," Ginty said of the changes made to EPA press releases. "It almost shakes your trust in the country when you think that a president would do that. I would just hope it was a lower functionary . . . that somebody eight levels below him just changed it without him seeing it. Because he was there. I was there when he came and he was with us, all the firemen, saying that he was going to get the people that did it and he'd make sure he'd take care of us. Now to find out at a later date like this that they were lying, it's very discouraging" (www.democracynow.org). The UFOA did not endorse Bush in 2004. Neither did the International Association of Fire Fighters.

10. See references cited in chapter 12, especially n. 29 below, the report by the EPA's Office of the Inspector General (OIG); and see the first book to address these issues, *Fallout*, by Juan Gonzales (New York: W. W. Norton & Co., 2002). Gonzales's series of columns in the *Daily News* regarding the EPA and Lower Manhattan represented a rare, almost solitary voice in the mainstream.

11. I have been unable to locate the television program from which this quotation from Raines is taken, but Raines told the story similarly to Greg Mitchell of *Editor & Publisher* in "Howell Raines on 9/11, and After, at 'The Times,'" 4/08/02 (www.editorandpublisher .com). For Raines's belief that "pictures are independent content," see "Raines Developed a Visual Legacy," by Kenneth F. Irby, 6/06/03 at (www.poynter.org).

12. Initialism for Counterintelligence Program. In 1976, domestic spying intended to neutralize political dissent was discouraged after a Senate committee known as the Church Committee issued a scathing report on these activities.

13. On 2/06/05 on the C-SPAN show *Q & A*, Brian Lamb asked Wisconsin senator Russ Feingold why he had voted against the USA PATRIOT Act. "I took an unusual step for a legislator," he said. "I read the bill." He called it "an old wish-list of the FBI" (www .qanda.org/Transcript/?ProgramID=1009).

14. See "Searing Memories, Etched in Art," by Randal C. Archibold, *New York Times*, 4/01/02: B1, B6.

15. The article by Dan Barry, "Determined Volunteers Camped Out to Pitch In," is in the *New York Times*, 9/23/01: B1, B11. An extraordinary article by C. J. Chivers, "September," in the September 2002 *Esquire* (138, no. 3: 144–157; 204–206), includes a memorable vignette about Kevin McCrary around St. Joseph's Chapel on September 13. Chivers, who was working for the *Times* on the 11th and was caught in both collapses, spent the next twelve days at Ground Zero. His eyewitness account, one of the best, is compellingly detailed and superbly illustrated with photographs by Edward Keating. See also Chivers's "Ground Zero Diary: 12 Days of Fire and Grit," *New York Times*, 9/30/01: A1, B9; and Chivers's "Looting Is Reported in Center's Tomblike Mall," *New York Times*, 9/21/01: A1, B11.

In an interview with reporter Steven Ward, Chivers, an ex-marine who was sent to cover the war in Afghanistan and is now in the *Times*'s Moscow Bureau, confirmed a story that Kevin McCrary had told me of when Chivers became embedded with the New York National Guard. Chivers: "After I got under the trade center ruins, into the subterranean space that survived the collapses, and wrote a story showing that some of the rescue workers were looting the mall down there, my source in Albany called to say that the administration went ballistic and was pressuring people at the Guard to have me tossed out. So I left. That was that." About the difficulties for journalists trying to cover the site, Chivers told Ward: "[T]he administration welcomed volunteers from every trade except ours, and . . . one of the messages was that somehow we weren't citizens of our own land. . . . I later heard that they said they were trying to protect us, but that was bunk, because when Mayor Giuliani went down there each day he made sure there were reporters in tow to put him on TV" (Steven Ward, "Spotlight: C. J. Chivers," 7/13/05, www.mediabistro.com).

16. These columns of smoke are captured on pp. 18–63 in *Above Hallowed Ground: A Photographic Record of September 11, 2001*, by Photographers of the New York City Police Department (New York: Viking Studio, 2002).

17. Kevin presented one of these business cards to the widow of its owner.

18. The image of O'Hara's, taken by Frank Schwere, is on p. 100 of *One Nation* (Boston: Little, Brown and Co., 2001). There is another shot of O'Hara's on p. 91 of *Above Hallowed Ground*.

19. The pictures of United Flight 175 as it enters the South Tower, printed from video by Evan Fairbanks, are on pp. 30–31 of *One Nation*.

20. Archbishop Williams wrote a book, *Writing in the Dust: After September 11* (Grand Rapids: Wm. B. Eerdmans Publishing Co., 2002), in which he makes a case against the rush to war. It compares interestingly with Giovanna Borradori's talk with Jacques Derrida (see n.2); with Jean Baudrillard's *Spirit of Terrorism* (London: Verso, 2002); and with the views of David Frank and James Creedon in this book.

21. See "Trading in Disaster," by Nityanand Jayaraman and Kenny Bruno, 2/06/02; and see "Dumping Potentially Hazardous World Trade Center Steel Debris Is Danger to People and Environment," by Dr. V. Suresh of the People's Union for Civil Liberties, Chennai, India, 1/29/02; both at www.corpwatch.org.

22. This conclusion can be drawn from the National Institute of Standards and Technology's *Federal Building and Fire Safety Investigation of the World Trade Center Disaster: Final Report of the National Construction Safety Team on the Collapses of the World Trade Center Towers (DRAFT)* (Washington, D.C.: U.S. Gov. Printing Office, 2005). This fascinating report disclaims accusatory conclusions, but it does say, for instance: "Although the impact of a Boeing 707 was stated by the Port Authority to have been considered in the original design of the towers, only one three-page document, in a format typically used for talking points, was found that addressed the issue. This document stated that such a collision would result in only local damage and could not cause collapse or substantial damage to the building. NIST was unable to locate any evidence to indicate consideration of the extent of impact-induced structural damage or the size of a fire that could be created by thousands of gallons of jet fuel" (p. 13).

23. See "Egress Provisions," pp. 57–59, in the NIST report cited above, n.22.

24. *Report from Ground Zero: The Story of the Rescue Efforts at the World Trade Center,* by Dennis Smith (New York: Viking, 2002), p. 241. Smith's important book is both an oral history of the 11th and an eyewitness journal of the aftermath.

25. Bush said this in the Oval Office on the morning of 12/21/01. See "President Highlights First-Year Accomplishments" (www.whitehouse.gov).

26. Bush said this on 3/13/02 in the James S. Brady Briefing Room of the White House (www.whitehouse.gov.news/releases/2002/03/20020313–8.html).

27. See, for example, "U.S. Congressman Jerrold Nadler White Paper: Lower Manhattan Air Quality," 4/12/02, at www.house.gov/nadler/wtc/docs/EPAWhitePaper.pdf.

28. For interiors of 125 Cedar Street (120 Liberty) soon after the attacks, see Edward Keating's photographs on p. 101 of *One Nation* and p. 149 of the September 2002 *Esquire*.

29. See *EPA's Response to the World Trade Center Collapse: Challenges, Successes, and Areas for Improvement,* issued by the EPA's Office of the Inspector General (OIG), 8/21/03: p. 8, p. i (www.epa.gov.oig/reports/2003/WTC_report_20030821.pdf), hereafter referred to as OIG report. A chronological resource of false health assurances, "Environmental Impact of 9/11," can be found at the Center for Cooperative Research (www.cooperativeresearch.org).

30. OIG report, p. ii. Toward the end of the report, on p. 111, it is stated more forcefully in the summary of a 12/02 report by Joel Shufro from *The American Journal of Industrial Medicine:* "The absence of strong enforcement and leadership on the part of EPA, OSHA, PESH [Public Employee Safety and Health Bureau], the New York City Department of Health and New York City Department of Environmental Protection resulted in unnecessary exposure of workers and community residents to toxic substances."

31. OIG report, p. 19, p. 17.

32. OIG report, p. 16.

33. OIG report, p. 17.

34. OIG report, p. i. The EPA and the New York City Department of Health objected to many points in the report, but interesting appendices show that the OIG, to its credit,

stood firm against their complaints. James Connaughton of the CEQ approved of one term. "The right word here is 'collaborate,'" he said. "We had to do some very dramatic and significant coordination." Quoted in "White House Sway Is Seen In E.P.A Response to 9/11," by Jennifer Lee, *New York Times*, 8/09/03: B3.

35. Whitman can be viewed making this statement in "Clearing the Air," a *Now with Bill Moyers* program broadcast on 9/19/03. A transcript of "Clearing the Air" is at www .pbs.org.

36. See n. 34, Lee article. The statement is on p. 19 of the OIG report and is reaffirmed on p. 132.

37. Quoted in "Asbestos Targeted in Cleanup Effort," by Hugo Kugiya, *Newsday*, 9/16/01 (www.newsday.com).

38. OIG report, p. 16. The CEQ required this quote by John Henshaw to be added to its 9/16/01 press release.

39. Both quotations are from chapter 11, "Knowledge or Certainty," *The Ascent of Man*, by J. Bronowski (Boston: Little, Brown and Co., 1973), p. 367.

40. Ibid.

41. Ibid, p. 374. Frames of Bronowski at Auschwitz are on p. 375.

42. The picture to which David is referring appears on p. 27 *A Nation Challenged: A Visual History of 9/11 and its Aftermath,* compiled by the staff of the *New York Times* (New York: The New York Times Company and Callaway Editions, Inc., 2002). It was taken by Suzanne Plunkett as the cloud from Tower Two—the first collapse—rushed toward St. Paul's Chapel at Fulton Street and Broadway.

43. *Stick and Rudder: An Explanation of the Art of Flying*, by Wolfgang Langewiesche (New York: McGraw-Hill Professional, 1990), was first published in 1944. William Langewiesche's own book on flying is called *Inside the Sky: A Meditation on Flight* (New York: Pantheon, 1998).

44. Kevin's picture shows the beam that was removed on 5/28/02 in the ceremony described in chapter 1. Tex's habit of captioning photographs is evident in the Polaroids he took on the 11th and in the immediate aftermath, to all of which he added handwritten phrases in quotations. On his picture of the collapse that knocked him to his knees, Tex wrote: "Going Down!"

INDEX

Page numbers of illustrations are boldface.

182–184, 189–191, 196, 198–199, 203, 204, 215, 271n3

120 Liberty Street (125 Cedar), 15, 59, 85–86, 156, **160**, 170, 175, 181, 194–195, 275n28

Liberty Street: Alive at Ground Zero (film, Josyph), 3, 8–9, 11–12, 14, 18, 29, 36, 38, 40, 45, 49–52, 57–63, 65, 72, 75–76, 81, 86, 96, 113, 120, 154, 177, 179, 183, 189, 191, 193, 213, 219, 233, 269, 271

Life (magazine), 117, 246–247

Lispenard Street, 8

Look (magazine), 247

Lost New York (Silver), 110–111

Lowe, Jacques, 56

"Luis" (story, Selzer), 189

Lyon, Danny, 271

MacArthur, Douglas James, 104, 198, 249

Machiavelli, Niccolo. See *The Prince*

Mad Max (film, Miller), 30

Maiden Lane, 9, 20, 47, 54, 125–127, 132–141, 180, 242

59 Maiden Lane, 132–134, 137–138

Manav (Indian language newspaper), 177

Manito (film, Eason), 29

54 Marienstrasse (Hamburg), 81

Marriot Vista Hotel. *See* Building Three

masks and respirators 4, 16–17, 19, 24, 30, 65, 85, 97, 137, 162, 170, 184–186, 193–194, 248, 259

Masoni, Stefania, 18–19, 40

Mayerowitz, Joel, 231, 233

Mazzone, Jason, 271n1

McCrary, Kevin, 62–63, 68, 77–79, **80**, 81–96, 98–108, 117, 119, 139, 146, 148, 154, 156, 163, 166–168, 171–172, 175–176, 184, 189, 203–204, 206, 214–215, 217, 240–241, 244–245, 247–249, 251, 274n15, 274n17, 276n44. *See also*

(for Kevin's cart) VIP's Taylor-Dunn transporter

McCrary, Tex, 19, 29, 62–64, 78, 87–89, 91, 98–102; 104–106, 139, 146, 156, 176, 183, 198, 206, 215, 276n44; view from Tex's new apartment, **64**; in conversation, 240–250; on origin of Battery Park City, 241; on Ground Zero and rebirth, 100, 241–242; on Hiroshima, 242, 244, 246–247, 249; on Kevin McCrary, 247; on personal motto 245; on 9/11, 244–245; on origin of the WTC, 242–244; on PHCQ (Picture, Headline, Caption, Quote), 247; on photographing the first collapse, 245–246; on hidden photography, 248–249; on Wall Street, 244; on WTC as community, 249–250; on WWII, 241, 242, 244, 246–247, 249

McGuinty, Steve, 249

McLaughlin, Jr., James A., (and Funeral Home), 100, 245

Melville, Herman, 44

Metalsmiths, 40

Miami Sub (Liberty Street), 77–78, 153–154, 163–166, 184

Mike (bartender), 83, 117

Miller, Henry, 25–26

Mohammed (fruitseller), 148

Morgan Stanley, 74, 204

Mount Sinai Medical Center, 186–187

Mueller, Stephan, 40–41, 89

Mulhern, Michael, 86

Munn, David, 40

Murphy, Cullen, 228

Murray, Scott, 32, 36–40

Museum of Jewish Heritage, 92, 149, 261

Nadler, Jerrold, 193, 275n27

Nagasaki, 198, 242, 244

Napoleon, 43